Hearing

Hearing
PHYSIOLOGY AND PSYCHOPHYSICS

W. LAWRENCE GULICK
Dartmouth College

New York
OXFORD UNIVERSITY PRESS
London   1971   Toronto

Figures 3.3, 3.4, and 3.7 modified from original drawing by Biagio J. Melloni, Director Medical Illustration, Georgetown University School of Medicine, published in *What's New,* No. 199, Spring 1957, by Abbott Laboratories, North Chicago, Illinois. By permission.

Figure 4.7 modified from Fig. 50, p. 138 in E. G. Wever and M. Lawrence, *Physiological Acoustics,* Princeton, N.J.: Princeton University Press, 1954, and *J. Acoust. Soc. Amer.,* 1938, *9,* 227-233. By permission.

Figure 4.11 modified from Fig. 103, p. 331 in E. G. Wever, *Theory of Hearing,* New York: John Wiley, 1949. By permission.

Figure 4.15 modified from R. K. J. Pfalz, Centrifugal inhibition of afferent secondary neurons in cochlear nucleus by sound, *J. Acoust. Soc. Amer.,* 1962, *34,* 1472-1477. By permission.

To my teachers

H. M. M.
AND
E. G. W.

Preface

This volume is a textbook written for students of sensory physiology and sensory psychology. I have selected from available data those facts necessary to the development of concepts and principles in the hope that coherence would be gained and the student's learning thereby advanced. Although limited to matters deemed central to an appreciation of the fundamentals of hearing, the treatment is sufficient in detail to prepare the careful reader for subsequent advanced study in specialized topics. I believe the book to be appropriate for use both by undergraduate and graduate students of hearing and sensory processes.

Mastery of the content is gained most easily by reading the chapters in order. The complexity of the material increases with progress through the book, and each chapter builds upon the concepts and principles considered in those preceding it. Foreknowledge of the fundamentals of nervous activity as well as of psychophysical methods will certainly aid comprehension.

Since this is a textbook, there are several emphases which serve to distinguish its character, and these should be made plain. First, an historical account of the evolution of major hypotheses is provided. Second, concepts and principles are considered as more important than the results of any single experiment except when the validity of the concept or principle is called into question. Third, special attention is given to auditory theories and the extent to which the major ones are able to handle the facts of hearing as they are now known. Finally, relationships between physiological and psychophysical data are examined.

I am indebted to a number of students who read and criticized drafts
of the manuscript. Particularly, I acknowledge the help of Gary Savatsky
who did his best to improve my logic. Portions of the penultimate draft
were read by Professors E. G. Wever and W. C. Patterson, and I am
grateful for their valuable criticisms and suggestions. I am indebted also
to Frank Romano for his execution of the line drawings. With great interest and skill, Howard S. Friedman converted my rough sketches of the
ear into clear and understandable illustrations. His drawings represent a
very substantial contribution to this book. Finally, my special thanks
are to Barbara Rikert, both for her good cheer and for her hard work in
typing so many drafts of the manuscript with such care.

Hanover, New Hampshire   W. L. Gulick
April 1970

Contents

Hearing

1
Introduction

A number of disciplines within science deal with one or more aspects of hearing, and together they provide converging lines of evidence on how sounds act upon the ears and nervous system so as to result in the unique experience of hearing. The treatment given in the chapters following includes evidence from physical acoustics, anatomy, neurology, sensory and nerve physiology, and auditory psychophysics. Of these, evidence pertaining to the two last-named topics is developed as the core of the book.

Before beginning with the formal treatment in the next chapter, we shall consider briefly three other topics which serve to introduce the student to the study of hearing. The topics are theory, history, and psychophysics. The chapter ends with a brief statement on the plan of the book.

Theory, History, and Psychophysics

THEORY

Although we have good reason to be pleased by the progress made in our knowledge of hearing, we must still recognize that a full understanding of hearing has not yet been gained. In earlier times, when the data were few, theories of broad scope were achieved more easily and each one of them could account satisfactorily for the major facts at hand. However, with the highly inventive advances in technology and the consequent yield of new information witnessed in recent years, the magnitude of the task for

3

theory is no less than staggering to the mind. Whereas one might hope that new facts would lead to a reduction in the number of alternative theories, this hope has not materialized. It would appear, therefore, that theories flourish when facts are either scarce or plentiful, but for different reasons. With but few facts one cannot critically choose among alternative theories. This, of course, gives impetus to research. Yet as new information is gained, the task of conceptual organization becomes more difficult and this is reflected today in the narrowing scope of theories. Where they once were broad and dealt with hearing, they are now narrow and deal only with aspects of hearing such as pitch or loudness or masking. Although reductions in the scope of theory may be an inevitable result of our expanding data, there is nevertheless a danger that theory will come to stand in the shadow of facts which are sought for themselves rather than for their significance.

The need for theory has always been apparent. In no other way can facts be brought together so meaningfully or their relationships so well examined. Yet in times like the present, when the yield of new data is high and the need for coherence is thereby made great, too little effort is being directed toward theory construction. How history will view our feverish efforts remains to be seen. Perhaps science, too, can suffer from affluence.

Despite the absence of a widely accepted grand theory of hearing, much can still be said of the importance of the role played by those that have been advanced thus far. Even though the concerns of modern theories overlap, each in its way has served to add some order to our facts. In this book several theories judged to have had a major influence on the development of contemporary views of hearing are examined in the light of evidence now available. In general, the examination is directed to the validity of the principles upon which they rest rather than to their detail. Because each is found to have liability in varying seriousness, the student may be left with an unsettled feeling about the present state of affairs in auditory theory. Perhaps this is not without some value. In any case, the alternative would have been to make light of some important contradictions and thereby decide for the reader about a preferred theory. This, even for the sake of pedagogy, does not seem justified. To find a theory wanting is not to deny its heuristic value.

A recognition of the importance of theory bears relevance to a general introduction to hearing in that it alerts the student to a pressing need, the alleviation of which may be far off. This is an important observation to make because many students in beginning their study assume that there is a single acceptable auditory theory.

HISTORY

Science does not advance by itself. Our knowledge of hearing has grown only through individual achievement. What students seldom appreciate are the inescapable limitations imposed upon scientific progress. Here we shall mention two. The first limitation operates on the individual himself and consists both of the compass of his foreknowledge and his habits of thought. The second operates on his discoveries to influence the extent to which they are accepted, and it consists of the habits of thought which characterize his scientific discipline at the time of the discovery. The latter limitation is sometimes referred to as the *Zeitgeist*. Needless to say, these two limitations interact in that each influences, and is influenced by, the other. Two examples of these limitations may be taken from the historical development of scientific thought on hearing.

Ancient ideas on the problem of knowing led slowly to a recognition of the importance of the senses. By the middle of the fifth century B.C. the belief was widely held that the senses somehow mirrored the external world by the *principle of likeness*. According to the principle, perception arises because activity in the external environment is met by activity within the sense organ of corresponding kind: *like is perceived by like.*

When the rudiments of the nature of sound as aerial disturbance and an elementary acquaintance with the anatomy of the ear came to be known, it is not surprising that, out of the context of the *principle of likeness,* Empedocles should have advanced his doctrine of "implanted air." According to the doctrine the middle ear contained a permanent refined air on which external aerial disturbances acted. Obviously, the limits of his knowledge determined what could plausibly be advanced as a "theory" of hearing, and its congruence with the prevailing way of looking at the nature of things assured its acceptance.

What needs especially to be pointed to is the way men, even men of science, view knowledge because this illustrates the interplay of history and scientific progress. When science reawakened in the 1500's a number of new discoveries were made, any one of which might have given sufficient cause for the abandonment of "implanted air," if the *principle of likeness* had not been so firmly established as an explanation of sensing the external world. For example, the discovery in 1564 by Eustachius (3) that the middle ear and throat are connected by a passage meant that the "implanted air" of Empedocles was not implanted, permanent, or refined. In 1566 Coiter (1) rejected the idea of "implanted air" in his *De auditus instrumento* by a careful account of the transmission of sound from the external meatus through the middle and inner ear to the nerve, but the essential conservatism of science did not allow his arguments to prevail. The doctrine lived on to gain new impetus in 1680 from the work of Perrault (5) who, by relocating the "implanted air" in the cochlea itself, was able to accommodate new facts without challenging science's conservatism. It took almost another century before evidence against this doctrine was sufficient to counteract the inertia of the *principle of likeness*. Wever treats this matter in detail, and he summarized it well when he wrote, "This idea of the 'implanted air' was destined to haunt the theory of hearing for two thousand years and more" (6, p. 6).

Let us consider now a contemporary case. In 1863 Helmholtz (4) advanced a theory of hearing which continues to be influential. The details of the theory we shall treat later in the book, but our purpose here is served by noting two important parallels to the doctrine of Empedocles. Helmholtz knew a good deal about physical acoustics and resonance, and when some of the finer structures of the receptor organ became known through the work of Corti (2), Helmholtz was able to formulate his resonance theory of hearing. Briefly, he proposed that each tonal frequency set into motion by sympathetic vibration one of a series of graded resonators located in the cochlea. He identified as resonators the "rods" of Corti, and by so doing he advanced the view that the ear operated as a peripheral analyzer with each pitch allocated to a place within the sense organ. His theory was accepted immediately because it extended the acknowledged facts about the physics of vibration as a solution to a physiological problem. Yet when it became clear later that the "rods" were in fact arches, and therefore unsuited as resonators, his resonance theory was not abandoned because it had become the habitual way of accounting for the facts of hearing. Instead of abandonment, different resonators were sought. This is certainly a close parallel to moving "implanted air" from the middle ear to the cochlea.

When the new resonators also were found unsuited to that function, the role of resonance as a principle to account for selective local action in the sense organ began to give way to consideration of alternatives, but the principle of resonance was not fully given up until the evidence against it was overwhelming. What has prevailed, however, is the view that different frequencies act selectively upon different places within the cochlea. The idea of local action continues to be held in contemporary auditory theories although the process by which it is brought about is no longer held to be resonance. As we shall see later, some evidence against the local action hypothesis in the cochlea can now be advanced, but such evidence is so alien to the current and prevailing view that its impact is almost bound to be modest. Whether or not adherence to the local action hypothesis is another parallel to "implanted air" only time will tell.

We see, then, that the habits of thought that characterize a period of time impose limits on the progress of a science. Only slowly do new discoveries effect change. A discovery too much ahead of its time is lost, perhaps to be rediscovered later on. Once firmly established, a theory is apt to exert an influence on scientific thought long after its usefulness ends. The problem for the student is how to be aware of the spirit of his own time so that he can work as a master of fact in a coherent context without being too much of it. Only those who solve this problem are likely to ask truly significant questions and to recognize significance in the experimental answers to those questions.

PSYCHOPHYSICS

Inasmuch as the reader is assumed to have a general acquaintance with the established methods of psychophysics and scaling we need do no more than state briefly a few concerns of particular importance to the material of this book.

Psychophysics and scaling take as their task the establishment of relationships between psychological and physical measures of a particular process. The advent of improved technology has aided greatly both our specification and our control of auditory stimuli; but as we shall see, full advantage of this happy state of affairs has not always been taken. For example, in experiments on hearing it is always better to measure the stimulus *as sound* at or near the ear than it is to measure it in terms of the electrical signals which drive acoustic transducers. Unfortunately this

is not always done. Confusion and error are added to experimental results more or less to the extent to which faithful transduction fails. The
fact that a sinusoidal voltage is applied to a speaker by an experimenter
does not assure him that he used pure tone stimuli. Such assurance can
come only by measuring the sound at the ear of his listener.

A second concern deals with the other side of the psychophysical equation. Since methods do influence results, it is imperative in assessing experimental data that a full account be taken of the nature of the task set
for the listener. For example, when a psychological scale of loudness is
obtained with the method of magnitude estimation, the mathematical
equation which describes it differs substantially from one which describes
the loudness scale obtained by integrating just noticeable differences in
loudness. While this is well known and may appear obvious, the general
case of the influence of a particular methodology is not always so readily
acknowledged. Needless to say, the extent to which a method influences
psychophysical relationships is often difficult to know, but to suppose
that the present fund of psychophysical data is independent of the methods which gave rise to it is unjustified.

The third matter, more an observation than a concern, deals with the
fundamental issue of what kinds of questions we should attempt to answer. Traditionally, psychophysics has dealt with relationships between
sensation and environmental energy, thus ignoring the mediation of
physiology. Because we know that sound does not act directly upon the
auditory nerve, but rather only indirectly after it is converted to an electrical trigger potential, perhaps we should attend more than we do to the
study of the relationships of sensation to measurable aspects of sensory
processes. One such relationship is developed in the book in connection
with intensity discrimination. The treatment given attempts to establish
a *psychophysiological* relationship rather than a psychophysical one.

Plan of the Book

Both physiological and psychophysical data are treated together in most
chapters of the book, but those chapters comprising the first half favor
sensory and nerve physiology whereas those comprising the second half
favor psychophysics. The relationships between these two major approaches to hearing are explicated first as part of the treatment of pitch

and loudness, and it is assumed that the reader is knowledgeable about the material presented earlier.

Since much of the psychophysical material is presented in relation to auditory theory, Chapter 5, Theories of Hearing, serves both as a central transition to the discussion of discriminative processes and as a means of providing a larger context for the interpretation of complex processes. Consideration of selected aspects of certain topics is sometimes delayed to a later chapter for the sake of coherence. For example, electrophysiological studies pertaining specifically to sound localization are presented as a part of that topic rather than as a part of the general topic of electrophysiology.

Experimental methodology is occasionally treated rather fully when by so doing divergent data can be explained or a reconciliation achieved. Terms and symbols judged to be unfamiliar to most readers are defined in the glossary at the end of the book. References are cited by number in the text and they are listed alphabetically at the close of each chapter. A full list of names of the men whose work is cited in the text appears in the author index.

References

1. Coiter, Volcher. *De auditus instrumento,* in *Externarum et internarum principalium humani corporis,* Noribergae, 1573, pp. 88-105.
2. Corti, Alphonse. Recherches sur l'organe de l'ouïe des mammifères, *Zeits. f. Wiss. Zool.,* 1851, *3,* 109-169.
3. Eustachius, Bartholomaeus. *Opuscula anatomica,* Venetiis, 1564, pp. 148-164.
4. Helmholtz, H. L. F. von. *Die Lehre von den Tonempfindungen als physiologische grundlage für die Theorie der Musik,* Braunschweig: Viewig u. Sohn, 1863.
5. Perrault, Claude. *Du bruit* (1680), republished in C. Perrault and P. Perrault, *Oèuvres diverses de physique et de méchanique,* Aleide, 1721.
6. Wever, E. G. *Theory of Hearing,* New York: Wiley, 1949.

2
Sound and Its Measurement

A basic acquaintance with the nature of auditory stimuli and the manner in which they are specified in terms of their physical characteristics is essential to an understanding of physiological acoustics and hearing. The treatment here is selective, and it is intended simply to provide the necessary background for the material of the chapters following.

Sound

Sound is a change in pressure propagated through an elastic medium. The change in pressure is related to fluctuations in the density of the medium that are brought about by a vibrating body within it. In treating the nature of sound we shall limit comment to sound in air since it is the usual medium for man. Further, it is illustrative of all elastic media whether gaseous, liquid, or solid.

Consider air as comprised of many small particles evenly distributed within a given volume. As long as the air particles remain evenly distributed within space, there can be no fluctuation in pressure and no sound. However, it is important to realize that the absence of sound is not equivalent to an absence of pressure since the atmosphere always exerts a pressure (about 1 million dynes/cm^2). Sound is a change in pressure around some null or reference pressure. When a vibrating body is introduced into an elastic medium, it will selectively displace some particles and thereby selectively change the density of the medium. *Sound pres-*

sure, or force per unit area, is a function of density. If the particles so displaced act to displace other particles and tend as well to return to their original location, then the change in density, and therefore pressure, will be propagated through the medium.

SOUND-PRODUCING BODIES

Sound is generated in air as a result of a vibrating body which has *elasticity* and *inertia.* The tuning fork, a simple sound generator, produces sinusoidal pressure variations known as pure tones, and these constitute sound in its least complex form.

When the prong of a tuning fork is struck, it moves from its position of rest in the direction of the force applied to it. However, the kinetic energy imparted to it by the blow is quickly spent as it encounters *elastic resistance* which is the tendency of molecules to resist distortion. When the motion of the prong ceases, the kinetic energy has been converted to potential energy contained in the distorted patterns of metal particles. The distorted particles exert an *elastic force* which acts to move the prong back toward its null position. *Inertia* carries the prong through its null position until, once again, displacement is halted by elastic resistance.

The tuning fork, therefore, performs the transfer of kinetic to potential energy and potential to kinetic energy over and over again. In so doing the vibrational energy is dissipated in two ways. Some is dissipated as heat through friction between the moving metal particles and through friction between the tuning fork and the air particles with which it comes in contact. The rest is dissipated as the sinusoidal transfer of kinetic energy from the tuning fork to the surrounding air particles. It is this latter form of dissipation which gives rise to sound. Both forms of dissipation ultimately bring the tuning fork to rest.

SOUND AND ITS PROPAGATION

The prong of a tuning fork in motion will push before it those particles with which it comes in contact. The *condensation* of particles leads to an increase in pressure above normal atmospheric pressure. Prong displacement in the opposite direction effectively separates the air particles in the same region. The reduction in density is called a *rarefaction,* and it is accompanied by a decrease in pressure with reference to normal atmospheric pressure.

One cycle refers to displacement of the vibrating body from its null to a maximum in first one and then an opposite direction followed by a return to the null position. Each cycle, therefore, includes a condensation and a rarefaction. Aerial sound is propagated because air particles in contact with the generator impart their motion to more distant particles that, in turn, impart motion to still more distant particles. It is the general disturbance in density that is propagated and not the air particles themselves. The actual displacement of air particles is minute, rapid, and oscillatory whereas density disturbances are propagated over long distances, at slower velocities, and in a direction away from the source. The velocity of propagation is determined by the *elasticity* and *density* of the medium and in air it is approximately 340 m/sec. In water the velocity is quadrupled. The leading condensation is called the *wavefront,* and the velocity of sound is usually calculated by measuring the time required for the wavefront to move a known distance. The linear distance between two successive condensations is the *wavelength* of the sound.

Propagation velocity is independent of the frequency, amplitude, and complexity of the vibratory motion of the sound source. However, as propagation continues through air, energy involved in the communication of particle movement is dissipated so that the magnitude of pressure fluctuations above and below the normal decreases with increasing distance from the source.

Three things happen when an advancing sound encounters an object. The sound is scattered (diffraction), reflected back (reflection), and propagated in the obstacle (penetration). The relative importance of these three depends primarily upon the size of the obstacle in relation to the wavelength of the sound and the density and elasticity of the obstacle relative to the medium. Objects smaller in linear extent than the wavelength of the sound striking them typically diffract the incident portion of the wave, but the wavefront closes around the obstacle and no sound shadow is cast. However, objects many times larger in linear extent than the wavelength of the impinging sound not only diffract it, but they also reflect it back to form a wave propagated in the opposite direction. Such obstacles cast sound shadows, and the shadow is best delineated when the impinging sound is made up of the shorter wavelengths.

In every instance some of the energy of the sound is transmitted into the obstacle. The amount of penetration is determined by the relationship of the elasticity and density of the obstacle to the elasticity and density of the medium. When they are alike, most of the energy is transmitted into the substance of the obstacle. When they are very different, most of the energy is reflected.

The matter of sound shadows is treated more fully in Chapter 9 in connection with the localization of sounds in space. Sound transmission from one medium into another is considered specifically in Chapter 3 in the discussion of the function of the middle ear.

THE PARAMETERS OF SOUND

Propagated condensations and rarefactions produce fluctuations in pressure which can be measured and recorded at any particular location in the medium. When pressure changes produced by a tuning fork are plotted as a function of time a *sine* wave results. In the absence of sound the sensing device records a straight line which, in effect, represents normal atmospheric pressure; but as the leading condensation approaches the location of the sensing device, an increase in pressure occurs which reaches its maximum as the middle of the condensation passes. It then falls back through normal to reach its minimum as the middle of the rarefaction passes after which it returns to normal atmospheric pressure. By convention, positive pressures are graphed above the normal pressure base line and negative pressures are graphed below it.

Frequency. The frequency at which a body vibrates is determined by the physical characteristics of the body and the pattern of energy acting upon it. The time required for one cycle to occur is called the *period* of the wave. Wavelength decreases as the frequency of vibration increases inasmuch as the speed of propagation of sound is independent of the frequency of vibration. A higher frequency simply puts the condensations and rarefactions closer together in space. It has proved convenient in acoustics to specify sounds in terms of cycles per second rather than in terms of wavelength. In this book frequency is denoted either by the abbreviation cps or the symbol $\wedge$.

Maintenance of a constant frequency seldom, if ever, occurs in sound-producing bodies outside the laboratory. Almost all sounds in the environment undergo progressive or patterned changes in frequency. This is especially the case for animal vocalizations, including human speech. Changes in the frequency of a continuously vibrating body are referred to as *frequency modulations.*

Amplitude. The distance through which a sound-producing body moves during vibration, measured from its null position, is a function of the force applied to it, and the fluctuations of pressure resulting from its vibration are correlated in magnitude with the extent of its displacement.

To measure the amplitude of sound one could consider the magnitude of *particle displacement,* but the distances involved are too small to lend themselves to direct measurement in practice. However, if one considers a single particle to be displaced sinusoidally about a null position as a consequence of a vibrating tuning fork, then it is clear that *particle velocity* (amount of displacement per unit time) increases as the force applied to the tuning fork increases because the particle moves over a greater distance in the same period of time. Although particle velocity could be used to indicate the magnitude of sound, it turns out in practice to be no less difficult to measure than particle displacement.

The practical resolution is to measure pressure. For a particle to change its velocity it must be accelerated, and this means that a *force* must be applied. While it is difficult to know the force required to displace or accelerate a single particle, it is relatively simple to measure a force acting upon a large surface. *Pressure* is force per unit area, and sound pressures are measured in dynes per square centimeter. For example, a pressure of 1 dyne/cm² is equivalent to a force of 50 dynes acting upon a surface whose area is 50 cm².

Amplitude of vibration is, of course, related to energy. Because energy is proportional to the product of the squares of frequency and amplitude ($E = kf^2a^2$), sounds of high frequency possess more energy than those of equal amplitude but lower frequency. Yet frequency and amplitude are independent parameters and each may be varied without alteration of the other. Just as with frequency, the amplitude of environmental sounds is far from constant, and progressive or patterned changes of it are referred to as *amplitude modulations.*

In Fig. 2.1 the essential properties of sine waves are illustrated. The prong of the fork is displaced back and forth between limits arbitrarily called ±1. Directly below on the left is shown the continuously changing

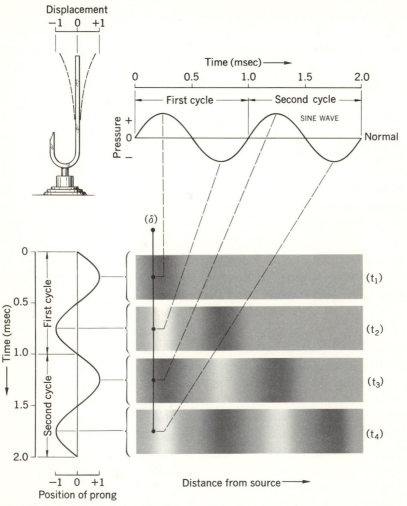

Fig. 2.1 A depiction of sinusoidal pressure changes occurring as a consequence of a vibrating tuning fork. See text for explanation.

position of the prong through time. During the first half-cycle the displacement to the right produces a condensation (t_1) whereas the second half-cycle produces a rarefaction (t_2). By the time the second condensation occurs (t_3), the first one will have advanced about 34 cm (340 m/sec = 34 cm/msec). The distribution in space of condensations and rarefactions is shown at each of four stages by the brightness patterns. Although sound could be depicted by the distribution of pressure through space at an instant in time (t_i), it is represented conventionally as pressure variations through time at a single locus. The sine wave shown in the upper portion of Fig. 2.1 represents the alternating condensations and rarefactions as they pass the single locus (δ) over a 2 msec period.

Complexity. Our discussion of sound has thus far dealt with pure tones because they serve best to make plain the fundamental nature of sound. Yet most sound sources do not generate sinusoidal (harmonic) waves. Although the human whistle approximates a pure tone, the voice and all musical instruments produce waves which are complex in nature.

During the displacement of a vibrating body, irregularities in the movement pattern often occur. An example is illustrated in Fig. 2.2. A speaker cone shown in the upper left moves back and forth between limits arbitrarily called ±1; but the direction of displacement is momentarily reversed during each condensation and rarefaction, as depicted on the lower left. This kind of movement would generate pressure variations shown by the brightness patterns. The complex wave (solid line) shown in the upper part of Fig. 2.2 would be obtained by measuring pressure changes at a single locus (δ) over a 2 msec period.

It is because bodies do not vibrate at a single frequency that complex sounds occur. In general, a body vibrates simultaneously at several frequencies which bear to one another the ratios of the integers 1, 2, 3, and so on. Body vibration as a whole generates the lowest frequency called the *fundamental.* Higher frequencies, *overtones,* occur as a result of vibration of the body in parts. For example, if the fundamental frequency be 1000∿, then simultaneous vibration of the body in two parts would produce an overtone with a frequency of 2000∿. Vibration in thirds would produce another overtone of 3000∿. In general, the amplitude of vibration is inversely related to frequency so that contributions to the total changes in pressure produced by complex vibration decrease from the fundamental to the highest overtone. Both the number of overtones and their relative amplitudes are determined by the physical properties of the vibrating body and the forces acting upon it.

Any complex wave can be analyzed into a specific series of sine waves according to Fourier's theorem. This fact is known as *Ohm's Acoustic*

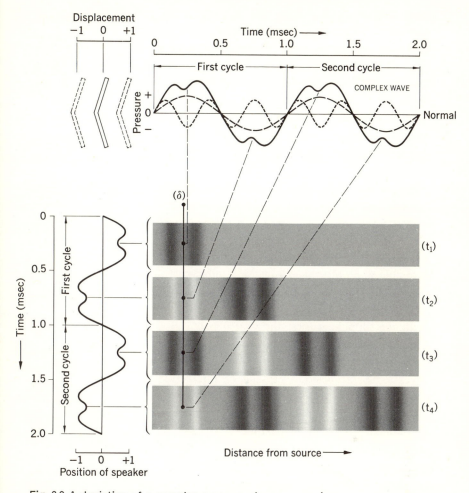

Fig. 2.2 A depiction of a complex pressure change occurring as a consequence of a moving loudspeaker. See text for explanation.

Law (*1*). Such an analysis yields a unique result since no other combination can produce the same complex wave. In Fig. 2.2 are shown the two sine waves (dashed lines) comprising the complex wave (solid line). In practice, Fourier analyses are seldom done because audiospectrometers can now do the task much faster. Complex signals fed into such an instrument result in an almost simultaneous *spectral analysis* printed in graphic form which includes not only specification of the frequencies involved but their relative contributions to the total amplitude as well.

The presence of a repeating pattern of pressure change from cycle to cycle is known as *periodicity* and it always results in *tones,* no matter how complex the waveform. However, when complex waves have no repeating pattern they are *aperiodic* and result in *noise.* When a broad band of frequencies is involved in the generation of a complex wave, the aperiodic result is called "white noise" because of its similarity to the complex form of white light.

Phase. Phase refers to the progress of a sinusoidal pressure change through one cycle. Since the projection of uniform circular motion is equivalent to sinusoidal motion, it has proved useful to specify the phase of a sound wave in terms of degrees. An example will help clarify the relationship. If one placed a thimble near the perimeter of a record turntable, then the shadow of the thimble cast upon the wall by a light on the other side of the room would move to the right and left on the wall in the same manner as that occurring with simple harmonic motion. With the thimble nearest the wall denoted as 0°, then a 90° rotation clockwise would cast the shadow to its extreme right position (peak of condensation) while rotation 270° clockwise would cast the shadow to its extreme left position (trough of rarefaction). The position of the shadow at any instant can be represented by the corresponding position of the thimble, in degrees. It is usually unnecessary to specify the phase of a simple sine wave (pure tone) in studies of hearing, but phase becomes important as a means of comparing the relative progress of two or more sounds.

When two tuning forks with the same vibrating frequency are struck simultaneously, their movements are exactly synchronous and the pressure waves they produce remain alike in phase at every instant. They are said to be *in phase.* However, if one fork is struck after the other has begun its cycle, then the waves from the two sources are different in phase. A phase angle difference of 180° indicates that the maximum condensation for one wave corresponds in time with the maximum rarefaction of the other.

Since pressures produced by bodies sounding simultaneously sum algebraically, the amplitude of the total combined pressure change is influenced by the phase relation of the two sources. For example, if each of two tuning forks has a frequency of 1000∿ and an amplitude of *p,* then the amplitude of the combined waves will equal 2*p* when the forks are in phase (phase angle $= 0°$) and zero when the forks are exactly out of phase (phase angle $= 180°$). Consider the same two forks again but with the amplitude of one reduced to 0.5*p*. The amplitude of the combined waves now will equal 1.5*p* when in phase and 0.5*p* when exactly out of phase. Here we may state a general rule: whenever the algebraic sum of two pressures produces a combined pressure which deviates from atmospheric pressure *more* than the larger of the individual pressures, then *reinforcement* is said to occur; and conversely, whenever their algebraic sum deviates from atmospheric pressure *less* than the larger of the individual pressures, then *interference* occurs. Reinforcement and interference reach their maxima at phase angles of 0° and 180°, respectively.

Two sources of slightly different frequency undergo constant phase changes through time, with the result that reinforcement and interference alternate. The number of times per second that the maximum effects of reinforcement and interference occur always equals the difference in the frequencies of the two sound sources. Assume that one fork has a frequency of 1000∿ and an amplitude of *p* while the other has a frequency of 1001∿ and an amplitude of 0.5*p*. If they are struck simultaneously, then at that instant they are in phase and their condensations add to give a total pressure change of 1.5*p*. After 0.5 sec, however, the waves are 180° out of phase and the algebraic sum of their pressures equals 0.5*p*. By the end of one second they will once again be in phase and the total pressure will be 1.5*p*. Thus, there occurs through time a fluctuation in amplitude of the total pressure change. In this example the amplitude of the complex wave undergoes modulation even though the amplitudes of the two sine components are constant.

RESONANCE

When a sound-producing body is coupled to another body, the motion of the first body is communicated to the second one. The coupling can be of two sorts: it may be *direct,* as when a vibrating tuning fork is pressed against another object, or it may be *indirect,* as when a vibrating tuning fork sets into vibratory motion a crystal glass on the other side of a room. When of the latter sort, the elastic medium itself constitutes the coupling. In either case, *resonance* occurs when the periodicity of the first body matches the natural frequency of the second. A tuning fork sounding with a frequency of 1000∿ will cause a second fork with the same natural frequency to vibrate. The amount of induced vibration (resonance) in a second body decreases as the frequency of the inducing body grows more discrepant.

In a simple vibrating system the nature of its oscillatory movement is determined primarily by three factors: mass, stiffness, and resistance. Its natural frequency is inversely related to mass and directly related to stiffness. Resistance determines the rapidity with which it comes to rest and is important to the concept of *damping*. In the extreme, a system can be so heavily damped that it will not vibrate. In other words, once displaced from its null, it simply returns to it without passing through it. This defines a *critical* level of damping.

From the foregoing it should be apparent that the degree of resonance in a second body is determined both by the relationships of its frequency to that of the first vibrating body as well as to its level of damping. The ear, taken as a whole, may have a natural frequency of vibration. Yet the complexity of its structures makes the specification of its resonant frequency impossible, for each part has its own resonance characteristics and the mechanical coupling of the parts is itself complex. Nevertheless, the concept of resonance is important to our understanding of the variations in auditory sensitivity as a function of the frequency of the stimulating tone. This matter is treated explicitly in Chapter 6.

DISTORTION

In our example of resonance in a tuning fork, the simple sinusoidal force acting to produce resonance did not lead to distortion in the resonating fork because its properties were such as to produce sinusoidal movement even if it had been left to vibrate freely. Stated differently, the tuning fork is a *linear* system in that its displacement from the null is proportional to the force applied to it (Hooke's law). For a system to be linear it must also be symmetrical. A system is symmetrical whenever the application of a given force in one direction displaces the body from its position of rest an amount equal to that produced when the same force is applied in the opposite direction.

In the context of our earlier discussion on the effects of displacement of a sounding body on the density of an elastic medium, one can readily appreciate that the absolute increase in density *above normal* (condensation) would not be the same in magnitude as the absolute decrease *below normal* (rarefaction) if displacement were asymmetrical. For the purpose of illustration, assume that an asymmetrical system gives rise to greater positive changes than to negative changes in density relative to normal. In this example, the area under the curve representing the condensation exceeds the area representing the rarefaction. The total pressure fluctuation would still look very much like the one shown at the top of Fig. 2.1, but the straight line representing the *normal* would be shifted downward. Such a fluctuation in pressure can be shown to result when to a simple sinusoidal wave is added another sinusoidal wave of higher frequency such that the higher frequency component always *adds* its condensation both to the condensation and rarefaction of the lower frequency component. This has the effect of enhancing the total positive change and reducing the total negative change since the addition is algebraic. Accordingly, asymmetrical systems give rise to distortion in that their responses contain frequencies not present in the sound acting upon them. To moderate and high intensity sounds the ear is a non-linear asymmetrical system, and we shall consider the details of the ear's distortion when we discuss the electrophysiology of the ear.

Sound Measurement

INTENSITY

As mentioned previously, sound intensity is most conveniently measured as the pressure exerted by vibrating particles upon a surface, and the unit of measure is the dyne per square centimeter. Since sound pressures are very small, often more than a million times smaller than atmospheric pressure, accurate measurement of them had to await the development of the *condenser microphone*. Such a microphone consists of two plates which comprise an electrical condenser. One of these plates is actually a thin metal diaphragm upon which the displaced particles impinge. Movement of the diaphragm changes the capacity of the condenser so that when a voltage is applied across the condenser, the change in capacity results in a change in current. Calibration involves establishing the relationships between the current, which is usually amplified in the head of the microphone, and known pressures. Normally, condenser microphones are calibrated in such a way that accompanying recording instruments indicate sound intensity in terms of *root mean square* pressure (rms).

Symmetrical pressure changes, such as occur with sinusoidal motion, would always give a *mean sound* pressure in one cycle equal to atmospheric pressure since the pressure changes are added algebraically. This difficulty is eliminated by using *rms* pressure. In this method each pressure change is first squared so that all values become positive. The *rms* pressure is the square root of the mean of the squared values. The formula follows:

$$rms \text{ pressure (dynes/cm}^2) = \sqrt{\frac{(p\text{-}p_1)^2 + (p\text{-}p_2)^2 + \cdots (p\text{-}p_n)^2}{N}},$$

where p is atmospheric pressure, p_1 through p_n are the sampled pressure changes during a cycle, and N is the number of samples. The *rms* pressure reflects accurately the pressure changes in complex waves whereas a peak pressure alone does not. In complex waves the peak pressure varies, depending upon phase relations, but the *rms* pressure is relatively stable. With sine waves the peak pressure and *rms* pressure bear a fixed relationship and the formula is simplified to,

$$rms \text{ pressure (dynes/cm}^2) = \frac{p}{\sqrt{2}},$$

where p equals the peak pressure.

Sometimes it is necessary to measure sound pressure at places that are inaccessible with a condenser microphone. At such times a probe tube of small diameter can be affixed to the head of the condenser microphone and inserted into the otherwise inaccessible place, such as the external meatus. However, the microphone must be recalibrated whenever a probe tube is used because the probe's presence seriously influences the pressures acting on the metal diaphragm of the microphone. Without calibration, errors of sound pressure measurement as large as two log units can occur. Since the probe has resonance characteristics of its own, it cannot be used satisfactorily to measure the pressure of complex waves because certain component frequencies will be emphasized relative to others.

Besides condenser microphones there are various kinds of sound level meters used to measure sound pressure. Most conform to the American Standards Association requirements and consist of a non-directional microphone, a calibrated attenuator, an amplifier, an indicating meter, and weighting networks. Typically, the meters are calibrated to give sound pressure in decibels relative to a standard reference.

Decibel Notation. Because the ear is sensitive to an enormous range of pressures (about 100,000-fold), it is more convenient to express sound intensity in terms of decibels than it is to express it directly in dynes per square centimeter. The advantage of the decibel scale is that it affords a means to express a large pressure range on a conveniently abbreviated scale.

Although the decibel scale can be applied to acoustic power, we shall limit our discussion to its application to sound pressure. The decibel formula for sound pressure is,

$$N(\text{db}) = 20 \log \frac{p_1}{p_2},$$

where N is the number of decibels, and p_1 and p_2 are the two pressures to be compared. Inasmuch as the system is based upon logarithms, the decibel scale has no zero reference point. Consequently, whenever two sound pressures are compared on this scale, one of them acts as a reference for the other.

By way of example, let us assume that we wish to specify the intensity of two different 1000∿ tones (A and B) used in an experiment. Their sound pressures are 0.2 (A) and 2.0 (B) dynes/cm². If the smaller pressure (A) serves as the reference (p_2 in the formula), then

$$N = 20 \log \frac{2.0}{0.2}$$
$$= 20 \log 10$$
$$= 20.$$

If the larger pressure (B) serves as the reference (p_2 in the formula), then

$$N = 20 \log \frac{0.2}{2.0}$$
$$= 20 \log 0.1$$
$$= -20.$$

Any two sounds with pressures bearing a constant ratio will be different by the same number of decibels, regardless of their absolute pressures. Therefore, the reference pressure must always be specified.

Common Decibel References. It is convenient in psychoacoustics to be able to compare readily the sound pressures used in different experiments. If sound pressures are expressed in decibels, as they usually are, this requires that a standard reference pressure be used by different experimenters. A standard now widely accepted is 0.0002 dyne/cm². This pressure was adopted because it approximates the least pressure required for the *average* human listener to hear a 1000∿ tone. Sound pressures specified in decibels relative to this reference are called *sound pressure levels* (SPL), and whenever a decibel notation is followed by SPL it may be assumed that 0.0002 dyne/cm² is the reference. This reference is used so commonly now that SPL is sometimes omitted. Therefore, unless otherwise indicated, decibels are always in reference to this standard.

In our earlier example with the two 1000∿ tones A and B, we expressed the sound pressure of each in decibels with reference to the other. We could have expressed them with reference to a standard pressure like 0.0002 dyne/cm², in which case A and B would have sound pressures of +60 and +80 db SPL, respectively. Note that they still differ by 20 db.

A second means of specifying sound pressure is sometimes used in psychoacoustics. Instead of using the pressure at absolute threshold for a 1000∿ tone as the reference for all other tones of whatever frequency, it is sometimes the case that the sound pressure for a tone of a given frequency is specified relative to the pressure at absolute threshold for that frequency. Since the pressure at threshold varies as a function of frequency, a different reference pressure is used necessarily for each frequency involved. While this may seem confusing, it has the advantage of allowing the experimenter to express sound pressures with reference to absolute thresholds rather than with reference to a single pressure. When the threshold is used as a reference, sound pressures in decibels are referred to as *sensation levels* (SL). It must be emphasized that decibels (SL) are expressions of sound pressure and not sensation.

In experiments in physiological acoustics in which the ear and the auditory system are treated primarily as physiological entities with no particular regard to psychological phenomena, it is common for convenience to use 1 dyne/cm² as a reference. In such instances the reference must be specified.

In general, these three references, 0.0002 dyne/cm² (SPL), absolute threshold (SL), and 1 dyne/cm² constitute the three common references against which other sound pressures are compared. They are not, by any means, the only references used.

One last word about decibels. Once the reference is known, one can easily approximate the sound pressure of a stimulus when it is given in decibels by the application of one or two simple rules of thumb. While they are no substitute for computation, they nevertheless allow one to approximate pressure without recourse to tables of logarithms or calculations. Given the reference, then for every 20 db increment move the decimal one place to the right and for every 20 db decrement move it one place to the left. For every 6 db increment double the sound pressure, and for every 6 db decrement halve it. For example, consider a tone 46 db SPL. ($46 = 20 + 20 + 6$). With reference to 0.0002 dyne/cm^2, move the decimal two places to the right and double the pressure (.04 dyne/cm^2). Again, consider a tone -48 db. ($-48 = [-20] + [-20] + [-20] + 6 + 6$). With reference to 1 dyne/cm^2, move the decimal three places to the left, double the pressure, and then double it again (.004 dyne/cm^2).

MEASUREMENT OF FREQUENCY AND COMPLEXITY

In modern acoustics electrical methods are available both to generate sounds and to measure their frequencies. When audio-oscillators are used to generate sinusoidal voltage fluctuations which then drive transducers, one can lead the oscillator output into an electronic frequency counter or display the oscillator output on the face of an oscilloscope with a calibrated sweep. The former method is considerably more accurate since the latter requires a visual judgment of the sinusoidal wavelength relative to the grid on the oscilloscope. The fact that the voltage driving a transducer is sinusoidal and of known frequency does not, of course, assure an experimenter that the sound thus produced is itself sinusoidal. Distortions can easily occur either as a consequence of the transducer or its direct or indirect coupling to other bodies.

In general it is always better to measure the sound produced by a transducer than to measure the voltage which drives it, and the closer the sound is measured to the location of the listener's ear the more accurately can it be specified. A microphone of known characteristics can be used for this purpose and its output can be fed into a counter.

The complexity of a sound is best determined if it is analyzed with an audiospectrometer. An audiospectrometer is simply a selectively tuned voltmeter the selectivity of which is determined by filter networks. Many of them have a device that allows them to sweep through a series of frequency bands so as to plot the relative contribution of each frequency band. The precision of the analysis is related primarily to the width of the frequency bands and the abruptness with which each is tuned. Relatively crude analyses can be made with octave-band analyzers, but the precision increases as the bandwidths become narrower. Some instruments have bandwidths as small as 3∿.

References

1. Ohm, G. S. Ueber die Definition des Tones, nebst daran geknüpfter Theorie der Sirene und ähnlicher tonbildener Vorrichtungen, *Ann. Physik,* 1843, *59,* 497-565.

3

The Ear and Auditory Pathways

Here we shall consider the basic structure of the auditory receptor and outline the major neural connections. More detailed consideration of particular aspects will be treated where appropriate in later sections of the book. Although some attention will be given in this chapter to the functions of the simpler parts of the ear, the major treatment of the receptor and neural processes underlying hearing occurs in the next chapter.

The Ear

The ear may be divided into three major divisions: the external ear, the middle ear, and the internal ear.

EXTERNAL EAR

The cartilaginous structure on the side of the head commonly called the ear is actually the *pinna*. In man it is without useful musculature so that it remains relatively immobile with reference to the head. It does not play any significant part in hearing in man except as a possible aid to the localization of sounds in space. In certain lower animals the pinna can be turned toward sources of sound, and in such instances it undoubtedly serves to improve sensitivity by reflecting or scattering sound toward the meatal opening.

Sound enters the head through a small canal known as the *external auditory meatus*. The meatus begins near the center of the pinna and

27

courses medially for approximately 2.6 cm. The longitudinal axis is nearly perpendicular to the side of the head, and in cross section the height of the meatus is slightly greater than its width. Its mean diameter is 0.7 cm. The distal third of the meatus has a cartilaginous wall whereas the remainder has a bony wall. The fact that the meatus is not bounded by uniform tissue makes its resonance properties rather complex. In general, however, it has a natural resonance frequency near 3500∿, and at the resonance frequency the sensitivity of the ear can be increased by as much as 8 db. This matter will be treated fully when the sensitivity of the ear is discussed.

At the proximal end of the meatus lies the *tympanic membrane,* the inner boundary of the external ear. The membrane, about 69 mm² in area, has the shape of a flat cone (altitude, 2 mm) with its apex pointed inward and its oval base held obliquely within the meatus by a bony ring. The walls of the conical membrane are slightly concave, and they are comprised of circular and radial fibrous layers superimposed one on the other.

Pressure fluctuations propagated through the meatus set the membrane in motion. Because of the complexity of its structure and the variable tensions upon it, the vibratory motion of the membrane is often complex. This is especially true for high frequencies when it is known to vibrate in segments (*2, 4, 26*). Nevertheless, the motions imparted by the membrane to the structures of the middle ear reflect with great fidelity the fluctuations in pressure of the acoustic stimulus (*22, 23*).

MIDDLE EAR

The basic anatomy of the middle ear is shown in Fig. 3.1. The tympanic membrane separates the external ear from the middle ear cavity which is situated in the mastoid region of the temporal bone. Air is admitted to this cavity from the pharynx through the *Eustachian* tube, which opens during the act of swallowing. This connection with the throat serves to equate air pressure in the middle ear to ambient pressure in the external meatus. As long as the pressures bounding both sides of the tympanic membrane are equal, the membrane vibrates normally. Inequality of pressures, however, has deleterious effects upon sound transmission through the middle ear (*13, 25, 26, 28*). Extreme pressure differences produce abnormal membrane displacement usually accompanied by pain.

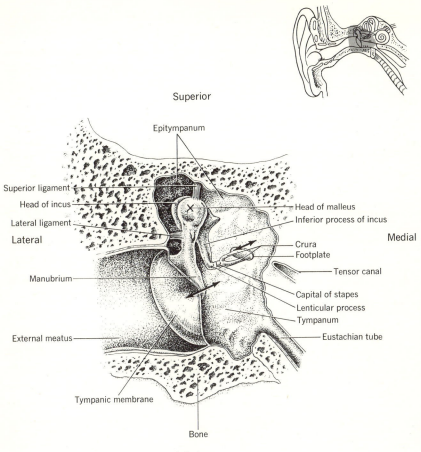

Superior

Epitympanum

Superior ligament
Head of incus
Lateral ligament
Lateral

Head of malleus
Inferior process of incus

Medial

Crura
Footplate

Manubrium

Tensor canal

Capital of stapes
Lenticular process
Tympanum

External meatus

Eustachian tube

Tympanic membrane

Bone

Inferior

Fig. 3.1 The general structures of the right middle ear seen in coronal view. The manubrium of the malleus, inferior process of the incus, and the stapes move to and fro along a medial-lateral line. The ossicular chain as a whole oscillates around an anterior-posterior axis through the head of the malleus and incus.

The middle ear cavity has a total volume of about 2 cc, and it is irregular in shape, being narrow in width but extended in anterior and posterior directions. The *tympanum,* the main part of the cavity, lies between the tympanic membrane and the lateral bony wall of the internal ear. Above lies the *epitympanum,* a smaller but continuous extension of the cavity. Suspended within the middle ear space, partly in the epitympanum and partly in the tympanum, is the conductive apparatus consisting of three small bones, the *malleus, incus,* and *stapes,* that bridge across the space from the tympanic membrane to the internal ear. Let us consider this bony chain in detail.

Ossicular Chain. The head of the malleus is situated in the epitympanum. From the head there originates an inferior process called the *manubrium* which extends downward into the tympanum. The manubrium is attached to the tympanic membrane in such a way as to pull it inward, thus giving the membrane its conical shape. The head of the incus lies posterior to that of the malleus. The heads of these two ossicles are fused together in a double saddle joint. Like the malleus, the incus also has an inferior process which projects downward into the tympanum. It is not as long, however, and near its terminus it bends medially for a short way to form the *lenticular process.* The stapes, the smallest of the ossicles, has the form of a stirrup. It is situated entirely within the tympanum. The lenticular process of the incus is attached by articular ligaments to the head or *capital* of the stapes. Two bony struts, the anterior and posterior *crura,* project medially from the capital and terminate on the stapedial *footplate,* a flat oval bone implanted in the *oval window,* which is an opening in the external wall of the internal ear. The footplate is held in place by an annular ligament. Beside the ligaments which hold the stapes in the oval window and the manubrium to the tympanic membrane, there are four major suspensory ligaments that hold the entire ossicular chain in the middle ear cavity. Together these ligaments determine the axis around which the chain oscillates.

Only two of the four suspensory ligaments (superior and lateral) are shown in Fig. 3.1. The x on the head of the malleus represents the head-on view of the axis of oscillation of the chain, and the arrows indicate the directions of movement of the manubrium and stapes. The vibrations of the tympanic membrane produced by aerial stimulation are imparted through the ossicular chain to the footplate of the stapes.

Intra-aural Muscles. In addition to the ossicular chain and its suspensory system, the middle ear contains two small muscles, the *tensor tympani* and the *stapedial* muscles. Their action is reflexive and bilateral and may

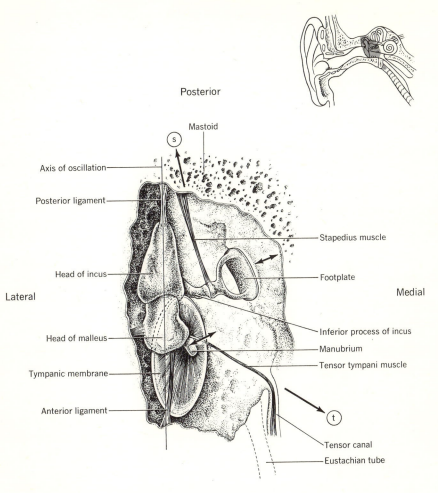

Posterior

Mastoid

Axis of oscillation

Posterior ligament

Stapedius muscle

Head of incus

Lateral

Footplate

Medial

Inferior process of incus

Head of malleus

Manubrium

Tensor tympani muscle

Tympanic membrane

Anterior ligament

Tensor canal

Eustachian tube

Anterior

Fig. 3.2 The general structures of the right middle ear seen in superior view. The manubrium of the malleus, the inferior process of the incus, and the tympanic membrane all are partly obscured in this view by the heads of the ossicles. The arrows **s** and **t** indicate the direction of tension imposed by the stapedius and tensor tympani muscles relative to the axis of ossicular oscillation.

be initiated either by moderate to intense acoustic stimulation or by irritation of the tissues of the external or middle ears or face *(7, 8, 10)*. The tensor tympani muscle is attached to the upper portion of the manubrium and courses diagonally across the tympanum into the tensor canal just superior to the Eustachian tube. It is supplied by a branch of the trigeminal nerve. The stapedial muscle is attached to the capital of the stapes and courses posteriorly. A branch of the facial nerve serves this muscle. The two muscles pull in very nearly opposite directions, both being more or less at right angles to ossicular articulation. In Fig. 3.2 a superior view of the middle ear is shown. The arrows s (stapedius) and t (tensor tympani) indicate the lines of force of the intra-aural muscles. The solid line through the head of the malleus and incus and in line with the anterior and posterior suspensory ligaments represents the axis of oscillation. The small arrows indicate the direction of movement of the manubrium and stapes.

A number of functions have been suggested for these muscles, but only two are now generally accepted (26). First, the muscles assist in maintaining the ossicular chain in its proper position (*fixation hypothesis*), and second, the muscles act to protect the internal ear from excessive stimulation by damping ossicular movement (*protection hypothesis*). The protective action apparently takes two forms: contraction of the tensor tympani attenuates sound transmission (3, 21, 24, 30), whereas contraction of the stapedius produces a rotary motion of the stapes footplate, thereby expending harmlessly the large amplitudes carried to it by the malleus and incus (1). Since the average reflex latency of the tensor tympani and stapedius is 150 and 60 msec respectively, these muscles do not offer effective protection against intense stimuli with steep wavefronts (11, 12). Some data indicate that the intra-aural muscles under moderate levels of tension and at certain stimulus frequencies enhance slightly the transmission of sounds by the middle ear (29), but more data are required before the protection hypothesis requires revision. Behavior of the middle ear muscles also has been implicated in stuttering (16).

Function of the Middle Ear. The anatomy of the middle ear makes apparent its general function: the transmission of the vibratory motions of the tympanic membrane to the internal ear. However, the action of the middle ear is not as simple as it first appears to be. Because the stapedial footplate in the oval window is bounded on its inward side by a fluid-filled cavity (internal ear), the energy which began as aerial sound in the external meatus must now be transferred to the fluids of the internal ear.

Whenever sound in a gaseous medium such as air impinges upon a fluid, most of the energy is reflected because of the difference in the *acoustic resistances* of the two media. Acoustic resistance (R) equals the square root of the product of the density (d) and elasticity (e) of a medium. The amount of energy transmitted (T) from one medium to another is determined by applying the following formula:

$$T = \frac{4r}{(r+1)^2},$$

where r is the ratio of the acoustic resistances of the two media. If aerial sound were to act *directly* upon fluids with properties like those of the internal ear, then 99.9 per cent of the energy would be reflected and hence lost to the internal ear. It is obvious, therefore, that the direct effects of aerial sound upon the internal ear would be negligible. The basic problem is one of obtaining a mechanical advantage so that the energy of aerial sound can be more effectively communicated to the internal ear. As an *acoustical transformer* the middle ear provides a solution to this problem.

Helmholtz (9) suggested three hypotheses for the securing of a mechanical advantage to aerial sound, as follows: a lever action of the tympanic membrane, a lever action of the ossicular chain, and an hydraulic action. Of these three, the first has been disproved (26). The other two have gained general acceptance.

The *lever action* of the ossicular chain becomes apparent when it is recalled that, relative to the axis of ossicular oscillation, the manubrium of the malleus is slightly longer than the inferior process of the incus, thereby allowing the larger movement of the manubrium to be converted into smaller, more forceful movement of the inferior process. The lever ratio is about 1.31 to 1 (4, 27).

The *hydraulic action* refers to the areal ratio of the tympanic membrane to the stapedial footplate. In man this ratio is approximately 21 to 1. However, as Wever (26) has pointed out, it is necessary to consider the fact that about one-third of the area of the tympanic membrane is ineffective as a vibrating diaphragm so that the corrected ratio is reduced to 14. The total transformer action equals the product of the two mechanisms $(1.31 \times 14 = 18.3)$. Thus it may be concluded that the middle ear acts not only to transmit sound energy, but it also acts as an acoustical transformer.

INTERNAL EAR

The internal ear is known as the *cochlea,* a part of the *bony labyrinth* concerned with hearing. It is situated completely within the petrous portion of the temporal bone at a site which is antero-medial to the middle ear cavity. The shape of the cochlea resembles a tube of decreasing diameter which is coiled ever more sharply upon itself two and three-quarters times. The cochlear spiral begins at the vestibule, a relatively large fluid-filled space on whose lateral side the oval window lies. The lateral bony wall of the vestibule separates the structures of the internal ear from those of the air-filled middle ear. The cochlea terminates blindly in its third turn at the *apex.* Taken as a whole, the conical spiral of the cochlea has a shape which approximates that of a cone, and the major axis of the cochlear spiral (altitude of the cone) lies in a horizontal plane and follows an antero-lateral direction, bisecting the mid-sagittal plane at an angle of 45°. The apex points forward and outward.

The spatial orientation of the cochlea of the right ear is shown in Fig. 3.3. The left portion of the drawing shows the tympanum of the middle ear and the Eustachian tube. The stapes, normally held within the oval window, is shown pulled away in order to facilitate conceptualization of the oval window. The semicircular canals have been omitted for the sake of simplicity. Notice that the cochlear spiral begins at the floor of the vestibule and coils to the apex. The line *ab* represents the axis of the cochlear spiral. On the right the cochlea is seen projected within an imaginary cone whose altitude, the cochlear axis, is seen to bisect the mid-saggital plane at 45°.

As mentioned previously in connection with the transformer action of the middle ear, the vestibule and cochlea are filled with fluid. The total volume of these structures is approximately 0.1 cc. Inasmuch as the fluids of the internal ear are virtually incompressible, the stapes could not move toward the vestibule unless a pressure relief point were provided. The *round window,* which is an elastic membrane that opens on the middle ear, serves this purpose. Movements of the oval and round windows, therefore, are reciprocal, as indicated by the solid and dashed arrows in Fig. 3.3.

Cochlear Canals. The cochlear tube is divided longitudinally into three canals, the *scala tympani,* the *scala vestibuli,* and the *scala media.* Be-

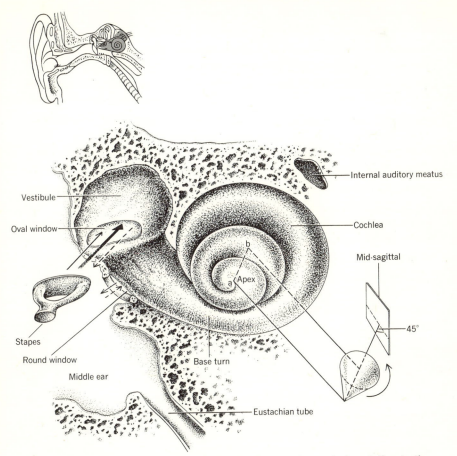

Fig. 3.3 The cochlea of the right ear showing the cochlear axis in relation to the mid-sagittal plane. After Melloni. By permission.

cause the scala media contains the final receptor mechanism for hearing, it will best serve our purpose to treat first the simpler canals.

Projecting from the internal wall of the cochlea all along its length is a bony shelf known as the *spiral osseous lamina*. Directly opposite is another shelf, the *spiral ligament*. In cross section the cochlear tube is approximately circular, and with this in mind, consider the spiral lamina and the spiral ligament as projecting toward the center of the circle from opposite ends of a diameter. The two shelves do not meet in the center, but between them lies the *basilar membrane*. Together these structures form the boundary between the scala tympani and the other two scalae. In man the basilar membrane varies in width about sixfold, being 0.08 mm at the basal end and 0.5 mm near the apex. Note that the width of the basilar membrane increases from base to apex even though the diameter of the cochlea decreases. The basilar membrane is absent at the apex and here the scala vestibuli and the scala tympani communicate through a small opening known as the *helicotrema*.

The vestibule and both of these canals contain *perilymph,* a watery fluid similar in viscosity to cerebrospinal fluid yet different from it in chemical composition. The origin of perilymph is not completely understood, but it is believed to be derived from cerebrospinal fluid. Perilymph probably enters the cochlea by way of a small aqueduct across which may lie an osmotic membrane. Filter action of the membrane and the selected withdrawal of some substances by cells of the perilymphatic scalae probably account for the difference in composition of the two fluids.

Motion of the stapedial footplate acting upon the oval window membrane establishes pressure waves in the perilymph of the vestibule, and these waves are propagated into the scala vestibuli. Once in this canal they produce a practically instantaneous motion all through the cochlea because of the speed of propagation of sound in fluid and the small dimensions of the cochlea. Although the scala vestibuli is continuous with the vestibule, the scala tympani is not, for its basal end terminates blindly in the petrous bone below the vestibule, as shown in Fig. 3.4. It is here at the base of the scala tympani that the round window opens upon the middle ear cavity.

The *scala media* is a small self-contained membranous canal containing a viscous fluid called *endolymph*. In cross section the scala media approximates a triangle. Its base is made up of the spiral lamina, the spiral ligament, and the basilar membrane. Taken together these structures separate it from the scala tympani. It is separated from the scala vestibuli by *Reissner's membrane.* A vascular area, the *stria vascularis,* serves as its third boundary along the external wall of the cochlea. It is believed that endolymph is secreted by the stria vascularis. In total volume this canal represents only 7 per cent of the cochlea and vestibule.

In Fig. 3.4 the spatial arrangement of the three cochlear canals is

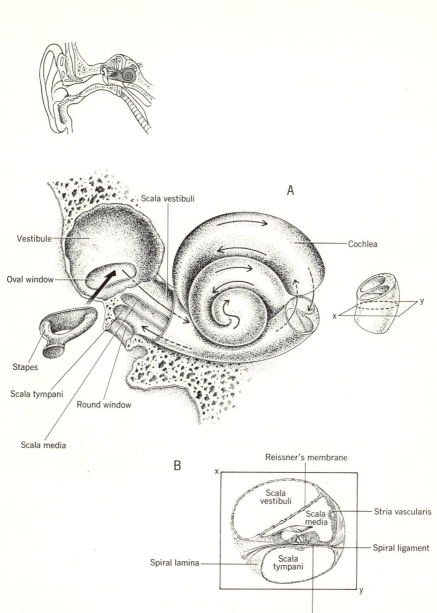

Fig. 3.4 A. The cochlea of the right ear showing the relative positions of the scala vestibuli, scala media, and scala tympani. Only the scala vestibuli communicates directly with the vestibule. The arrows show possible paths of sound. B. A cross section of the cochlear tube. After Melloni. By permission.

shown. In part A the cochlea is shown cut away at its origin at the floor of the vestibule and again in its first turn. The scala vestibuli may be seen to be continuous with the vestibule whereas the scala tympani is not. The arrows indicate possible pressure waves beginning in the vestibule and traveling through the scala vestibuli to the apex. It is commonly assumed that they pass through the helicotrema and return to the round window through the scala tympani. Part B of this figure shows the cochlea in cross section at the plane *xy*.

Pressure changes in the perilymphatic canals initiated by the movement of the stapedial footplate are readily communicated to the structures of the scala media. The acoustic properties of perilymph and endolymph are sufficiently similar to allow effective transmission through the two membranes that serve as boundaries for the scala media. Reissner's membrane contains only two cellular layers and probably offers little resistance to sound transmission. The basilar membrane is flexible.

Organ of Corti. Resting upon the basilar membrane and projecting into the scala media is a group of structures collectively called the *organ of Corti*. The organ is shown in cross section in Fig. 3.5. The most prominent structure is the *arch of Corti* which is shaped like an inverted V with its internal foot resting upon the edge of the spiral lamina and its external foot resting upon the basilar membrane. When viewed longitudinally the adjacent arches form a tunnel which extends the length of the basilar membrane, a distance of about 32 mm.

Situated against the medial surface of the tunnel is a single row of specialized epithelial cells called the *inner hair cells.* In the human cochlea there are approximately 3,400 inner hair cells which extend in a row from the base to the apex of the cochlea. Extending in a similar manner close to the lateral surface of the tunnel of Corti are three or four rows of *outer hair cells,* numbering about 12,000 in man. The inner and outer hair cells are inclined toward each other and are held in place in three ways. First, cells of *Claudius, Boettcher,* and *Hensen* serve as a lateral buttress for the external hair cells and the *phalangeal cells* serve the same purpose for the inner hair cells. Second, a *reticular membrane* embraces the upper ends of the hair cells and assists in maintaining their alignment. Third, the base of each hair cell rests within a cup made of an arborized

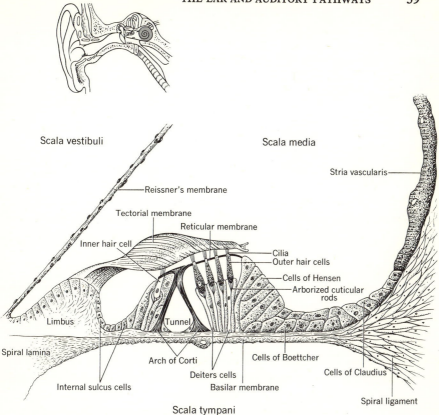

Fig. 3.5 Cross section of the scala media showing the organ of Corti.

cuticular rod whose foot rests upon the basilar membrane. These cuticular rods are part of the *Deiters cells* which form the main vertical supportive mechanism. Cilia emerge from the upper surface of the inner and outer hair cells to penetrate the tectorial membrane which extends from the spiral lamina to form a roof over the organ of Corti.

Inasmuch as the high potassium content of endolymph would inhibit action potentials in nerve fibers which make contact with the hair cells, it has been suggested that the spaces immediately surrounding the hair cells and the tunnel of Corti contain *cortilymph,* a fluid of extracellular properties similar to perilymph (5). It is possible that all inner spaces of

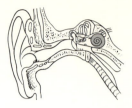

Inner hair cell

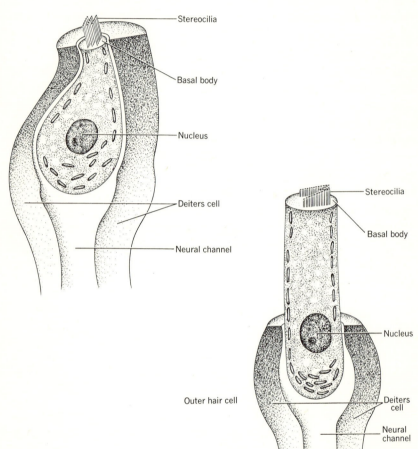

Stereocilia

Basal body

Nucleus

Deiters cell

Neural channel

Stereocilia

Basal body

Nucleus

Outer hair cell

Deiters cell

Neural channel

Fig. 3.6 Cross section of an inner and an outer hair cell of the organ of Corti. Whereas the stereocilia are arranged in parallel rows on the inner hair cells, they show an incredibly regular W pattern on outer hair cells. In both the stereocilia are rooted in a cuticle. Nerve terminals reach the bases of the hair cells by way of the neural channel.

the organ of Corti actually contain cortilymph with endolymph restricted to the remainder of the scala media. The results of chemical microanalysis have not yet determined if cortilymph is a fluid other than perilymph, but it seems fairly certain that the hair cells are not bathed by endolymph. The upper surface of each inner hair cell consists of a plasma membrane below which is a cuticle into which the bases of the stereocilia are rooted. In addition to the parallel rows of stereocilia on each cell there is found a single basal body (6).

The upper surface of the outer hair cell is similar except that there are more stereocilia and they are arranged on each cell in the shape of a W. The basal body lies at the bottom of the W. For a number of years it was assumed that each hair cell also had a kinocilium emerging from its basal body, but electron-microscopy has, so far, failed to support this assumption. Apparently, the basal body apparatus in the hair cells of the organ of Corti is excited by movement of the cuticular plate as a result of the microlever action of the stereocilia. The essential characteristics of the inner and outer hair cell are shown in Fig. 3.6.

The hair cells play a critical role in the transduction of acoustic energy into a graded electrical trigger potential which initiates neural impulses in the auditory nerve. We shall return in subsequent chapters to consider further what is known about the role of the hair cells in hearing.

The Auditory Pathways

The acoustic neurology is best considered in four phases: the innervation of the organ of Corti and the projection of nerve fibers to the primary auditory nuclei of the medulla; the connections of these nuclei with other neural centers within the brain stem; the projection on the auditory cortex; and finally, the efferent connections.

INNERVATION OF THE ORGAN OF CORTI

Nervous connections between the organ of Corti and the medulla of the brain stem are made without synapse by bipolar cells which form the *cochlear branch* of the eighth cranial nerve. The cell bodies of these fibers form the *spiral ganglion,* as shown in Fig. 3.7A. In this drawing all the bony structures have been removed so that only the scala media remains. The distal processes of the bipolar cells leave the scala media and lead directly to their cell bodies within the spiral ganglion. Twisted

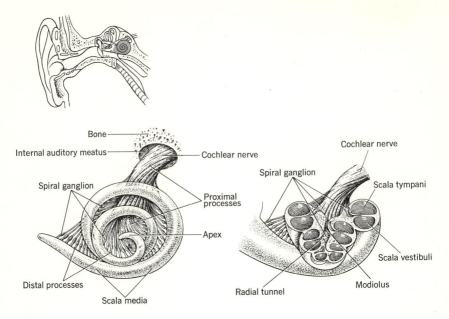

Fig. 3.7 A. The neurology of the right cochlea. The scala vestibuli, scala tympani, and all surrounding bone are removed, thus leaving only the membranous scala media. The distal neural endings connect with the spiral ganglion from which the proximal endings twist upon each other and run medially through the internal auditory meatus to synapse in the medulla.

B. The right cochlea shown in horizontal section. The distal neural endings enter and leave the scala media through small radial tunnels in the spiral lamina. Their cell bodies form the spiral ganglion which lies in an irregular bony cavity, the modiolus, located about the cochlear axis. After Melloni. By permission.

one upon another, their proximal processes project through the *internal auditory meatus* to the medulla where the primary auditory nuclei are found.

The twisted nature of the nerve innervating the organ of Corti probably comes about from embryological development: rudimentary neural connections to the internal ear are present before the cochlea takes its spiral form. Notice that the apical fibers take a central course through the nerve whereas the others are added to the periphery. Those fibers coming from the basal turn of the cochlea make up the outermost segment.

The number of nerve fibers innervating the organ of Corti in a particular region varies according to its location along the longitudinal extent of the organ. The greatest innervation density occurs about the middle of the cochlea.

The drawing in Fig. 3.7B shows a horizontal section of the bony cochlea. Although only isolated portions of the spiral ganglion are visible, the irregular bony cavity surrounding the cochlear nerve is shown and is known as the *modiolus*. From the modiolus numerous small radial tunnels penetrate the spiral lamina, and it is through these tunnels that the distal processes of all auditory bipolar cells find their way to or from the organ of Corti.

The manner in which the distal processes of the bipolar cells make contact with the hair cells of the organ of Corti is shown schematically in Fig. 3.8. Innervation follows a pattern, and it is best considered by dividing the neural endings into three major groups: the radial bundles, the internal spiral fibers, and the external spiral fibers. The inner row of hair cells is innervated by neurons of the *radial bundles* and the *internal spiral*. Distal processes of the radial bundle fibers lie near the bases of the inner hair cells. Generally the terminals are arborized so that several adjacent hair cells are served by the same fiber. Moreover, each hair cell is probably served by the arborized endings of several fibers. The radial bundle fibers exit through tunnels that lie close to the hair cells which they innervate. Fibers of the internal spiral group do not exit immediately, but rather send their processes basally for about one-quarter of a turn before entering one of the radial tunnels. As these fibers run basally below the inner row of hair cells, many of them pick up collaterals. Innervation of the inner hair cells is, therefore, both specific (radial bundle) and diffuse (internal spiral bundle).

The outer hair cells are innervated by the *external spiral* fibers. The fibers in this group are best characterized by their tortuous and circuitous route through the organ of Corti. Beginning just beneath the outer hair cells, the distal processes of these fibers run apically over as much as one third of the length of the basilar membrane before turning to make their exit. Along the way they pick up collaterals from many of the hair cells that they pass. Often they make abrupt swings medially during their apical course so that a particular fiber sometimes serves numerous hair cells in several or all of the parallel rows of outer hair cells. Once turned

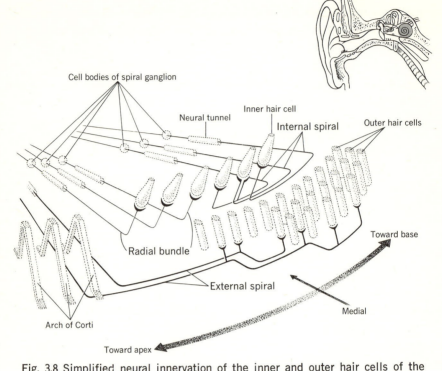

Fig. 3.8 Simplified neural innervation of the inner and outer hair cells of the organ of Corti. The inner and outer hair cells are inclined toward each other, and all other structures have been removed. All neurons first project downward to the basilar membrane and then follow various courses as described in the text.

finally toward the cochlear axis, they pass between adjacent pillars of the arches of Corti, thus transecting Corti's tunnel, after which they join the radial bundles beneath the inner row of hair cells to follow a course with them toward their cell bodies located in the spiral ganglion. External spiral fibers do not pick up collaterals from the bases of the inner hair cells. The innervation of the outer hair cells is much more diffuse and overlapping than is the case for the inner hair cells. Neurons serving the inner hair cells are smaller in diameter than those serving the outer cells.

It is now established that the inner and outer hair cells are served by both afferent and efferent fibers. The neural endings for the afferents (type 1) are small and sparsely granulated, whereas the efferents (type

2) are large, vesiculated, and densely granulated (6). The major differences are depicted in Fig. 3.9, where an outer hair is shown cut away. Along its lateral boundaries are the efferent terminals. Where they ap-

Fig. 3.9 A section of an outer hair cell with its base in the cup of the Deiters cell. Between the two cells are found the afferent and efferent neural connections.

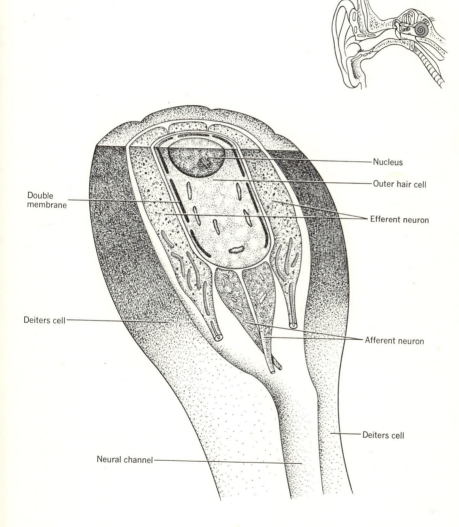

pear, the hair cell has a double membrane inside its plasma membrane. The double membrane is absent at the origin of the afferent fibers along the base of the hair cell.

From the spiral ganglion the proximal processes of the bipolar cells, twisted one upon another as already described, enter the medulla near the inferior border of the pons. Between the cochlea and the medulla the fibers of the cochlear nerve pass through the skull via the internal auditory meatus. Because the internal ear lies close to the brain stem, the cochlear nerve in man is only about 5 mm long.

Upon entering the medulla, each acoustic fiber bifurcates and sends a branch to each of two primary cochlear nuclei. The ventral branch divides again to penetrate the anterior and posterior divisions of the *ventral cochlear nucleus* and the dorsal branch penetrates the *dorsal cochlear nucleus*. Within all of these primary nuclei there is preserved an orderly arrangement of cellular endings which corresponds generally with the locus within the cochlear spiral of the hair cells that they innervate. The branches of fibers serving hair cells in the apical region terminate in the ventral portions of both nuclei, whereas those that serve the hair cells in the middle and upper basal turns end in the dorsal portions of both nuclei. Some violation of this orderly pattern occurs for the fibers serving the lower basal end of the cochlea. These fibers show a more diffuse distribution within the nuclei.

It is here, within the primary auditory nuclei, that the first auditory synapses occur. Some synapses are made with second-order neurons that pass to other acoustic centers of the brain stem. However, many first-order neurons synapse with small neurons contained within the primary nuclei. Thus, the neural network allows complex cellular interaction, much of which is appreciated though not yet fully understood.

SECONDARY ACOUSTIC CENTERS OF THE BRAIN STEM

The projection of auditory neurons from the medulla to the mesencephalon and the thalamus is by way of acoustic pathways in the *lateral lemnisci*. There are, however, three principal tracts within the medulla which are used to gain access to these ascending pathways. Of these, two are dorsal tracts, those of Monakow and Held, and one is a ventral tract, the trapezoid body (see Fig. 3.10).

The *tract of Monakow* is the larger of the two dorsal tracts and origi-

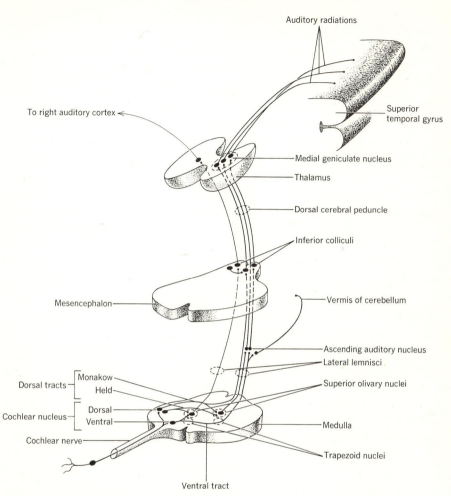

Fig. 3.10 Schematic arrangement of the major ascending auditory pathways.

nates from cells in the dorsal portion of the dorsal cochlear nucleus. These neurons decussate through the floor of the fourth ventricle and reach the contralateral superior olivary nucleus, to which they send off collaterals before coursing upward in the lateral lemniscus. The smaller dorsal *tract of Held* originates in the ventral portion of the dorsal cochlear nucleus and sends fibers to both contralateral and ipsilateral superior olivary nuclei. Here they synapse with fibers which ascend the acoustic pathways of the lateral lemnisci.

The *ventral tract* originates from cells in the ventral cochlear nucleus. These fibers lead to the trapezoid nuclei. Of those fibers which cross the mid-line to the contralateral trapezoid nucleus, some synapse in the nucleus with third-order neurons which ascend the acoustic pathways while others simply send off collaterals to the nucleus and then turn upward to enter the acoustic pathways. This arrangement is similar in that portion of the ventral tract which projects to the ipsilateral trapezoid nucleus. Some fibers in the ventral tract also send off collaterals to the superior olivary nuclei as they pass by to enter the lemnisci.

The acoustic pathways in the lateral lemnisci contain fibers which eventually project via higher-order neurons to the auditory cortex. There are, however, two important collateral pathways. One of these involves auditory projections to the vermis of the *cerebellum* where coordination of impulses with those from other sense modalities occurs. *(17)*. The second collateral route is more diffuse and involves the reticular formation of the brain stem. Most of the ascending fibers have collateral processes which penetrate this formation.

The majority of axonal processes of the fibers leading from the lower acoustic centers synapse in the *inferior colliculi*. The others send off collaterals to the colliculi and synapse in the *medial geniculate bodies* of the thalamus. Some fibers that failed to decussate in the medulla do so at the collicular level where the cross-connections are complex and sometimes involve visual centers in the superior colliculi as well as the auditory centers of the inferior structures. No decussation occurs at the level of the geniculate bodies of the thalamus, and all auditory fibers make synapse there regardless of the locus of their origin, be it the inferior colliculus or the lower centers. From the medial geniculate bodies impulses are transmitted to the auditory cortex by way of the *auditory radiations*.

The specific functions of many of the auditory centers within the brain stem are unknown. Because the superior olivary nuclei are intimately connected with motor centers, it is believed that they are important in mediating certain eye and head movements in response to sound. The inferior colliculi may also function as centers for auditory reflexes.

PROJECTION ON THE AUDITORY CORTEX

In each cerebral hemisphere the fibers comprising the auditory radiations originate in the medial geniculate body and project to the *superior temporal gyrus* by way of the ventral portion of the internal capsule. In man the auditory cortex lies partly within the Sylvian fissure and it probably has two major divisions, auditory areas I and II. It should be mentioned that most of our knowledge about human acoustic neurology at the level of the cortex comes to us from isolated clinical cases and from extensions of data from experimental investigations on animals. It has been established in the cat, dog, and monkey that there are at least two auditory areas. Moreover, each area seems to be served by a relatively independent projection system, each of which arises from different cellular layers of the geniculate body (*15, 20*). The human auditory cortex is probably similar.

Each ear projects bilaterally with the contralateral ear favored slightly. The final pathway through the internal capsule contains fibers which are at least of the fourth-order. There is evidence to indicate that different areas within the auditory cortex receive impulses originating from selected regions along the basilar membrane, with the spatial order reversed in auditory area II (*18, 19, 31*). This matter is considered in detail later in the book when electrophysiological data are discussed.

THE CENTRIFUGAL AUDITORY SYSTEM

The descending pathways follow a course very similar to the ascending ones, and although their presence has been known for a number of years the manner in which they function in hearing is still not entirely clear. What is known of their functional significance will be considered in the next chapter.

The centrifugal fibers originate in the auditory areas of the cortex, particularly in the insular region, and descend to the medial geniculate body, the inferior colliculus, the dorsal nucleus of the lateral lemniscus, and the superior olivary nucleus. From the latter nucleus there arises the *olivocochlear bundle* which decussates through the floor of the fourth ventricle and follows the reverse course of the first-order fibers of the cochlear nerve. The efferent dendrites are in intimate relationship with other cells of the olivary nucleus and trapezoid body, both of which function in the efferent system. The olivocochlear bundle, although mainly contralateral in origin, does contain some ipsilateral fibers. The axonal processes enter the cochlea and send branches to the bases of the hair cells of the organ of Corti. The number of efferent (type 2) endings on the hair cells suggests that there may be additional efferent tracts since the olivocochlear bundle is not believed to be of sufficient size to account for all of the type 2 fiber endings that have been found in the organ of Corti (*14*).

References

1. Békésy, G. von. Zur Physik des Mittelohres und über das Hören bei fehlerhaftem Trommelfell, *Akust. Zeits.*, 1936, *1*, 13-23.
2. Békésy, G. von. Ueber die Messung der Schwingungsamplitude der Gehörknöchelchen mittels einer kapazitiven Sonde, *Akust. Zeits.*, 1941, *6*, 1-16.
3. Bornschein, H., and F. Krejci. Bioelektrische Funktionsanalyse der Intraauralmuskulatur, *Mon. f. Ohrenheilk. Laryngo-Rhinol.* (Vienna), 1952, *86*, 221-229.
4. Dahmann, H. Zur Physiologie des Hörens; experimentelle Untersuchungen über die Mechanik der Gehörknöchelchenkette, sowie über deren Verhalten auf Ton und Luftdruck, *Zeits. f. Hals-Nasen-Ohrenheilk.*, 1929, *24*, 462-497.
5. Engström, H. Electron micrographic studies of the receptor cells of the organ of Corti, in *Neural Mechanisms of the Auditory and Vestibular Systems*, G. L. Rassmussen and W. F. Windle (Eds.), Springfield, Ill.: C. C. Thomas, 1960.
6. Engström, H., H. W. Ades, and J. E. Hawkins. Cellular pattern, nerve structures, and fluid spaces of the organ of Corti, in *Contributions to Sensory Physiology*, W. D. Neff (Ed.), Vol. 1. New York: Academic Press, 1965.
7. Hammerschlag, V. Ueber den Tensorreflex, *Arch. f. Ohrenheilk.*, 1899, *46*, 1-13.
8. Hammerschlag, V. Ueber die Reflexbewegung des Musculus tensor tympani und ihre centralen Bahnen, *Arch. f. Ohrenheilk.*, 1899, *47*, 251-275.
9. Helmholtz, H. L. F. von. *Die Lehre von den Tonempfindungen als physiologische Grundlage für die Theorie der Musik.* Braunschweig: Viewig u. Sohn, 1863.
10. Kato, T. Zur Physiologie der Binnenmuskeln des Ohres, *Pflüg. Arch. ges. Physiol.*, 1913, *150*, 569-625.
11. Kobrak, H. Zur Physiologie der Binnenmuskeln des Ohres, *Passow-Schaefer's Beitr. zur. Anat. Physiol. des Ohres.*, 1930, *28*, 138-160.
12. Perlman, H. B., and T. J. Case. Latent period of the crossed stapedius reflex in man, *Ann. Otol. Rhinol. Laryngol.*, 1939, *48*, 663-675.
13. Rahm, W. E., Jr., W. F. Strother, G. Lucchina, and W. L. Gulick. The

effects of air pressure on the ear, *Ann. Otol. Rhinol. Laryngol.,* 1958, *67,* 170-177.

14. Rasmussen, G. L. Further observations of the efferent cochlear bundle, *J. Comp. Neurol.,* 1953, *99,* 61-74.

15. Rose, J. E., and C. N. Woolsey. Cortical connections and functional organization of the thalamic auditory system of the cat, in *Biological and Biochemical Bases of Behavior,* H. F. Harlow and C. N. Woolsey (Eds.), Madison: University of Wisconsin Press, 1958.

16. Shearer, W. M. Speech: behavior of middle ear muscles during stuttering, *Science,* 1966, *152,* 1280.

17. Snider, R., and J. Stowell. Receiving areas of the tactile, auditory, and visual systems in the cerebellum, *J. Neurophysiol.,* 1944, *7,* 331-357.

18. Tunturi, A. R. Audio-frequency localization in acoustic cortex of dog, *Amer. J. Physiol.,* 1944, *141,* 397-403.

19. Tunturi, A. R. Further afferent connections to the acoustic cortex of the dog, *Amer. J. Physiol.,* 1945, *144,* 389-394.

20. Waller, W. H. Thalamic degeneration induced by temporal lesions in the cat, *J. Anat.* (London), 1939, *74,* 528-536.

21. Wever, E. G., and C. W. Bray. The tensor tympani muscle and its relation to sound conduction, *Ann. Otol. Rhinol. Laryngol.,* 1936, *46,* 947-961.

22. Wever, E. G., and C. W. Bray. Distortion in the ear as shown by the electrical responses of the cochlea, *J. Acoust. Soc. Amer.,* 1938, *9,* 227-233.

23. Wever, E. G., and C. W. Bray. The locus of distortion in the ear, *J. Acoust. Soc. Amer.,* 1940, *11,* 427-433.

24. Wever, E. G., and C. W. Bray. The stapedius muscle in relation to sound conduction, *J. Exper. Psychol.,* 1942, *31,* 35-43.

25. Wever, E. G., C. W. Bray, and M. Lawrence. The effects of pressure in the middle ear, *J. Exper. Psychol.,* 1942, *30,* 40-52.

26. Wever, E. G., and M. Lawrence. *Physiological Acoustics,* Princeton, N. J.: Princeton University Press, 1954.

27. Wever, E. G., M. Lawrence, and K. R. Smith. The middle ear in sound conduction, *Arch. Otolaryngol.,* 1948, *48,* 19-35.

28. Wever, E. G., M. Lawrence, and K. R. Smith. The effects of negative air pressure in the middle ear, *Ann. Otol. Rhinol. Laryngol.,* 1948, *57,* 418-428.

29. Wever, E. G., and J. A. Vernon. The control of sound transmission by the middle ear muscles, *Ann. Otol. Rhinol. Laryngol.,* 1956, *65,* 5-14.

30. Wiggers, H. C. The functions of the intra-aural muscles, *Amer. J. Physiol.,* 1937, *120,* 771-780.

31. Woolsey, C. N., and E. M. Walzl. Topical projection of nerve fibers from local regions of the cochlea to the cerebral cortex of the cat. *Bull. Johns Hopkins Hosp.,* 1942, *71,* 315-344.

4

Electrophysiology of the Auditory System

Investigations of bio-electrical potentials have resulted in significant advances in our understanding of two old problems: namely, the nature of cochlear action as a trigger for the auditory nerve, and the manner in which the various parameters of acoustic stimuli are coded by the auditory nervous system. Only recently have investigators realized the importance of complex stimuli and begun to study them seriously in the laboratory. This change is due to a growing sophistication in experimental methodology and to a realization that a sensory system does not necessarily encode only those first-order parameters of stimulus energy which have been for so long the sole matters of study. There is, after all, a fundamental difference between a pure tone and the honk of a horn. In short, auditory systems are not simply for sensing sound: they are for hearing, and this implies utility as an organism behaves purposefully in its normal environment.

With this caution in mind, let us turn to examine electrophysiological evidence concerning the relationship of structure and function in the auditory system. The matter is best considered in four stages: the electrical potentials of the cochlea; the electrical responses of the cochlear nerve and auditory nuclei of the brain stem; the electrical activity of the auditory cortex; and finally, centrifugal inhibition.

Electrophysiology of the Cochlea

Two specific problems arise when electrical potentials are recorded from the cochlea. The first is the specification of the particular structure which gives rise to the potential being recorded, and the second is the identification of the source of its energy. Although these problems always exist in electrophysiology, the first is especially troublesome in connection with cochlear activity because of the presence of electrically conducting fluids which surround the tissues that generate the various potentials. Specification of a particular potential's origin in the cochlea is complicated further because of complex layers of insulating tissue. The source of energy for the electrical activity of the cochlea is not understood very well, but it is safe to say that it depends upon oxygen transport through endolymph from the *stria vascularis* to the hair cells. Békésy (*4*) has shown the cochlea to be more than a simple transducer by his calculation that the mechanical energy of sound cannot account for all the electrical energy present.

There are two general kinds of potentials detectable within the cochlea, not including action potentials. The first kind includes dc resting potentials which occur in the absence of acoustic stimulation. The second kind is the *trigger potential* which occurs only during acoustic stimulation.

RESTING POTENTIALS

There are two resting polarizations of possible significance to cochlear action. The first is an intracellular potential, not unlike that found very generally in physiology. The hair cells of the organ of Corti have interiors which are negative (20 to 70 mV) relative to the surrounding fluid by which they are bathed. As mentioned previously, we are not certain whether the fluid is endolymph or cortilymph. The second resting potential, the *endocochlear* potential, refers to the fact that the endolymph of the scala media is positive (50 to 80 mV) relative to the perilymph of the two surrounding canals.

Both of these dc potentials are believed to have oxidative metabolism as a primary factor in their generation. The proposal that the endocochlear polarization reflects the differences in sodium and potassium ion concentration between endolymph and perilymph is almost certainly wrong. The same fluids are found in the non-auditory labyrinth and yet no similar polarization has been detected. Indeed, the endocochlear potential may be unique since the *stria vascularis* appears essential to it.

The precise role of the dc polarizations is not at all clear, but they no doubt serve generally as an energy pool for cochlear action even though the trigger potential can be detected in their absence over restricted courses of time.

TRIGGER POTENTIAL

The neural trigger is the *cochlear potential* (CP). The CP follows the wave form of the acoustic input while having a magnitude proportional to the intensity of the stimulus. In the higher animals, most particularly the mammals, a *summation potential* (SP) also has been observed, but it is now believed that the SP plays no role in triggering the nerve. This latter potential is generally recorded as a negative dc potential (relative to perilymph), and it may be produced by the inner hair cells of the organ of Corti (6) or some other cells.

Cochlear Potential. In 1930 Wever and Bray (48) were astonished to find that the amplified signals from the cochlear nerve of a cat were intelligible as speech when one experimenter spoke into the cat's ear. After additional study of this phenomenon by Wever and Bray, and later by others, it became apparent that the signal from the nerve included much more than nervous action potentials. Indeed, the major component was a faithful transduction of sound energy which they called the cochlear potential. The discovery of the CP, sometimes called the *Wever-Bray* effect, has been of immense value in studies of physiological acoustics, as we shall see. While Stevens and Davis (40) argued that the CP was an epiphenomenon and a simple microphonic, Wever has maintained that the CP is a biological trigger potential. Wever's early interpretation now is widely accepted, and Davis has come to place greater significance on the role of the CP in hearing than he once did (5, 6).

The CP arises from the hair cells of the organ of Corti when they undergo mechanical bending. The site of origin has been determined by showing that the degeneration of the auditory nerve has no effect on the CP, that the CP is reduced in proportion to hair cell damage, and that in certain animals without organs of Corti the potential is wanting (47).

Békésy (*1, 2*) has shown that bending of the outer hair cells in a radial direction (perpendicular to the longitudinal axis) is most efficient in generating the CP. The magnitude of the CP is directly and linearly related to the intensity of stimulation, and it demonstrates an incredibly faithful transduction of wave form. Not only does a sinusoidal pressure wave give rise to a sinusoidal electrical potential, but a complex pressure wave is also reflected in the potential, at least within the limits described later (see pp. 62-68). Apparently the ear operates somewhat like a microphone, a fact which explains the initial observations of Wever and Bray.

Comparison of CP and Nerve Impulse. There are marked differences between the trigger and neural responses. First, the CP has no absolute threshold. Its magnitude remains a linear function of intensity down to a level limited by the apparatus used to record it. The lower measurable limit has been extended downward to about 0.0001 μV. By contrast, neurons have thresholds. Second, the trigger potential is local whereas the nerve impulse is propagated. Third, the trigger potential is graded and does not follow the all-or-none law of neural behavior. Fourth, the CP does not show fatigue, whereas neurons do. Finally, neural responses are affected earlier by the course of hypothermia and anoxia.

COCHLEAR MECHANICS AND ELECTRICAL ACTIVITY

Movement of the stapes produces pressure changes in the cochlear fluids which displace the basilar membrane and thus produce mechanical bending of the hair cells of the organ of Corti. The nature of the mechanical stimulation of the hair cells is extremely complex, but the essentials are depicted in Figs. 4.1, 4.2, and 4.3.

In Fig. 4.1 the vestibule is shown cut away. Inward movement of the stapes produces a pressure wave which travels from the vestibule toward the apex while displacing the basilar membrane downward, and the pressure finds relief at the round window membrane. In Fig. 4.2 the displaced basilar membrane is shown, but for graphic clarity only half the width of the membrane is included. Displacement along the longitudinal axis (base-apex) is less along p than q because it is nearer radially to the locus of suspension. This will be important when we consider the inner and outer hair cells. There is also displacement on the radial axis, r. The

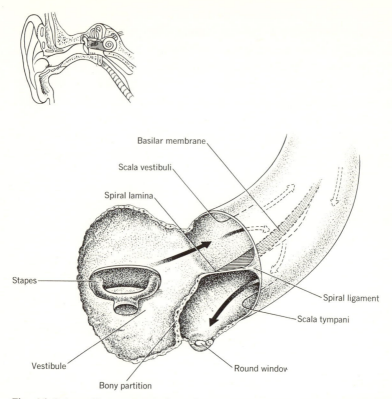

Fig. 4.1 Schematic representation of cochlea with the vestibule cut away. Inward movement of the stapes leads to outward movement of the round window. The arrows show the direction of pressure changes with their consequent displacement of the basilar membrane. When the stapes moves outward, pressure gradients and basilar membrane displacement are reversed.

consequences of these displacements for the motion of the arches of Corti is critical to our understanding of the origin of the trigger potential.

Since the pillars which form the arches of Corti are not articulated at their vertexes, the arches are believed to move as a whole. In Fig. 4.3A the solid and dashed lines indicate basilar membrane displacement from the null at the longitudinal axes p and q, respectively. Below is shown the longitudinal movement of the vertex of one arch at the locus y. At a null position the arch is vertical. The line p' is perpendicular to the membrane on axis p at the base of the inner pillar, and q' is perpendicular to the membrane on axis q at the base of the outer pillar. The resultant displacement of the vertex apically is through angle ϕ. Movement of the arch in a transverse plane is shown in part B of the same figure.

With the bases of the hair cells in the Deiters cups and their cilia in contact with the tectorial membrane above, the longitudinal and radial forces produced by arch displacement operate on both the inner and outer hair cells. The supporting tissue surrounding the inner hair cells conveys longitudinal displacement to the hairs more effectively than is the case for the less densely supported outer hair cells. Radial force, how-

Fig. 4.2 A longitudinal and transverse cross section of the basilar membrane during stimulation. For clarity only half the membrane is shown.

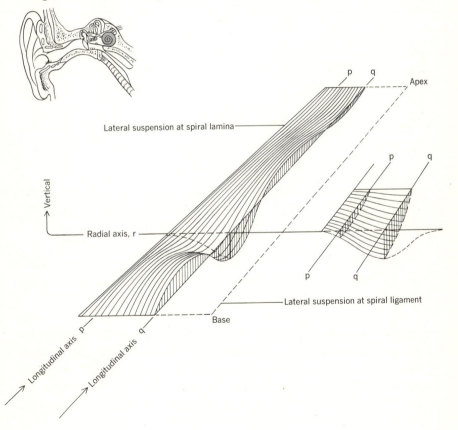

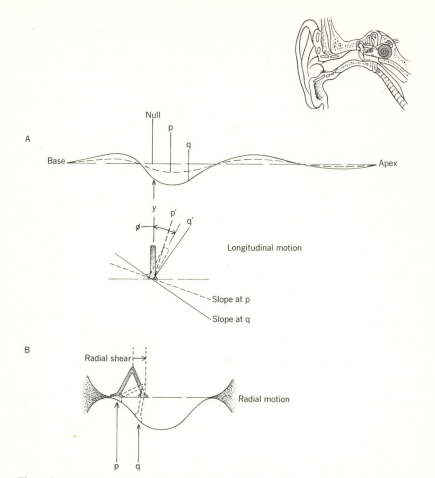

Fig. 4.3 A. Longitudinal motion of arch of Corti at locus **y**. See text for explanation.
B. Radial motion of arch of Corti at locus **y**. See text for explanation.

ever, is more efficient for the outer hair cells because of the shearing motion produced by the interaction of the fulcrums of the arches and the tectorial membrane. This matter is clarified schematically in Fig. 4.4. When the fluid pressure displaces the organ of Corti downward, the movement of the vertex of the arch provides a shearing force against the outer hair cells. Upward movement, however, does not shear the inner

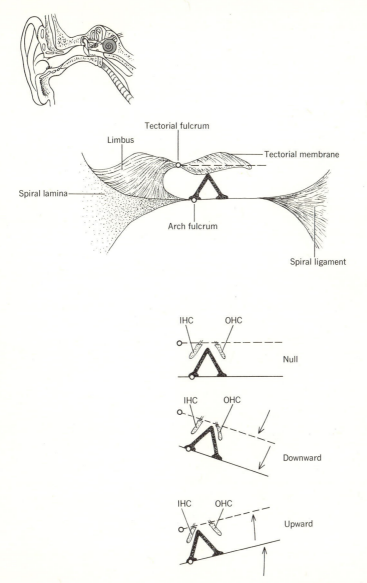

Fig. 4.4 Radial motion of the vertex of the arch of Corti produces a shearing force which bends the outer hair cells when the basilar membrane moves downward. Upward movement also is believed to bend the outer hair cells, probably as a consequence of the movement of the supporting cells which comprise their lateral buttress.

hair cells very much because of the location of the fulcrum of the arch.

Both the inner and outer hair cells undergo mechanical bending along longitudinal and radial axes, but the favored direction differs between them. Békésy (4) has shown that vertical distortion (see Fig. 4.2) does not influence the CP, and so we may conclude that it is the *shearing* force that is necessary to the transduction of mechanical to electrical energy.

The analysis of cochlear mechanics offered here has been simplified greatly to illustrate the main effects. It should be noted, however, that there are two important factors which serve to complicate the matter rather substantially. First, the various cellular structures of the organ of Corti are coupled in such a way as to prohibit simple independent movement of any particular one (3, 54). Second, the elasticity of the basilar membrane increases one-hundredfold from base to apex (1), and this fact clearly complicates the nature of cochlear mechanics.

Role of the Cilia. We have previously described the cilia protruding from the upper surfaces of the hair cells (Chapter 3). Recall that the geometrical arrangement of the cilia is different on inner and outer hair cells. In both kinds of cell they serve as microlevers to impart by their own movement a graded displacement of the cuticular plate from which they arise. The upper portions of the cilia actually are embedded in the gelatinous undersurface of the tectorial membrane, and they are moved by it during acoustic stimulation. Although the arrangement of cilia varies somewhat in various regions of the cochlea, the cilia always comprise a directional transducer. Unlike the hairs of the vestibular organ which have one kinocilium and many stereocilia, there is no evidence of kinocilia in the hair cells of the cochlea (14, 22). This is an important fact for an understanding of cochlear mechanics because the absence of a kinocilium is responsible for the directional aspects of the transduction process. A schematic analysis of cochlear transduction as proposed by Hawkins (22) is shown in Fig. 4.5. The stereocilia in contact with the tectorial membrane move the cuticular plate which, in turn, probably effects an ion exchange through the plasma membrane of the basal body. The reticular lamina serves as a boundary between the endolymph of the *scala media* and the cortilymph surrounding the hair cells. The plasma membrane therefore may be critical to an ion exchange between the

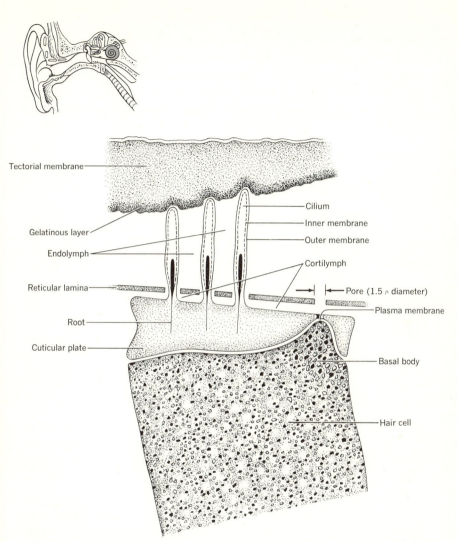

Fig. 4.5 Cross section of an outer hair cell showing relation of the cilia to the tectorial membrane and cuticular plate. Microlever action of the cilia moves cuticular plate alternately toward and away from the basal body.

potassium-rich endolymph and intracellular contents. This appears especially likely inasmuch as the basal body contains a large number of mitochondria, Golgi membranes, and granules. Since knowledge of the chemoelectrical events of the transduction is wanting, the conception is necessarily speculative. In detailed studies of the relationship between hair cell structure and function there is one important matter which commonly goes unrecognized: namely, the effective microlever action of the stereocilia is as readily accomplished by hair cell movement as by tectorial movement. The critical factor is that *relative* motion occur between them.

PROBLEMS OF DISTORTION

Ideally a transducer of acoustic energy should not use up energy or change the character of the vibrations which impinge upon it. Yet these requirements are never met because every transducer imposes its own charactristics upon the energy transformation. The ear is no exception. The mass, friction, and elasticity of the structures of the ear combine to produce distortions of phase, frequency, and amplitude. Knowledge of the nature of these distortions is of major importance to an understanding of hearing because coding in the cochlear nerve is determined by the trigger potential and it reflects all the distorting factors which precede its generation.

Wever and his colleagues have made extensive studies of distortion by comparing the CP with the measurable aspects of the action of earlier processes (*53*). In turn, we shall consider each of the major kinds of distortion. It will become apparent that they are interrelated.

Phase Distortion. If the ear were a perfect transducer, then the phase of the trigger should match that of a tonal stimulus at the tympanic membrane. Failure of the receptor to meet this requirement constitutes phase distortion. By comparing the phase of the CP with the phase of the aerial stimulus, Wever and Lawrence (*51, 52*) found that in the cat the CP lagged between 0° and 40° for tones from 100 to 5000∿. At higher frequencies the phase lag was more varied, but generally it increased with frequency to beyond 180° at the highest frequency studied. These data taken together with the study of relationships in phase between the CP and the stapedial footplate with the ossicular chain removed suggest that phase distortion occurs from processes within the cochlea and within the middle ear. The important point is that phase distortion is not constant: it depends upon the frequency of the stimulating tone. We shall have more to say about this when we consider the localization of sounds in space.

Frequency Distortion. Frequency distortion is more complex than phase distortion because its effects are often measured in terms of amplitude. The ear transduces acoustic energy more efficiently at some frequencies than at others. Consequently, a complex wave is altered in composition by the transmission and transduction processes so that the relative magnitudes of the components as reflected in the CP depart from their original values. This departure constitutes frequency distortion.

It is convenient to measure frequency distortion by determining the sound pressure required at each of many frequencies to produce a CP of constant magnitude. Such a relationship for the cat is shown in the upper portion of Fig. 4.6, where an arbitrary CP magnitude of 30 μV was selected as a criterion. If there were no frequency distortion, then the function would appear as a straight line with a slope of zero. The obtained function indicates that the ear handles the middle frequencies more successfully than it does the extremes.

There is another way to conceptualize frequency distortion. In the lower portion of Fig. 4.6 five intensity functions are shown where the CP in microvolts is given as a function of sound pressure in decibels. Note that shifts of these functions to the right signify a reduction in the efficiency with which the hair cells convert acoustic energy into a graded electrical trigger (CP). A 30 μV response to a 3000$\sim$ tone occurred with an intensity of -20 db (re: 1 dyne/cm^2), whereas it was necessary to increase intensity to obtain an identical response magnitude to frequencies above and below 3000$\sim$. When viewed in this way it is clear that frequency distortion is evident throughout the intensity range and that any CP magnitude would serve equally well as a criterion value.

Amplitude Distortion. Amplitude distortion arises from the non-linear relationship between the response of the ear and sound acting upon it. Although the CP shows a remarkably faithful transduction over extensive ranges of intensity, linearity fails at the higher intensities. This may be seen in all the intensity functions shown in the lower portion of Fig. 4.6. For example, consider the function for a 3000$\sim$ tone. The CP rises linearly with sound pressure up to a limit of about 300 μV. Thereafter it departs from linearity to become negatively accelerated. In general, intensity functions reach a final asymptote beyond which further increases in intensity result in a reduced CP, probably as a consequence of injury

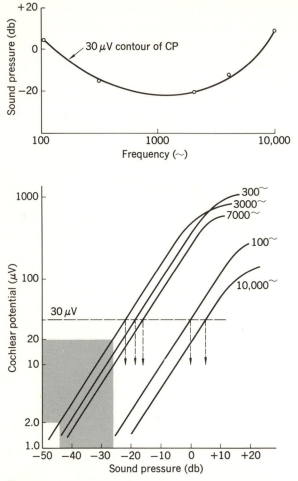

Fig. 4.6 The upper graph depicts frequency distortion by showing the sound pressure in decibels (re: 1 dyne/cm²) required to generate a CP of constant magnitude (30 μv) as a function of frequency. The lower graph shows a series of intensity functions where the CP in microvolts is plotted against sound pressure in decibels (re: 1 dyne/cm²) for each of five frequencies. This is another way in which frequency distortion can be represented. Data from the cat.

inflicted to the hair cells by their violent motion. The range of linearity varies with frequency and is increasingly restricted as frequency rises. Note that within the range of linearity the slope of intensity functions approximates 1.0. In other words, a tenfold increase in sound pressure

(20 db) results in a tenfold increase in the CP (20 db). This is illustrated for the 3000∿ function by the shaded portion of the graph in Fig. 4.6.

We have already suggested that the destruction of hair cells accounts for the reduction in the magnitude of the CP when intensity exceeds that level at which the asymptote is reached. Under such circumstances the ear may be said to be *overloaded,* and injury thus sustained is permanent. However, the initial departure from linearity, up to asymptote, is not attributable to hair cell damage, but rather to two other factors.

The first of these is a diversion of energy into *aural* harmonics. Wever and Bray (*50*) stimulated the cat's ear with a 1000∿ tone especially filtered to ensure its purity, and then successively measured all components present in the resulting CP by means of a wave analyzer used as a selective voltmeter. As expected, they found the prominent component of the CP to have a frequency of 1000∿, but they were also able to measure components of other frequencies, some as high in frequency as the 16th harmonic. Representative data are shown in Fig. 4.7.

Clearly, cochlear transduction is complex because the CP has harmonics, none of which are in the stimulus. The numbers on the curves indicate order in the harmonic series. Each harmonic, like the fundamental, has a linear portion, thus showing itself to be a power function. The slopes tend to increase with the harmonic series whereas their magnitudes decrease. Aural harmonics become prominent only at the higher intensities, and the question arises as to whether they alone account for the departure from linearity of the intensity function for the stimulating pure tone.

To answer this question Wever and Bray, using the root-mean-square method, summed the voltages of all harmonics present at each of several sampled intensities and then added these sums to the function for the fundamental tone at the same intensities. Although linearity was approached, it was not restored by the addition of energy which had been diverted into aural harmonics. This suggests that a second factor is involved in amplitude distortion, but before we leave the matter of aural harmonics we should say a word about the site of their generation. By studying them with the ear intact and with the middle ear excluded, Wever and Lawrence (*53*) showed that they arise within the cochlea.

The second factor which accounts for amplitude distortion is a failure of the cuticular rods of the Deiters cells to remain rigid under the forces

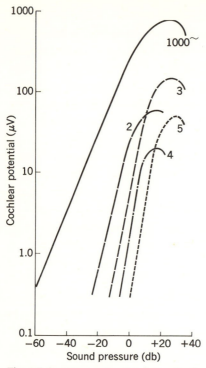

Fig. 4.7 Cochlear potential intensity function for a 1000∿ pure tone as a function of sound pressure in decibels (re: 1 dyne/cm²), showing the presence of overtones in the CP not present in the stimulus. See text for explanation. After Wever and Lawrence (**53**, p. 138). After Wever and Lawrence. By permission.

acting upon them during intense stimulation. Their own bending would reduce the distortion of the hair cells and thus contribute to non-linearity of the transduction process.

Amplitude Distortion with Multiple Tones. There is another form of amplitude distortion which occurs when two or more pure tones stimulate the ear simultaneously, and it is known as *interference*. In its simplest form it appears as a reduction in the CP to one tone on the presentation of another. Interference does not occur when the second, or interfering, tone is of low intensity, but at moderate or high intensities it can reduce the magnitude of the CP to the first tone by as much as 30 db. Although interference can occur between any pair of tones of whatever frequency, it is greater when the tone interfered with is within the frequency range to which the ear is most sensitive: namely, the middle frequency range. Somewhat like the diversion of energy into aural harmonics, interference can be accounted for by the occurrence of combination tones of which there are two kinds, *summation tones* and *difference tones*. If the two stimulating tones are designated as *h* (higher frequency) and *l* (lower frequency), then the first-order combination tones are $(h+l)$ and $(h-l)$. The former is the summation tone and the latter is the difference tone. For example, simultaneous stimulation with 2800∿

Fig. 4.8 Summary of the kinds of distortion produced by the ear. On the left are the stimuli and on the right are the resultant cochlear potentials.

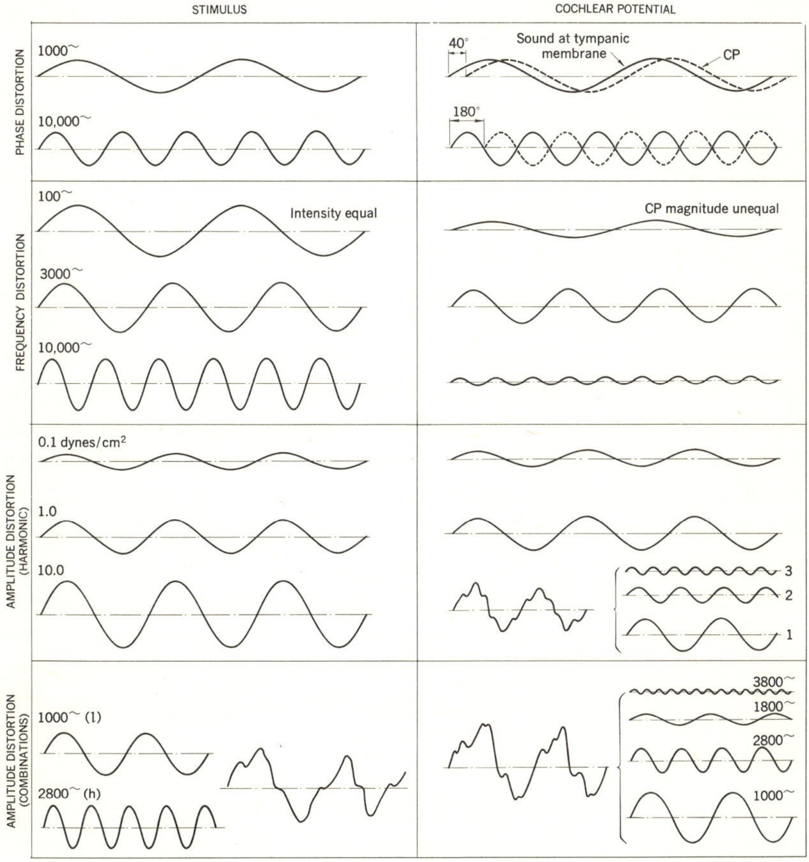

(h) and 1000$\backsim$ (l) tones would give rise to a CP with components of 2800$\backsim$ and 1000$\backsim$ as well as 3800$\backsim$ ($h+l$) and 1800$\backsim$ ($h-l$). With very high intensities one can isolate second-order combination tones ($h+2l$), ($2h+l$), ($h-2l$), and ($2h-l$).

In Fig. 4.8 the major forms of distortion which have been discussed are summarized. The left column shows the acoustic stimulus and the right column shows the cochlear potential. At the lower frequencies the CP lags only slightly in phase behind the stimulus, whereas at high frequencies it lags appreciably. Frequency distortion is illustrated by the fact that the three frequencies 100, 3000, and 10,000$\backsim$, all of equal intensity, do not produce potentials of equal magnitude. The middle frequency is handled more efficiently. Amplitude distortion in the form of a diversion of energy into aural harmonics is illustrated at high intensity (10 dynes/cm^2) by a CP of complex waveform analyzed into the fundamental and the first two harmonics. Finally, combination tones are illustrated. Here a complex stimulus (1000$\backsim$ and 2800$\backsim$ together) gives rise to a very complex potential analyzed into four frequencies: namely, the two fundamentals of 1000$\backsim$ and 2800$\backsim$, a first-order difference tone ($h-l$) of 1800$\backsim$ and a first-order summation tone ($h+l$) of 3800$\backsim$.

Electrical Activity of the Auditory Nerve and Nuclei

Although the last few decades have witnessed the appearance of several hypotheses as to how the neurons of the cochlear nerve are excited, the overwhelming evidence now is that the electrical trigger (CP) acts directly upon the unmyelinated dendrites of the afferent neurons found at the sides and bases of the hair cells.

FIRST-ORDER NEURONS

There are two general approaches that have been taken in investigations of the cochlear branch of the eighth cranial nerve. One approach uses gross recording electrodes to give information on the compound nerve potential, whereas the second uses microelectrodes to study the behavior of single units. We shall treat each in turn.

Compound Recordings. From an electrode placed on the round window membrane or from one wrapped around the cochlear nerve between its

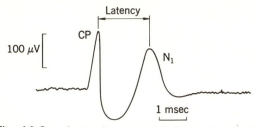

Fig. 4.9 Sample tracing recorded from the round window membrane of the guinea pig. The stimulus was an acoustic click. The CP appears first, followed by the compound action potential N_1.

exit from the internal meatus and its entrance into the medulla, it is possible to record simultaneously both the trigger potential and the compound action potential. The former placement favors the trigger whereas the latter favors the action potential. A typical recording from some of our experiments is shown in Fig. 4.9. Here the stimulus was an acoustic click delivered to the tympanic membrane of a guinea pig. Note that the CP appears first, followed by the compound action potential. The low magnitude of the action potential, hereafter called N_1 to denote a nerve response from first-order neurons, is due to the fact that the recording electrode rested on the round window membrane, thus being relatively distant from the nerve.

In a study of the relationship between the intensity of an auditory click and the electrical responses of the cochlea and auditory nerve, Gulick, Herrmann, and Mackey (21) found in the guinea pig that the CP and N_1 responses followed a power function, as shown in Fig. 4.10. In general, the slopes of the functions plotted for individual animals exceeded 1.0, thus providing evidence that the function is actually positively accelerated when plotted directly in voltages. Since with auditory clicks the N_1 magnitude is determined primarily by the number of active neurons, one would expect, given a normal distribution of fiber thresholds, that a linear increase in the CP would give rise first to a positively accelerated N_1 response followed at the higher intensities by negative acceleration. The data plotted in Fig. 4.10 cover only a limited range of 20 db, beginning with threshold values of N_1, but they are consistent with the expectation that the nerve would show positive acceleration near thresh-

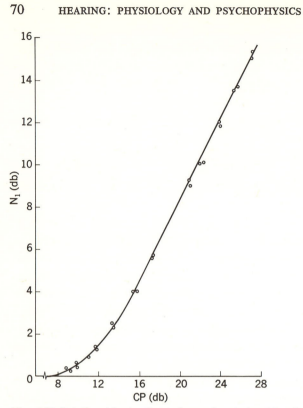

Fig. 4.10 Relationship in the guinea pig of the CP trigger to N_1 magnitude. Stimuli were acoustic clicks. Both CP and N_1 responses are shown in decibels relative to noise level. From Gulick **et al.** (21, p. 63).

old. Data on the effects of high intensity clicks on N_1 show the compound action potential to become negatively accelerated (*37*). The latency of N_1 to acoustic clicks varies from about 2.0 msec at low intensity to 1.2 msec at high intensity (*21, 37*).

Beside the compound nerve potentials elicited by clicks, it is also possible with round window electrode placement to obtain the nerve response to pure tones of low frequency. When thus obtained, N_1 appears as an abrupt irregularity on the rising slope of the CP on every cycle. A sample trace from a guinea pig appears in Fig. 4.11. The stimulus was a 60∿ tone of moderate intensity. As frequency is increased the locus of N_1 is progressively shifted until it appears on the falling slope of the CP.

One can note, therefore, an increasing lag in the appearance of N_1 with reference to the phase of the CP as the frequency of the stimulating tone is increased. However, this relationship does not necessarily produce a change in N_1 latency with reference to stimulus *onset* because the period of the wave becomes shorter as frequency increases. The synchrony noted here for low frequencies between discharge of the auditory nerve and stimulus frequency does not extend over the entire auditory range, and this fact represents a complication for the coding of pitch.

Inasmuch as intense pure tones lead to the generation of aural harmonics, the question arises as to whether the harmonic components of the CP also can serve to trigger the cochlear nerve. Wever (*47*, p. 331) reports that they can. When a 60∿ tone at 10 dynes/cm² was used to stimulate the ear of a guinea pig, there appeared two nerve discharges in each cycle, a large one superimposed on the peak of the CP, and a smaller one superimposed on its trough. The trough of the CP shown in Fig. 4.11 actually corresponds to the peak of the first overtone (120∿). Presumably, had the wave analyzer been tuned to 120∿, the N_1 discharge would have appeared on the peak of the CP. Further, as shown in the figure, N_1 superimposed on the peak should be the sum of the discharges produced by the fundamental (60∿) and the first overtone.

Considering these data, it seems reasonable to accept Wever's conclusion that the aural harmonics do act to trigger first-order neurons. In all likelihood the higher partials would lead to components in the CP of too meager amplitudes to surpass neural thresholds, but that matter remains

Fig. 4.11 Sample tracing recorded from the round window membrane of the guinea pig showing the CP to a 60∿ pure tone on which N_1 is superimposed near the crest. A second N_1 discharge produced by the first harmonic of the CP appears less visibly in the trough. Stimulus intensity was 10 dynes/cm². After Wever (**47**, p. 331). By permission.

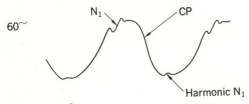

60~

N_1 CP

Harmonic N_1

10 dynes/cm²

to be resolved by experimental study. In any case, the fact that the cochlear nerve has been shown to discharge in a pattern reflecting the effects
of cochlear distortion emphasizes a point already made: the nerve is
coded according to the trigger acting upon it and not by an undistorted
aerial stimulus.

Single-Unit Recordings. Single-unit recordings with microelectrodes give a
very detailed account of the action of first-order neurons, but only when
invariant patterns of neural activity emerge do we come to realize their
significance. Recognition of such patterns is made difficult by the incredible
variety of activity which has been noted thus far in single-unit studies. Our
purpose here will be to present as coherent a statement of the known
classes as possible and to suggest enough of the variety to make clear the
magnitude of the challenge before the electrophysiologist.

Historically, auditory theorists proposed a nervous system which encoded only frequency and intensity. There prevailed a persistent faith
that the coding of complex sounds was by way of *neural addition* involving multiple and parallel neural channels. For example, a broad-band
noise containing frequencies from 1000 to 5000∿ was assumed to be
coded by the simultaneous action of independent channels, each of which
responded to a particular frequency. By far the most profound effect of
recent single-unit work has been to challenge this view. We know now
that there are auditory neurons which by themselves serve as noise detec-
tors. These fibers are unresponsive to pure tones, thereby demonstrating
that the concept of *neural addition* is not necessary. Furthermore, fibers
have been found which are specifically responsive to abrupt transients,
such as clicks. Facts like these have revolutionized our conception of the
auditory system: it has apparently evolved in a manner which makes it
directly sensitive to many complex acoustic signals.

In 1954 Tasaki (*41*) reported that individual fibers of the auditory
nerve of the guinea pig showed a degree of frequency specificity in that
each single-unit studied responded most vigorously to a particular stimulus frequency. When stimulus frequency was raised above the frequency
at which the unit responded most vigorously, it became inactive. Thus, a
critical *cut-off frequency* was established for each unit, and Tasaki found
that the value of the critical cut-off was related to the site of origin of the
single-unit within the cochlea. Fibers arising from the apical end had

low-frequency cut-offs whereas those arising from the basal end had high-frequency cut-offs. Based upon this and other work (*44*), Tasaki concluded that the *critical cut-off frequency* was the neural counterpart of the spatial distribution of the CP within the cochlea. His conclusion is difficult to accept because the loss of neural responsiveness to frequencies slightly higher than the critical cut-off frequency is considerably more abrupt than could be expected on the basis of the CP gradient within the cochlea. Nevertheless, the fact of rudimentary frequency tuning in first-order neurons remains, and it has been found in other animals as well (*26, 28, 42*). Single-unit studies have raised serious difficulties for those who hold the view that frequency is encoded by the rate of neural discharge in single auditory neurons (*40*) or in the nerve as a whole (*49*). The theoretical implications of frequency tuning will be treated fully in the next chapter.

The degree of frequency specificity shown by a given fiber is most easily described by its *response area,* a graphic representation of the combinations of frequency and intensity which are sufficient to the production of action potentials or a modification of the rate of its firing. Hypothetical response areas for each of three first-order neurons are shown in Fig. 4.12.

Fig. 4.12 Hypothetical response areas for three neurons showing the combinations of frequency and intensity sufficient to stimulate them. The precision of tuning falls off with increasing intensity. Type I neurons have asymmetrical response areas whereas Type II have symmetrical ones.

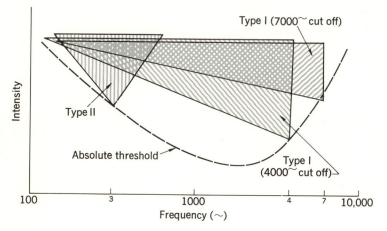

Each fiber has a frequency to which it is most sensitive, but the bandwidth of frequencies to which it responds widens markedly with intensity from a rather precise tuning near threshold to a very broad one at high intensity. Type I fibers are distinguished by two characteristics: they show *best-tuning* to the high frequencies and their response areas are clearly asymmetrical with responsiveness falling off abruptly to frequencies higher than *best-tuned* but only gradually to those lower. Type II fibers also show the *best-tuned* characteristic, but they are tuned to low frequencies and their response areas are more nearly symmetrical. Type II fibers have been studied extensively in the cat and monkey by Katsuki and his colleagues (*26, 27*). He has hypothesized that Type I and II fibers serve the inner and outer hair cells, respectively. Experimental data make it clear that there are many fibers with the same *best-tuned* frequency, but they have different thresholds. The implication is important, for it suggests that fibers are not tuned to frequency alone, but rather *to frequency within some particular intensity range.*

HIGHER-ORDER NEURONS AND NUCLEI

There are several important differences in neural action which distinguish the higher pathways from the auditory nerve. First, a comparison of response areas of second-, third-, and fourth-order neurons shows that the tuned character remains and improves because the decline in sensitivity to frequencies above and below the *best-tuned* frequency becomes increasingly more abrupt. Apparently tuning is sharpened in some way by synaptic processes. Based upon the work of Katsuki (*26, 27*), Tasaki and Davis (*43*), Galambos and Davis (*18*), and Galambos (*16*), the general change in response areas as a function of location within the projection system is illustrated in Fig. 4.13. To assist in localization of the levels cited, Fig. 3.10 may be consulted. For purposes of comparison, these hypothetical response areas are shown as all having the same *best-tuned* frequency and threshold. The point illustrated is the remarkable improvement in tuning.

Second, there is greater variety of response patterns among higher-order units than among those of the first-order. Moushegian, Rupert, and Galambos (*31*), in a study of the cochlear nucleus of the cat, reported some single-units which had more than one response area. Still others were observed to be inhibited from their normal "spontaneous

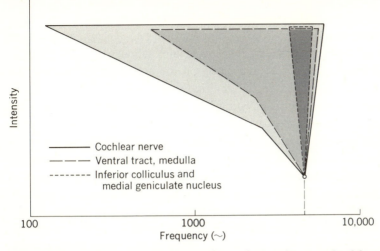

Fig. 4.13 Hypothetical response areas of four single-units at each of four neural levels. For purposes of comparison their thresholds have been equated. Note that tuning improves as the auditory pathway is ascended.

activity" when stimuli of particular frequency-intensity combinations were introduced to the cat's ear. This kind of unit, therefore, had an *inhibitory* rather than an excitatory response area.

Third, these same experimenters also showed that a particular unit excited by a stimulus with a specific frequency-intensity combination could be inhibited during the presence of the excitatory stimulus when a second tone of a particular frequency was introduced. Neural interaction of this sort undoubtedly is responsible for the improved tuning depicted in Fig. 4.13 (*19*).

Fourth, extensive studies of the inferior colliculus show these higher-order cells to be similar in response patterns to other sense modalities in that they demonstrate "on," "off," and "on-off" behavior (*25, 36*).

Auditory Cortex and Tonotopic Organization

Auditory projections from the medial geniculate nuclei of the thalamus terminate primarily in the superior temporal gyri of the cortex (see Fig. 3.10). The complexity of the projection in man is not fully revealed at present, but observations obtained from lower animals suggests that each ear is projected on the cortex in multiple fashion.

In 1942 Woolsey and Walzl (*56*) identified two general cortical areas in the cat which responded to electrical stimulation within the cochlea. One of these areas (A-I) is located on the ectosylvian gyrus and the other (A-II) is located on the anterior and posterior ectosylvian gyrus and on part of the pseudosylvian gyrus. As shown in Fig. 4.14, A-I and A-II are contiguous. Woolsey and Walzl observed that the rostral section of A-I responded most vigorously when electrical stimulation was applied to the basal end of the cochlea while the caudal section responded most vigorously to apical stimulation. The reverse pattern occurred in A-II. These observations, depicted in the figure by the letters *a* (apical) and *b* (basal), suggested that the spatial organization of the basilar membrane might be preserved in the cortical projections. This suggestion gained some support from the work by Tunturi (*45*) who, by employing tonal stimuli, demonstrated tonotopic frequency localization in A-I in the dog. *Tonotopic frequency localization* refers to the spatial contiguity on the cortex of cells maximally responsive to stimuli of slightly different frequency. If tonotopicity in the cortex could be demonstrated unequivocally, then one would have to entertain seriously the role of cortical loca-

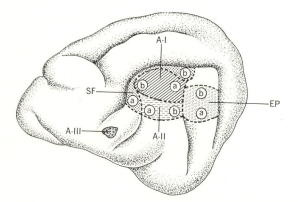

Fig. 4.14 Lateral aspect of the left hemisphere of the cat showing the five auditory areas responsive either to electrical stimulation of first-order neurons within the cochlea or to tonal stimuli. A-I, A-II, EP, and SF are specifically auditory in nature, and each shows selective responsiveness to basal (**b**) and apical (**a**) stimulation. A-III is polysensory.

tion as a means of frequency coding. We shall treat this matter in the next chapter.

Tunturi did not find tonotopicity in A-II, and therefore concluded that it was not a primary auditory area. In a second study, Tunturi (46) described a third area (A-III) responsive to auditory stimulation. More recently two additional auditory areas have been described which show selective responsiveness to basal and apical stimulation (13, 55). One of them is located on the posterior ectosylvian gyrus (EP) and the other is located on the suprasylvian fringe area (SF). These, too, are shown in Fig. 4.14. Auditory cells in the suprasylvian fringe area show "on," "off," and "on-off" behavior similar to that found in the inferior colliculi (27).

The studies just cited suggest that there are five auditory areas in the cortex of the cat and dog. Of these, all but Tunturi's A-III appear to have some spatial representation of the cochlea. A-III now is believed *not* to represent simple auditory projections, but rather to be illustrative of one of many *polysensory receiving areas*. Mickle and Ades (30) have shown that A-III responds to vestibular and somaesthetic as well as to acoustic stimuli. Accordingly, the area is probably fed by relay fibers from a variety of primary projection areas. A second polysensory area responsive to auditory and visual stimuli has been reported in the insular region of the cat by Desmedt and Mechelse (8).

The distinction between primary and secondary cortical areas was at one time considered obvious. Those areas receiving projections from the sensory nuclei of the thalamus were classified as primary whereas those receiving cortico-cortical fibers were classified as secondary. In recent years, however, evidence of multiple projections of specific and general sorts has made such a distinction open to question. On the basis of cyto-architectural characteristics, Rose (34) has proposed that A-I, A-II, EP, and SF are exclusively auditory in nature; yet the fact of basal-apical organization in each of them does not, by itself, give assurance that they are independent of one another. Indeed, there is some evidence to the contrary. Kiang (29) showed a clear functional relationship between A-I and EP, and he concluded that, at the very least, EP receives projections from A-I as well as from the ipsilateral medial geniculate nucleus. By cutting thalamo-cortical fibers, Kiang also established that A-II receives primary projections.

The suprasylvian fringe area of the cortex of the cat has been shown to have an orderly arrangement for frequency by Hind (*23, 24*) and Woolsey (*55*). The frequency of tuned units increased from low to high as the fringe was traversed anteriorly.

We may conclude, therefore, that in the cat and dog there are four cortical areas centrally concerned with hearing, and while each shows tonotopicity they are not fully independent of each other.

TONOTOPICITY

If the auditory cortex shows a spatial organization in parallel with the basilar membrane, as data seem to make plain, then one might profitably ask whether or not the same principle of organization characterizes the entire pathway. That this is not essential is made clear from the following. Recall, for example, that although the cutaneous system is organized spatially at the skin (dermatome) and cortex, the projection pathways in the spinal cord and brain stem ignore both the site of origin and terminal projection in favor of functionally organized tracts. What can be said of the auditory system?

There is very convincing evidence of tonotopic organization at the level of the cochlear nucleus. Rose, Galambos, and Hughes (*35*), employing threshold intensities, found that single-units were arranged in an orderly fashion with reference to their characteristic tuned frequency. However, along a single electrode tract they found occasional abrupt reversals in frequency ordering which led them to conclude that the cochlear nucleus of the cat has three distinct tonotopic representations, one in the dorsal cochlear nucleus, one in the posteroventral nucleus, and one in the anteroventral nucleus (see Fig. 3.10). Their findings agree with what is known from histological studies of the first-order terminations. Rose and his colleagues (*36*) also have shown tonotopic organization at the inferior colliculus where, when moving the electrode in a medial direction, the frequencies were represented from high to low as the external nucleus was traversed and from low to high as the central nucleus was traversed.

Efforts to find similar patterns in the olivary nuclei and trapezoid bodies have met with less impressive success (*20*), but considering the fact that many fibers by-pass these structures on their way to higher centers, failure to obtain clear evidence of frequency ordering is not totally unexpected. Furthermore, the olivary and trapezoid regions are known to have central roles in centrifugal connections and in phase coding, and the nature of coding for these functions might be different.

Based on the work presented here, we may conclude that there is a fairly specific tonotopic representation in the auditory system from the medulla to the cortex and that this functional organization derives from the anatomical specificity of the projection itself. Whether or not the regular order of frequency evident in the tuned units of the cochlear nucleus has a counterpart in the sites of origin along the basilar membrane of the cochlea presently is not established. Generally, it has been assumed that units in the medullary nuclei responsive to low frequencies originate in the apical region of the cochlea whereas high frequency units originate from the basal region. There is, of course, some anatomical evidence that this is so, but the anatomical arrangement is less well ordered than the functions known from electrophysiological studies would indicate (27). We shall return to this matter when we discuss the *place* principle in auditory theory.

Centrifugal Inhibition

It should be recalled from our treatment of the centrifugal pathways in the previous chapter that each cochlea receives efferent fibers by way of the *tract of Rasmussen* (olivocochlear bundle) which originates in the superior olivary complex of the medulla. In the cat there are about 500 efferent fibers to each cochlea, with 80 per cent arising contralaterally to decussate across the floor of the fourth ventricle, where they are joined by those arising ipsilaterally.

Galambos (17) was the first to show that electrical stimulation of the tract of Rasmussen could suppress a click-evoked N_1 action potential. The conditions of suppression depended upon both the strength and rate of shocks to the olivary complex as well as the temporal delay between shock onset and auditory click. Suppression occurred only when a restricted portion of the olivary complex was stimulated and the effect was shown to be independent of the action of the middle ear muscles. The CP from the hair cells appeared unaltered, but the demonstrated inhibition of afferent activity at so peripheral a locus served to raise a series of questions about the functional significance of the centrifugal system for such aspects of hearing as pitch and attention through some selective filtering or focusing device.

Following destruction of one cochlea of the guinea pig, Pfalz (32) was able to demonstrate inhibition in second-order neurons of the cochlear nucleus on the homolateral side by acoustic stimulation of the contralateral ear. Since the cells from which he recorded did not have any afferent input, he concluded that suppression of their spontaneous activity was due to centrifugal fibers. That the pathway from which he recorded was really de-afferented was supported by his experimental method of destruction, by the total absence of any excitatory activity from sound stimulation, and by the long latency of the inhibiting effect. Latencies varied from 11 to 500 msec.

If one considered the combinations of frequency and intensity of the acoustic stimulus which produce inhibition of spontaneous firing in second-order cells, then one would have a *response area of centrifugal inhibition*. Pfalz described two major inhibiting patterns in second-order cells as a result of pure tone stimulation of the contralateral intact cochlea. He referred to the patterns as "best" and "worst" frequency of inhibition. The "best" frequency effect has a response area like those already describd in that there is a characteristic frequency which produces inhibition at low levels of intensity. As intensity is raised, the bandwidth of frequencies which produce inhibition widens asymmetrically, as shown in Fig. 4.15. The "worst" frequency pattern is also shown in this figure. Note here that the response area appears inverted, thus showing that at low levels of intensity a broad band of frequencies can inhibit second-order activity with frequency-specific inhibition occurring only at very high intensity levels. These two patterns, therefore, are exactly opposite. These data are in good agreement with the work of Fex (15), who showed that the centrifugal olivocochlear bundle has an exclusively inhibitory effect on afferent fibers and that its effects are apparent only when stimulus intensity is 60 db SPL or higher.

Pfalz concluded that the inhibitory patterns that make certain secondary neurons "prefer" and others "reject" particular frequencies probably have different origins within the centrifugal system. The mechanisms for preferred frequencies may arise from centrifugal tracts coming from the higher neural levels, as described by Rasmussen (33), whereas the rejected frequencies may arise from the olivocochlear bundle. From the

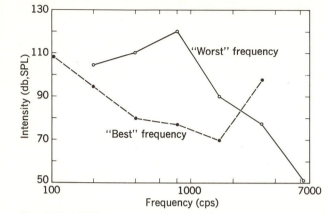

Fig. 4.15 Inhibitory response areas of second-order auditory neurons showing the combinations of frequency and intensity of tonal stimuli which inhibit their spontaneous activity. Two types of area are shown. "Best frequency" represents a second-order neuron whose inhibition is finely tuned at low intensity, whereas "worst frequency" is finely tuned only at high intensity. After Pfalz (32, p. 1476). After Pfalz. By permission.

work of Galambos and Pfalz it would appear that the olivocochlear bundle works directly upon both the primary and the secondary afferents. The inhibitory mechanism is, no doubt, chemical in nature at both levels (*38, 39*).

Desmedt and his colleagues have performed a number of studies of the efferent auditory system (*7, 9-12*). Here again the evidence points to an inhibitory function for the centrifugal system. In one study Desmedt (*7*) stimulated the olivocochlear bundle in the cat by stereotaxic electrode implantation and then determined the magnitude of its inhibitory influence at various sites along the acoustic pathway from the cochlea to the cortex. His measure of influence was obtained by determining the increase in stimulus intensity required during olivocochlear activation which would give the same potentials as those obtained with sound stimulation alone.

The inhibitory effects on N_1 showed that stimulation of the olivocochlear bundle was equivalent to reducing the stimulus intensity 20 db. That is, the click intensity had to be increased by a factor of ten during centrifugal stimulation in order to effect an N_1 potential of constant magnitude. Desmedt also noted, as had Fex (*15*) before him, a small but regular augmentation of the CP (4 db) during centrifugal stimulation. This, of course, is paradoxical in that while the CP is augmented, N_1 is reduced. The enhancement of the CP is very modest but its regular occurrence may provide some insight into the synaptic mechanisms of first-order neurons. It has been suggested that this potentiation depends on the release by centrifugal axons of an hyperpolarizing chemical transmitter in the vicinity of the hair cells.

The inhibition of N_1 did not end abruptly with the termination of centrifugal stimulation, but rather it showed itself to continue at progressively more modest levels over time, finally to disappear only after periods often as long as 500 msec.

When N_1 inhibitory effects are compared with those demonstrated at the ipsilateral cochlear nucleus, the superior olive, the contralateral inferior colliculus, and the auditory cortex (A-I), an impressive pattern emerges, as follows: regardless of the level of inhibition of N_1 (expressed as db equivalents), a proportional reduction is found at every level of the acoustic pathway. For example, if the parameters of stimulation of the olivocochlear bundle are such as to be equivalent to a 10 db reduction in click intensity for N_1, so also will the effects at all levels be equivalent to a 10 db reduction in click intensity. Different neural levels, therefore, clearly work in parallel. In behaving animals, acoustic afferents may be influenced by other filter gates, or perhaps even booster stations; but the importance of the centrifugal system is clearly established.

In our treatment of the electrophysiology of the auditory system, primary attention has been given to the classical pathways as well as the centrifugal system. There are, of course, many other aspects of auditory function which have been explored electrophysiologically. We shall return to a few of them in other contexts where electrophysiological data apply to particular auditory phenomena such as the localization of sounds in space.

References

1. Békésy, G. von. Elasticity of the cochlear partition, *J. Acoust. Soc. Amer.*, 1948, *20*, 227-241.
2. Békésy, G. von. Shearing microphonics produced by vibrations near the inner and outer hair cells, *J. Acoust. Soc. Amer.*, 1953, *25*, 786-790.

3. Békésy, G. von. Simplified models to demonstrate the energy flow and formation of traveling waves similar to those found in the cochlea, *Proc. Natl. Acad. Sci.*, 1956, *42*, 930-944.

4. Békésy, G. von. *Experiments in Hearing*, New York: McGraw-Hill, 1960.

5. Davis, H. Recent observations and interpretations of cochlear action, *Physiological Psychology*, 2nd Sympos., ONR Report ACR-30, March 1958, pp. 197-209.

6. Davis, H., C. Fernandez, and D. R. McAuliffe. The excitatory process in the cochlea, *Proc. Natl. Acad. Sci.*, 1950, *36*, 580-587.

7. Desmedt, J. E. Auditory-evoked potentials from cochlea to cortex as influenced by activation of the efferent olivo-cochlear bundle, *J. Acoust. Soc. Amer.*, 1962, *34*, 1478-1496.

8. Desmedt, J. E., and K. Mechelse. Corticofugal projections from the temporal lobe in cat and their possible role in acoustic discrimination, *J. Physiol.* (London), 1959, *147*, 17-18.

9. Desmedt, J. C., and K. Mechelse. Sur un phenomène d'inhibition centrifuge dans la voie acoustique centrale chez le chat, *Compt. Rend. Soc. Biol.*, 1957, *151*, 2209-2212.

10. Desmedt, J. E., and K. Mechelse. Suppression of acoustic input by thalamic stimulation, *Proc. Soc. Exper. Biol. Med.*, 1958, *99*, 772-775.

11. Desmedt, J. E., and K. Mechelse. Mise en évidence d'une quatrième aire de projection acoustique dans l'écorce cérébrale du chat, *J. Physiol.* (Paris), 1959, *51*, 448-449.

12. Desmedt, J. E., and P. Monaco. Mode of action of the efferent olivo-cochlear bundle on the inner ear, *Nature*, 1961, *192*, 1263-1265.

13. Downman, D. B. B., C. N. Woolsey, and R. A. Lende. Auditory areas I, II, and EP: cochlear representation, afferent paths and interconnections, *Bull. Johns Hopkins Hosp.*, 1960, *105*, 127-146.

14. Engstrom, H., H. W. Ades, and J. E. Hawkins, Jr. Structure and function of the sensory hairs of the inner ear, *J. Acoust. Soc. Amer.*, 1962, *34*, 1356-1363.

15. Fex, J. Auditory activity in centrifugal and centripetal cochlear fibers in cat, *Acta Physiol. Scand.*, Suppl. 189, 1962, *55*, 1-68.

16. Galambos, R. Microelectrode studies on medial geniculate body of cat: response to pure tones, *J. Neurophysiol.*, 1952, *15*, 381-400.

17. Galambos, R. Suppression of auditory nerve activity by stimulation of efferent fibers to the cochlea, *J. Neurophysiol.*, 1956, *19*, 424-437.

18. Galambos, R., and H. Davis. The response of single auditory nerve fibers to acoustic stimulation, *J. Neurophysiol.*, 1943, *6*, 39-57.

19. Galambos, R., and H. Davis. Inhibition of activity in single auditory nerve fibers by acoustic stimulation, *J. Neurophysiol.*, 1944, *7*, 287-304.

20. Galambos, R., J. Schwartzkopff, and A. Rupert. Microelectrode study of superior olivary nuclei, *Amer. J. Physiol.*, 1959, *197*, 527-536.

21. Gulick, W. L., D. J. Herrmann, and P. E. Mackey. The relationship between stimulus intensity and the electrical responses of the cochlea and auditory nerve, *Psychol. Rec.*, 1961, *11*, 57-67.
22. Hawkins, Jr., J. E. Cytoarchitectural basis of cochlear transducer, *Cold Spring Harbor Sympos. Quant. Biol.*, 1965, *30*, 147-157.
23. Hind, J. E. An electrophysiological determination of tonotopic organization in auditory cortex of cat, *J. Neurophysiol.*, 1953, *16*, 475-489.
24. Hind, J. E. Unit activity in the auditory cortex, in *Neural Mechanisms of the Auditory and Vestibular System*, G. L. Rasmussen and W. F. Windle (Eds.), Springfield, Ill.: C. C. Thomas, 1960.
25. Hind, J. E., J. M. Goldberg, D. D. Greenwood, and J. E. Rose. Some discharge characteristics of single neurons in the inferior colliculus of the cat. II. Timing of the discharges and observations on binaural stimulation, *J. Neurophysiol.*, 1963, *26*, 321-341.
26. Katsuki, Y. Neural mechanism of auditory sensation in cats, in *Sensory Communication*, W. A. Rosenblith (Ed.), Cambridge: MIT, 1961, pp. 561-584.
27. Katsuki, Y., N. Suga, and Y. Kanno. Neural mechanism of the peripheral and central auditory system in monkeys, *J. Acoust. Soc. Amer.*, 1962, *34*, 1396-1410.
28. Katsuki, Y., T. Sumi, H. Uchiyama, and T. Watanabe. Electric responses of auditory neurons in cat to sound stimulation, *J. Neurophysiol.*, 1958, *21*, 569-588.
29. Kiang, N. Y. S. An electrophysiological study of cat auditory cortex, *Thesis*, University of Chicago, 1955, No. 3028.
30. Mickle, W. A., and H. W. Ades. A composite sensory projection area in the cerebral cortex of the cat, *Amer. J. Physiol.*, 1952, *170*, 682-689.
31. Moushegian, G., A. Rupert, and R. Galambos. Microelectrode study of ventral nuclei of the cat, *J. Neurophysiol.*, 1962, *25*, 515-529.
32. Pfalz, R. K. J. Centrifugal inhibition of afferent secondary neurons in the cochlear nucleus by sound, *J. Acoust. Soc. Amer.*, 1962, *34*, 1472-1477.
33. Rasmussen, G. L. Descending or "feed-back" connections of auditory system of the cat, *Amer. J. Physiol.*, 1955, *183*, 653-660.
34. Rose, J. E. The cellular structure of the auditory region of the cat, *J. Comp. Neurol.*, 1949, *91*, 409-439.
35. Rose, J. E., R. Galambos, and J. R. Hughes. Microelectrode studies of the cochlear nuclei of the cat, *Bull. Johns Hopkins Hosp.*, 1959, *104*, 211-251.
36. Rose, J. E., D. D. Greenwood, J. M. Goldberg, and J. E. Hind. Some discharge characteristics of single neurons in the inferior colliculus of the cat. I. Tonotopic organization, relation of spike-counts to tone intensity, and firing patterns of single elements, *J. Neurophysiol.*, 1963, *26*, 294-320.
37. Rosenblith, W. A. Some quantifiable aspects of the electrical activity of

the nervous system, in *Biophysical Science,* J. L. Oncley (Ed.), New York: Wiley, 1959, Chapter 57, pp. 534-535.
38. Rossi, J. L'acétylcholinesterase au cours du développement de l'oreille interne du cobaye, *Acta Oto-Laryngol.,* Suppl., 170, 1961.
39. Schuknecht, H. F., J. A. Churchill, and R. Doran. The localization of acetylcholinesterase in the cochlea, *Arch. Otolaryngol.,* 1959, *59,* 549-559.
40. Stevens, S. S., and H. Davis. *Hearing,* New York: Wiley, 1938, pp. 398-400.
41. Tasaki, I. Nerve impulses in individual auditory nerve fibers of guinea pig, *J. Neurophysiol.,* 1954, *17,* 97-122.
42. Tasaki, I. Hearing, *Ann. Rev. Physiol.,* 1957, *19,* 417-438.
43. Tasaki, I., and H. Davis. Electric responses of individual nerve elements in cochlear nucleus to sound stimulation, *J. Neurophysiol.,* 1955, *18,* 151-158.
44. Tasaki, I., H. Davis, and J. P. Legouix. The space-pattern of the cochlear microphonics (guinea pig) as recorded by differential electrodes, *J. Acoust. Soc. Amer.,* 1952, *24,* 502-519.
45. Tunturi, A. R. Audio frequency localization in the acoustic cortex of the dog, *Amer. J. Physiol.,* 1944, *141,* 397-403.
46. Tunturi, A. R. Further afferent connections to the acoustic cortex of the dog, *Amer. J. Physiol.,* 1945, *144,* 389-394.
47. Wever, E. G. *Theory of Hearing,* New York: Wiley, 1949, pp. 135-137.
48. Wever, E. G., and C. W. Bray. The nature of acoustic response; the relation between sound frequency and frequency of impulses in the auditory nerve, *J. Exper. Psychol.,* 1930, *13,* 373-387.
49. Wever, E. G., and C. W. Bray. Present possibilities for auditory theory, *Psychol. Rev.,* 1930, *37,* 365-380.
50. Wever, E. G., and C. W. Bray. Distortion in the ear as shown by the electrical responses of the cochlea, *J. Acoust. Soc. Amer.,* 1938, *9,* 227-233.
51. Wever, E. G., and M. Lawrence. The transmission properties of the middle ear, *Ann. Otol. Rhinol. Laryngol.,* 1950, *59,* 5-18.
52. Wever, E. G., and M. Lawrence. The transmission properties of the stapes, *Ann. Otol. Rhinol. Laryngol.,* 1950, *59,* 322-330.
53. Wever, E. G., and M. Lawrence. *Physiological Acoustics,* Princeton, N. J.: Princeton University Press, 1954.
54. Wever, E. G., M. Lawrence, and G. von Békésy. A note on recent developments in auditory theory, *Proc. Natl. Acad. Sci.,* 1954, *40,* 508-512.
55. Woolsey, C. N. Organization of cortical auditory system, in *Sensory Communication,* W. A. Rosenblith (Ed.), Cambridge: MIT Press, 1961.
56. Woolsey, C. N., and E. M. Walzl. Topical projection of nerve fibers from local regions of the cochlea to the cerebral cortex of the cat, *Bull. Johns Hopkins Hosp.,* 1942, *71,* 315-344.

5

Theories of Hearing

Phenomena of hearing are of sufficient complexity that no single theory thus far advanced has attempted a full account of all the facts. Nevertheless, the older theories tended to be more comprehensive than modern ones because there were fewer facts of which theories had to take account. Accordingly, the early theories of hearing stand now more as testimony of the ingenuity of their originators than as useful reflections upon facts made coherent. But science has matured, and in the process theories have become more rigorous and a great deal more limited in scope. We shall confine our treatment to the modern era which began in 1863. After two influential classical theories are presented and criticized, contemporary statements of them are given. These are followed by a careful examination of data which bear directly on the tenability of the principles upon which they are based.

The Classical Theories

There are two major kinds of classical theories. *Place theories* argue that the analysis of sound occurs in the peripheral sense organ whereas *frequency theories* argue that analysis occurs centrally. This different emphasis is illustrated best by the manner in which pitch perception is handled. Place theories hold that each audible frequency (the physical counterpart of pitch) stimulates a specific region or "place" along the basilar membrane, thus initiating neural action along specific pathways.

Pitch, therefore, is coded by the place of origin of nervous activity. Frequency theories, on the other hand, do not generally posit local selective action along the basilar membrane, but instead view the entire sense organ as active for every audible frequency. Pitch is coded by the rate of nervous discharge which is said to be in synchrony with stimulus frequency. For example, first-order neurons would show ten-thousand bursts per second to a 10,000∿ tone, and this synchrony would be maintained all the way to the auditory cortex where analysis finally occurs.

PLACE THEORY: HELMHOLTZ

In 1863 Helmholtz (20) published his *Tonempfindungen* in which he stated fully a theory of hearing to which he had alluded earlier in public lectures. Some aspects of his theory were modified in revisions of his book, and our consideration will be limited to its final form, as stated in 1877.

Helmholtz conceived the basilar membrane as comprised of a series of transverse, independently tuned resonators. He was fully aware of the fact that the width of the basilar membrane increased from base to apex, and so he concluded that low tones resonated the transverse fibers near the apical end whereas high tones resonated transverse fibers near the basal end. Stimulus intensity was represented by the magnitude of vibration of the tuned resonators which then determined the magnitude of the nerve discharge. The ear performed a Fourier analysis to account for timbre. A complex sound wave simply would stimulate the several resonators tuned to the frequencies present in the stimulus.

FREQUENCY THEORY: RUTHERFORD

In 1886 Rutherford proposed a theory of hearing which ignored the place principle (24, 25). His theory, no doubt, grew out of a growing dissatisfaction with the concept of resonance. Against this concept he brought the full force of new anatomical evidence as a rebuttal. However, the theory of Helmholtz was so widely accepted that his arguments did not immediately prevail.

Rutherford proposed that the entire sense organ was active for all sounds and that the frequency, amplitude, and wave form (complexity) all were directly represented in "nerve vibrations." A single nerve cell, therefore, could simultaneously represent by the frequency, magnitude, and shape of its action potential the basic parameters of sound while an appreciation of them was left to the higher centers.

CLASSICAL THEORIES CRITICIZED

With reference to Helmholtz, modern work has shown the transverse fibers of the basilar membrane to be neither independent nor under tension. Inasmuch as resonance cannot occur in them under these circumstances, his resonance theory is untenable. Wever (29) argues convincingly that, even if one were to grant the matters of independent suspension and tension, the variation in fiber length and mass is so restrictive as to limit resonance to a range of frequency which is only a small fraction of the total to which we respond. It may be said, then, that the proposed resonators are both unsuited by their physical properties to the function ascribed to them and insufficient in number to provide enough "places."

Even if some other resonators were found, there remains a serious difficulty with the principle of resonance as a means to account for frequency discrimination. Let us suppose for a moment that there are resonators in the cochlea. If so, they would have to be tuned in such a way as to account not only for the absolute range of audible frequencies but for differential pitch discrimination as well. It is known that the manner of operation of a resonator is greatly influenced by the level of damping to which it is subjected. Only lightly damped resonators show a high degree of frequency discrimination. To account for our ability to discriminate frequency we would need a series of resonators with practically no damping at all. However, if the ear had such resonators we would be unable to distinguish rapidly successive changes of pitch, such as occur in music, because lightly damped resonators are slow in coming to rest after the driving frequency is withdrawn. Our ability with successive discriminations requires resonators with very heavy damping. Resonance, therefore, is not a particularly satisfactory concept because any hypothetical resonators in the ear cannot be at once lightly and heavily damped as the data on hearing require.

Although the full argument against resonance was not immediately offered in criticism of Helmholtz, part of it was. His theory came under attack because of the fact that a pure tone would cause resonance in a broad region of the cochlea rather than in a specific transverse fiber.

Thus a pure tone would signal simultaneously many "places" and therefore many pitches. In 1900 Gray (*17*) offered his hypothesis of maximum stimulation to counter this objection. He proposed that the exactly tuned resonator would always show maximum resonance, and it was this fiber alone which signaled the "place." However, he claimed that with intense stimulation many resonators would be responding at their practical maxima, and since the precision of the "place" would be lost under these conditions, he predicted that differential pitch sensitivity would worsen as a function of intensity. Psychophysical data show the opposite to be true.

There is another difficulty with Gray's hypothesis. To illustrate it, let us consider further his view that the exactly tuned resonator shows maximum resonance, with adjacent ones showing less and less resonance as their mis-tuning increases. According to him a pure tone stimulus would produce a gradient of resonance along the basilar membrane approximating a normal distribution with the peak alone signalling the "place" as the code for pitch. If a local lesion in the cochlea were present at the site of the normal maximum, then the gradient of resonance would be bimodal with two maxima signaling two "places" and two pitches. A human with a local lesion about the normal "place" for a given tone does not hear two tones as Gray's hypothesis predicts.

Finally, Helmholtz assumed that variations in stimulus intensity produced similar variations in impulse magnitude. However, the work of Adrian (*1*) on the all-or-none property of neural action emphatically denied his assumption.

Turning now to the frequency theory of Rutherford, the same evidence of all-or-none action of the nervous system also makes his theory untenable. He admitted that his theory demanded a great deal of the acoustic nervous system, yet it must have been disappointing, nevertheless, when the facts showed clearly that the size of the neural impulse was not a direct function of stimulus intensity, that the shape of the neural action potential did not mirror the stimulus wave pattern, and that the recovery cycle did not allow rates of response sufficient to cover the audible frequency range. Furthermore, the work of Forbes and Gregg (*12*) added a serious complication when it showed that the rate of response in a nerve fiber was a monotonic function of stimulus intensity. As stimulus intensity was increased, fibers responded earlier and earlier in their relative refractory periods up to a limit approaching the absolute refractory period. The practical maximum rate of response was set at about 500 impulses per second. The embarrassment for frequency theory thus took two forms: first, if individual nerve fibers could not respond beyond five hundred times per second, then synchrony with stimulus frequency could not be maintained to twenty-thousand cycles per second, as the theory proposed; and second, if rate of neural firing is a function of stimulus intensity, then rate could not easily serve to code frequency as well.

Current Theories

In spite of the evidence against the classical theories of Helmholtz and Rutherford, the major principles upon which they were based have continued to find expression in auditory theory. Rejection of resonance does not necessarily invalidate the place principle if another means consistent with the facts can be advanced to account for local stimulation along the basilar membrane. In similar manner, rejection of the frequency principle on the grounds that it cannot adequately account for all audible frequencies does not mean that it might not account for some of them. Let us consider two modern theories which grew out of the earlier ones.

TRAVELING-WAVE THEORY: BÉKÉSY

In 1928 Békésy (4) stated the essential case for his traveling-wave theory, and since that time he has continued to elaborte upon it (7). His theory offers an alternative to resonance while accepting the principle of place. According to the theory, the basilar membrane is thrown into wave motion during acoustic stimulation. The to and fro movement of the stapes forces the basal end of the membrane downward and then upward because of sudden fluid pressure changes. In turn, this leads to a wave which travels longitudinally along the membrane, rising in amplitude as it moves apically to reach a maximum, after which it falls rapidly toward zero because of heavy damping in the apical region. Data from hydraulic models of the cochlea and from actual specimens show that the location of maximum membrane displacement varies systematically with frequency. Low tones peak near the apex, high tones near the base. In the upper part of Fig. 5.1 is shown the position of the basilar mem-

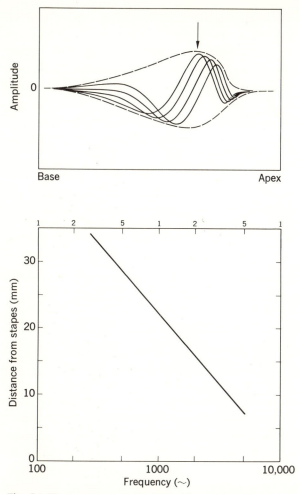

Fig. 5.1 The upper part depicts with exaggeration the position of the basilar membrane at each of four instants during low tone stimulation. The dashed line describes the envelope and the arrow signifies the "place" of maximum membrane displacement. After Békésy (7, p. 499).

The lower part shows the relationship between the frequency of the stimulus and the location of the "place" of maximum displacement of the basilar membrane. Data from cochlear models. From Békésy (7, p. 440).

brane at each of four instants during stimulation with a low frequency tone. The dashed line represents the envelope of membrane movement during a full inward-outward cycle of the stapes and the arrow shows the "place" of maximum displacement. The lower graph shows how the "place" varies as a function of frequency (7). Based upon measures of the phase lag of various structures in the *scala media,* Békésy has shown that the membrane is not resonating, but rather is responding more passively. It is not clear whether the membrane itself is responsible for transmission of the traveling wave, as in a rope under tension fixed at one end and shaken at the other, or whether it is displaced passively by pressure waves traveling in the cochlear fluid. The first alternative is suggested by the theory.

The traveling-wave theory of Békésy is concerned exclusively with the question of how the ear acts to discriminate pitch (7, p. 539). An alternative theory presented next addresses itself both to pitch and loudness.

FREQUENCY-PLACE THEORY: WEVER

Wever (29) has offered a theory which invokes both the frequency and place principles, and in this regard it is unlike any other major theory. Based upon his extensive studies of auditory receptors in organisms at different phylogenetic levels, Wever concluded that the simpler auditory systems allowed frequency discrimination by coding according to the *frequency* principle. However, in more complicated systems, usually of a later evolutionary stage, he concluded that some degree of selectivity to local stimulation was possible because of enlarged receptor surfaces and more elaborate means of stimulating them. In his view, therefore, *place* as a code for frequency is a late evolutionary development which serves to complement rather than to replace the earlier one. According to Wever, both *frequency* and *place* operate in man, and neither alone is sufficient to give an acceptable account of the major experimental facts.

His theory utilizes the frequency principle, as classically put forth, to account for the coding of low tones from 20 to about 400∿. Within this range there is evidence that individual fibers of the cochlear nerve can respond at each cycle of the stimulus tone. Recall that the hair cells of the organ of Corti transduce the sound pressure changes into a trigger potential (CP) which follows exactly the frequency of the stimulus. Apparently, neurons whose thresholds are surpassed depolarize on each peak of the CP with the result that each active neuron initiates as many impulses per second as there are cycles per second in the tone. This synchrony continues until the interval between the peaks of the CP becomes too brief to allow the neuron sufficient recovery time.

For the low frequencies, loudness is represented by the number of active neurons. An increase in stimulus intensity produces a proportional increase in the CP which, in turn, leads to an increase in the total number of neurons contributing to each synchronous burst.

For the frequency range from 400 to about 5000∿, Wever presents evidence that synchrony is maintained in the cochlear nerve as a result of neural volleying even though any particular fiber is limited in response rate to a maximum of about 400 impulses per second. The auditory nerve as a whole can continue to respond in synchrony with the stimulus up to about 5000∿ because the individual fibers stagger their responses to form platoons. For example, to a low tone of 300∿ every fiber whose threshold is surpassed would respond at each energy peak, whereas at 600∿ each would respond at every other peak, with some taking the even and others the odd numbered peaks. That all fibers would halve response rates and take *only* even (or odd) peaks is precluded by individual variations in recovery rates and excitability. With further increases in stimulus frequency, individual fibers would respond on every third, fourth, or fifth peak, and so on.

Where volleying occurs, loudness continues to be represented by the number of fibers contributing to each synchronous burst. An increase in intensity has two effects: first, more fibers are activated; and second, those already active are forced to respond earlier in their relative refractory periods so that a fiber which might have been responding on every fourth peak would respond now on every third peak. Both of these effects increase the number of impulses per burst. According to Wever, "it is possible for one kind of temporal variation to operate for pitch and another for loudness without essential contradiction" (*29,* p. 191).

For the audible range above 5000∿ the theory invokes the place principle. Place operates to some extent, along with volleying, up to about 5000∿ at which limit volleying fails and place becomes the sole basis for pitch. The number of impulses per second still represents loudness even though the rhythm of volleying is lost and the total discharge displays asynchrony.

With the essential aspects of the theories of Békésy and Wever before us, let us determine the extent to which current data are consistent with them.

Assessment of the Place Principle

There are two logical requirements which must be met if the place principle is to continue to serve as a basic tenet of auditory theory. First, the manner of selective activation along the receptor surface must be sufficiently precise to give rise to enough "places" to account for the number of discriminable pitches known to exist within the frequency range for which the place principle is said to operate. Second, stimulation of local places on the receptor must find adequate representation in the auditory nervous system, at least up to the neural level necessary for pitch decoding. There would be no value in a *receptor-place* if it were not coupled with a *neural-place* (fiber specificity). Evidence for frequency-tuned neural units and tonotopic organization has already been considered, and so we may conclude that *neural-place* is an acceptable tenet. It is to the matter of receptor-place that we shall devote major attention. In so doing we would do well to remember that *although receptor-place logically requires neural-place, the reverse is not true*. Localization of trigger processes may, indeed, give rise to tonotopic organization, but so too could other characteristics of the trigger beside its place if neurons were selectively responsive to those characteristics. For example, suppose that the dendrites of the afferent auditory neurons had membrane thicknesses which differed as a function of their location along the longitudinal axis of the cochlea. If the cochlea potential initiated neural impulses by effecting the transfer of selected cellular contents across the membrane, then the transfer would depend upon the frequency of the cochlear potential and the thickness of the membrane. This could account for fiber tuning without requiring that the trigger potential be applied at a "place" within the cochlea. In any case, a simple one-to-one template from receptor-place to neural-place is prohibited by the complexity of the ear's innervation.

Inasmuch as basilar membrane displacement is relatively broad, particularly at frequencies below 800∿, traveling-wave theory has been criticized on the grounds that membrane displacement is too coarse a means to establish specific "places." Several hypotheses have been offered to counter this criticism, and we shall consider three of them.

Békésy proposed that the cochlear nerve is stimulated by local *vortex movements* of the cochlear fluids rather than by membrane displacement itself. The vortex hypothesis serves the purpose of sharpening the place of stimulation because vortex movements are limited strictly to the region of maximum membrane displacement. To maintain the advantage of the hypothesis with reference to sharpening, one is forced to assume that there is something unique about vortical movements so that they alone serve as a cochlear trigger. This assumption does not seem justified.

Another hypothesis to sharpen "places" has been advanced by Békésy. This one, the *law of contrast,* operates within the nervous system. It is based upon lateral inhibition and is essentially a form of what he has elsewhere referred to as funneling (*8*). Although we have already considered evidence of improved tuning at the higher neural centers where lateral inhibition probably takes place, it is difficult to see how the phenomenon of neural sharpening can account for frequency-specific behavior *in first-order neurons*. Relegation of sharpening to higher centers does not answer for the failure of the place principle on the receptor surface.

The third hypothesis relating to sharpening was offered by Huggins (*21*) in 1950. He suggested that the basilar membrane communicates its effects to the tectorial membrane which itself has the properties of a rigid beam. The tectorial membrane was thought to stimulate the hair cells according to a pattern which reflected its beam characteristics. The advantage of his hypothesis is that stimulation is in proportion to the fourth derivative of displacement and this derivative under certain limiting conditions shows sharper maxima than displacement itself. Unfortunately the properties of the tectorial membrane do not meet his requirements.

Traveling-wave theory also runs into difficulty when several forms of hearing abnormalities are considered. In presbyacusia, which is a progressive loss of high tone sensitivity with advancing age, the basal end of the basilar membrane becomes calcified. Although the association of high tone loss with dysfunction of the basal end of the membrane has been taken as evidence of place for the high tones, it also raises a problem for traveling-wave theory in that the single most important determinant of membrane wave patterning is membrane stiffness (*30*). Traveling-waves, therefore, would be appreciably different under circumstances of presbyacusia, including a shift in the location of maxima; yet pitch perception for the middle and low frequencies remains normal.

In a second abnormality, clinical high-tone deafness in one ear due to selective basal lesions, a high frequency tone inaudible at moderate intensity becomes audible at a higher intensity, presumably because the increased intensity produces a broader spread of action on the basilar membrane and thus stimulates the normal area beyond the lesion. When binaural pitch matches are made, the pitch is the same in spite of the fact that the "places" in the normal and impaired ear are necessarily different.

The final line of clinical evidence which leads us to question the invariant relationship of pitch and place comes from instances of conductive deafness. In such cases the impairment is the result of some abnormality in the external or middle ears which blocks or alters the transmission of sound to the cochlea. The cochlea remains normal and hearing can occur by bone conduction. The cochlear capsule is shaken when the temporal bone is made to vibrate. The fluid contents lag behind the bony capsule because of their inertia, and thus the hair cells are bent as a result of relative motion. Stimulation by bone conduction results in normal pitch discrimination even though the pattern of membrane displacement would differ from normal.

STRUCTURAL PLACE

In our assessment of receptor-place we have raised a number of limitations of traveling-wave theory, but there remains a body of evidence which indicates clearly that the ear, to varying degrees, does respond differentially as a function of stimulus frequency. We need now to examine the extent to which the cochlea demonstrates the place principle so that we can then consider its functional significance.

In Fig. 5.1 we have already shown that the region of the maximum membrane displacement changes systematically with frequency. In addition to the direct observations of Békésy, the fact of differential action is fully consistent with the physical conditions of elasticity, friction, and mass which obtain in the cochlea. Nevertheless, the matter of localization of the maximum is not as simple as it might appear to be in Fig. 5.1 because the very same physical properties which allow the localization also complicate it. Beside changes in the location of the maximum as a function of frequency, there are also changes in the shape, skew, and slope of membrane displacement. The character of the "place" changes regularly from broad localization at low frequencies to relatively narrow localization at high frequencies (6). Let us consider two lines of evidence which support this conclusion.

In animal experiments in which very intense tones of prolonged duration are used to injure the organ of Corti (*stimulation deafness*), low frequencies were shown to damage almost the entire length of the organ. Increases in stimulus frequency injured areas which were progressively more restricted and displaced basally in a systematic fashion (2, 3, 26, 27). The areas of injury for the middle and high frequencies corresponded well with Békésy's data on wave patterns.

Further supportive data come from studies in which the CP was recorded at each of several sites from base to apex in order to measure its gradient along the longitudinal axis of the cochlea. This approach has an advantage over stimulation-deafness experiments in that tones within the normal intensity range can be used. The results were that low tones gave essentially a flat gradient with no localization whereas high tones gave a gradient with the greater CP magnitude in the apical region (9, 10, 18, 19).

From the study of traveling-waves, stimulation-deafness, and CP localization, we can conclude that the entire organ of Corti does not function in a simple manner with all of its regions equally responsive. Rather, it responds in a differential manner of a rather crude sort, with localized regions of activity absent for low tones, present but broadly defined for the middle tones, and more narrowly defined for the high tones. The structural characteristics of the ear give rise to patterns of action which suggest that the possibility of receptor-place is limited to the high tones. Evidence of place for the middle tones is questionable and for low tones absent. From this analysis one would expect that pitch discrimination would improve with frequency, being most acute for the highest tones where the "places" are best defined. Psychophysical data contradict this expectation.

FUNCTIONAL PLACE

Theories of hearing which rely upon receptor-place to account for pitch perception have failed so far to consider the functional significance of the differential patterns of cochlear action brought about by structural factors. If, as we now suppose, the cochlear nerve is triggered by an electrical graded potential (CP), then it must be shown that the trigger also behaves in a localized fashion. Many of the difficulties for place theories would be eliminated, or their seriousness reduced, if it could be shown that the trigger was more localized than the evidence so far presented would suggest. On the other hand, evidence of an extremely diffuse trigger would not only add to the liabilities of these theories; it could, in the extreme, deny their tenability altogether.

There is good reason to believe that the CP is diffuse. Consider the following argument from Wever (29). In measures of CP magnitude as a function of stimulus intensity, the relationship is linear over extensive ranges regardless of the stimulating frequency. The CP is, of course, a composite potential of all the active hair cells, but from it we can consider the behavior of the individual hair cell. The input-output relationship for a single hair cell might reasonably be expected to show positive acceleration, zero acceleration (linearity), or negative acceleration. The first is rejected because it could not lead to a linear composite. The third alternative is also rejected because the only circumstances under which a linear composite could result would be if, as intensity increased, additional hair cells became active at a rate which exactly compensated for the negative acceleration of the composite. That this would obtain over an intensive range of a thousandfold for most frequencies is too unlikely to invite further consideration. Therefore, Wever concludes that individual cells respond linearly. Since the composite function is linear it also follows that *all hair cells must be activated by all tones* because if the population of hair cells grew with intensity, then the composite would show positive acceleration. However, to say that all hair cells are active to every tone is not to say that all are equally active. The intent here is simply to show that hair cell involvement cannot be present in one place in the cochlea and totally absent in another.

The magnitude of the CP at a specific locus is determined both by the level of activity in its hair cells and by the amount of potential spreading to it from other loci. Functional receptor-place is tenable only if the final gradient is sufficiently steep so as to be of suprathreshold magnitude in a very restricted region. This requirement is shown in Fig. 5.2. In the upper part are shown hypothetical CP gradients for a 2000$\curvearrowright$ tone at each of two intensities (CP_1 and CP_2). In both cases, the CP surpasses N_1 threshold in a narrow region, and this would lead to selective neural

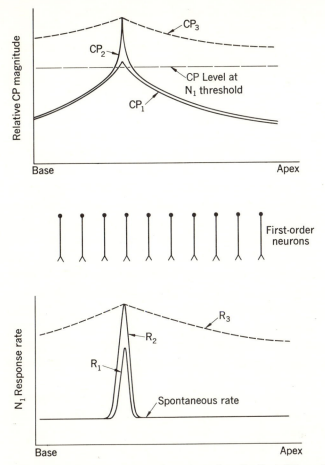

Fig. 5.2 The upper graph depicts three hypothetical CP gradients to a 2000∿ tone. Two are steep (CP_1 and CP_2) and surpass N_1 threshold in a restricted region only. The other (CP_3) is broad and is suprathreshold throughout the cochlea. The effects of these gradients on N_1 response rates are shown in the bottom graph.

stimulation, as shown in the lower graph (R_1 and R_2). On the other hand, if the CP gradient were very broad (CP_3), then there would be little selective neural stimulation (R_3). Clearly, we need to know which of these two situations obtains. Fortunately, some data are available to help us answer this question.

Wever and Lawrence (*31*) reported a series of experiments from which they concluded that for any particular frequency of moderate intensity the CP trigger was present throughout the length of the cochlea. Recording the CP simultaneously from the apex and base of the cat cochlea, they found there was no appreciable difference in CP magnitude between these sites for frequencies up to 800∿. As frequency was raised above 800∿, the apical position gave a relatively larger response which grew progressively more favorable as a function of increasing frequency. However, at no frequency investigated (up to 10,000∿) did the difference in CP magnitude between apical and basal sites exceed 20 db. The significance of these findings is made clear in Fig. 5.3. In the upper graph, basilar membrane displacement is shown for two frequencies according to Békésy. The lower graph gives the CP gradients for these same two frequencies, as determined from the studies already cited. The gradients are given in decibels relative to apical magnitude. There seems to be little doubt that the distribution of the CP trigger is extremely wide, and cochlear transduction makes "places" less rather than more precise. It can be argued that the gradients shown in Fig. 5.3 are broader than they ought to be because they were determined from measurements made in perilymphatic canals rather than in the endolymph of the cochlear canal (*7*). While this is probably true, the error involved is not large enough to raise serious doubt about the conclusion offered here.

Because the CP gradient for the 5000∿ tone indicates that the trigger is stronger near the basal end, let us consider it further in the light of an experiment by McGill.

McGill (*23*) studied behavioral thresholds of hearing in cats at each of several frequencies. Afterward, he determined the magnitude of the CP at threshold intensities for the same frequencies in the same cats. The CP values at the threshold were found to be incredibly low, on the order of 0.01 μV. Since cats can discriminate frequency at intensities at least 80 db above absolute threshold, we are left with a dilemma. Given the linearity of the CP intensity function, a tone 80 db SL would give a CP of 100 μV if the threshold (0 db) gave a CP of 0.01 μV, as observed by McGill. If we take Wever's figure of 20 db as the maximum attenuation of the CP with distance along the basilar membrane, then we must conclude that the cat can discriminate among pitches (even high ones), in spite of the fact that the CP produced by any single tone exceeds the

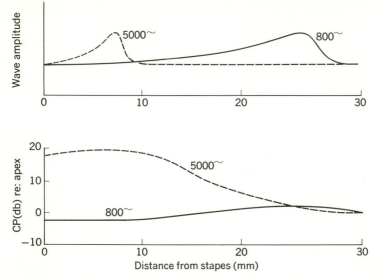

Fig. 5.3 The upper graph shows basilar membrane displacement for 800 and 5000∿ tones according to Békésy. Below, the CP gradients are given for the same two tones. Each gradient is expressed in decibels relative to the level measured at the apex.

neural threshold value at *all* other "places" by as much as a thousandfold.

The structure of the ear gives rise to a crude receptor-place for middle and high frequency tones, but no clear case can be made at present for a functional receptor-place principle. Accordingly, one has either to posit a local trigger other than the CP, or one has to consider some other means beside "place" whereby a particular neural unit is made sensitive to the electrical trigger.

Assessment of the Frequency Principle

We have already seen that the frequency principle must be rejected when considered in the context of more recent information on the behavior of the cochlear nerve and its higher projections. Restricting its use to the lower frequencies, as Wever has proposed, can only be acceptable if an accurate frequency code is maintained from first-order cells all the way to the higher centers. Precisely to what level of the acoustic projections we would have to have neural synchrony with stimulus frequency is not altogether clear, but a number of ablation studies are suggestive. Although discrimination among temporal acoustic patterns of some complexity requires the cortex (11, 13), there is evidence that simple frequency discrimination can occur in the cat after extensive bilateral lesions of the auditory cortex (14, 15). Whether or not impairment of the cortex alters the DL for pitch is unknown. However, Goldberg and Neff (16) have shown that frequency discrimination is lost when the medial pathway of the brachium of the inferior colliculus is sectioned bilaterally. Some clinical evidence from a human confirms this conclusion (22).

The results of these studies suggest that the inferior colliculus and all lower centers must be intact if pitch is to be discriminated. Inasmuch as direct following is not especially characteristic of nerve fibers of the higher orders, the frequency principle appears to be inadequate even though synchrony has been demonstrated for low tones in first-order fibers. The multiplicity of neural pathways and the number of synapses intervening between the cochlea and the inferior colliculus certainly would work against the maintainance of good synchrony. Furthermore, the single-unit work on frequency tuned fibers previously presented makes the concept of tuning an attractive alternative to the frequency principle. Admittedly, there have been relatively few fibers observed which are tuned to very low tones, but there have been some, at least down to 200∿. One would expect that at extremely low frequencies, say below 100∿, the matter of synaptic delay would be less troublesome for the frequency principle, particularly if broad regions of the cochlea were involved as Wever has proposed. There is, then, some likelihood that the frequency principle operates at the lowest extreme, but from 100∿ upward the possibility seems to grow more remote.

We have previously referred to response areas in our discussion of the electrical activity of the acoustic nervous system. A hypothetical response area is shown at the left of Fig. 5.4. Regardless of the level of the neuron within the projection system, the range of frequencies to which it responds increases with intensity. Yet when rate of response is plotted as a function of frequency and intensity, as in the right part of Fig. 5.4, we see from the shape of the surface that at every intensity level the neuron responds maximally to the best-tuned frequency. Therefore, it is not altogether accurate to state, as many do, that tuning becomes lost

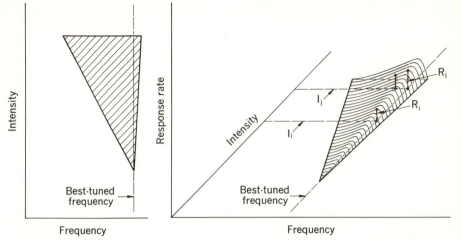

Fig. 5.4 The left portion depicts a hypothetical response area, giving the combinations of frequency and intensity sufficient to increase the rate of neural firing above the spontaneous level. The right portion depicts the same response area with response rate added as a third dimension. Note that response rate at every intensity level is always at its maximum to the best-tuned frequency. See text for explanation.

as intensity rises. The response pattern suggests that pitch information continues to be carried by the fiber itself rather than by its rate of response. On the other hand, there is a degree of ambiguity about the tuning. When intensity is raised from I_i to I_j, then the rate of response increases from R_i to R_j for the best-tuned frequency. However, a slight mis-tuning downward can reduce R_j to equality with R_i. Accordingly, two slightly different frequencies at two different intensities can effect the same response rate in this hypothetical neuron. The extent to which this can occur is a measure of loss of precision in frequency tuning. It also follows from this kind of analysis that the higher the rate of response at I_i, the *smaller* is the downward change in frequency required to keep the rate of response constant at I_j.

VOLLEYING

The volley principle may be considered a modification of Rutherford's earlier principle, and as we have seen, it has been used to extend the frequency principle well beyond the limit imposed by the behavior of single neurons. Volleying seems now well-established as a phenomenon of neural behavior, and Wever (29) has summarized evidence of it in a number of sensory systems. However, there may be difficulty with the volley principle as it has been applied in auditory theory. The seriousness of the difficulty is not established at present because the data which bear upon it are both incomplete and contradictory.

If one were to measure the magnitude of the compound action potential in the cochlear nerve, one would expect it to decrease as the frequency of the stimulating tone increased because the number of neurons contributing to each volley would grow smaller. The critical question deals with the nature of the decrease. The results of two studies aimed at determining the nature of the reduction in the compound action potential are shown in Fig. 5.5.

Stevens and Davis (28) found that the compound action potential recorded from the cochlear nerve of the cat changed very abruptly at certain frequencies, whereas data from our laboratory showed the change to be more gradual. Let us consider the implications of these findings.

The solid line in Fig. 5.5 shows that the initial size of the compound action potential remains constant with frequency change up to about 800∿. A further increase in frequency results in a precipitous drop in response magnitude, presumably because at 800∿ the active fibers begin to fire alternately, thus halving the number contributing to each volley. At 1600∿ another drop occurs, again suggesting that at this frequency active fibers divide into thirds. If these data from Stevens and Davis (28) are accurate, then Wever's use of the volley principle leads to a contradiction. He states that with volleying, the rhythm of the volleys codes pitch while the number of active fibers contributing to each volley codes loudness. Accordingly, we should have to conclude that the progressive change of frequency across each critical region (750-900∿ and 1500-1600∿) would lead to an abrupt change in loudness since the number of neural units contributing to each volley would be reduced suddenly. Yet a sweep through the frequencies from 100 to 3000∿ does not produce any sudden discontinuities in loudness.

Data from our laboratory, also shown in Fig. 5.5, indicate no sudden changes in response amplitude. We interpret the gradual reduction as reflecting the fact that all active neurons do not begin alternate firing at the same frequency. Instead, some begin alternation early and some late

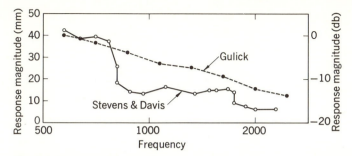

Fig. 5.5 The relationship between frequency and the magnitude of the compound action potential in the cochlear nerve of the cat. The solid line is from Stevens and Davis (**28**, p. 395) and should be read against the left ordinate. The dashed line represents data obtained in our laboratory and it should be read against the right ordinate where response magnitude is given in decibels with reference to 50 mV.

with the result that the reduction in the number of fibers contributing to each volley grows progressively, rather than suddenly, smaller as frequency rises. Whether or not our results raise an embarrassment for the volley principle cannot be answered until response magnitude is measured under stimulus conditions where intensity is adjusted at each frequency so as to effect equality in loudness.

Our review of theories and their principles was not intended to be exhaustive. Rather, we wished to point out the major limitations of them. Without doubt each theory has helped to organize some of the data on hearing, but the final word on theory has still to be written.

After considering the basic facts of hearing in the remaining chapters, we shall, perhaps, see more clearly the immensity of the task of conceiving a truly general theory.

References

1. Adrian, E. D. The all-or-none principle in nerve, *J. Physiol.*, 1914, *47*, 460-474.
2. Alexander, I. E., and F. J. Githler. Histological examination of cochlear structure following exposure to jet engine noise, *J. Comp. Physiol. Psychol.*, 1951, *44*, 513-524.
3. Alexander, I. E., and F. J. Githler. Chronic effects of jet engine noise on the structure and function of the cochlear apparatus, *J. Comp. Physiol. Psychol.*, 1952, *45*, 381-391.

4. Békésy, G. von. Zur Theorie des Hörens; Die Schwingungsform der Basilarmembran, *Physik Zeits.*, 1928, *29*, 793-810.
5. Békésy, G. von. Physikalische Probleme der Hörphysiologie, *Elekt. Nachr. Techn.*, 1935, *12*, 71-83.
6. Békésy, G. von. Ueber die Frequenzauflösung in der menschlichen Schnecke, *Acta Oto-Laryngol.*, 1944, *32*, 60-84.
7. Békésy, G. von. *Experiments in Hearing,* New York: McGraw-Hill, 1960.
8. Békésy, G. von. *Sensory Inhibition,* Princton, N. J.: Princeton University Press, 1967.
9. Culler, E. A. Symposium: is there localization in the cochlea for low tones?, *Ann. Otol. Rhinol. Laryngol.*, 1935, *44*, 807-813.
10. Culler, E. A., J. D. Coakley, K. Lowy, and N. Gross. A revised frequency-map of the guinea-pig cochlea, *Amer. J. Psychol.*, 1943, *56*, 475-500.
11. Diamond, I. T., and W. D. Neff. Ablation of temporal cortex and discrimination of auditory patterns, *J. Neurophysiol.*, 1957, *20*, 300-315.
12. Forbes, A., and A. Gregg. Electrical studies in mammalian reflexes, *Amer. J. Physiol.*, 1915, *39*, 172-235.
13. Goldberg, J. M., I. T. Diamond, and W. D. Neff. Auditory discrimination after ablation of temporal and insular cortex in cat, *Fed. Proc.* (Baltimore), 1957, *16*, 47.
14. Goldberg, J. M., I. T. Diamond, and W. D. Neff. Frequency discrimination after ablation of cortical projection areas of the auditory system, *Fed. Proc.* (Baltimore), 1958, *17*, 55.
15. Goldberg, J. M., and W. D. Neff. Frequency discrimination after bilateral ablation of cortical auditory areas, *J. Neurophysiol.*, 1961, *24*, 119-128.
16. Goldberg, J. M., and W. D. Neff. Frequency discrimination after bilateral section of the brachium of the inferior colliculus, *J. Comp. Neurol.*, 1961, *113*, 265-282.
17. Gray, A. A. On a modification of the Helmholtz theory of hearing, *J. Anat. Physiol.*, 1900, *34*, 324-350.
18. Hallpike, C. S., and A. F. Rawdon-Smith. The Helmholtz resonance theory of hearing, *Nature* (London), 1934, *133*, 614.
19. Hallpike, C. S., and A. F. Rawdon-Smith. The "Wever-Bray" phenomenon, *J. Physiol.*, 1934, *81*, 395-408.
20. Helmholtz, H. L. F. von. *Die Lehre von den Tonempfindungen als physiologische Grundlage für die Theorie der Musik,* Braunschweig: Viewig u. Sohn, 1863.
21. Huggins, W. H. Theory of cochlear frequency discrimination, *Quart. Progr. Rept.,* MIT Res. Lab. Elect., Oct. 15, 1950, 54-59.
22. Landau, W. M., R. Goldstein, and F. R Kleffner Congenital aphasia: a clinico-pathologic study, *Neurol.*, 1960, *10*, 915-921.

23. McGill, T. E. Auditory sensitivity and the magnitude of the cochlear potential, *Ann. Otol. Rhinol. Laryngol.*, 1959, *68*, 1-15.
24. Rutherford, W. *The Sense of Hearing*, Lecture at Birmingham, Eng., Sept. 6, 1886, privately printed.
25. Rutherford, W. A new theory of hearing, *J. Anat. Physiol.*, 1886, *21*, 166-168.
26. Smith, K. R. The problem of stimulation deafness: II. Histological changes in the cochlea as a function of tonal frequency, *J. Exper. Psychol.*, 1947, *37*, 304-317.
27. Smith, K. R., and E. G. Wever. The problem of stimulation deafness: III. The functional and histological effects of a high-frequency stimulus, *J. Exper. Psychol.*, 1949, *39*, 238-241.
28. Stevens, S. S., and H. Davis. *Hearing*, New York: Wiley, 1938, p. 395.
29. Wever, E. G. *Theory of Hearing*, New York: Wiley, 1949.
30. Wever, E. G. Development of traveling-wave theories, *J. Acoust. Soc. Amer.*, 1962, *34*, 1319-1324.
31. Wever, E. G., and M. Lawrence. *Physiological Acoustics*, Princeton, N. J.: Princeton University Press, 1954.

6

Sensitivity of the Ear

Our treatment so far has emphasized some major facts pertaining to physiological acoustics. The previous chapter and this one serve together as a bridge between the physiological processes which underlie hearing and the psychophysical and psychological data on hearing. Special attention is given to the relationship of receptor processes to the discrimination of intensity and frequency differences.

Intensitive Thresholds

The absolute sensitivity of the ear is measured as the least sound pressure which leads to a sensation of hearing. We have already seen through our discussion of cochlear distortion that the ear is differentially sensitive to pure tones of different frequencies. Accordingly, one cannot speak of a single intensitive threshold because each frequency has its own. Although several psychophysical methods have been employed in the study of intensitive thresholds, a much more important influence on sensitivity measures has been the manner in which the tones are delivered to the ear. The transducer may be placed tightly against the pinna (*closed-ear method*), or it may be located at a distance (*open-ear method*).

In the closed-ear method the sound pressure at threshold is either calculated from displacement of the transducer diaphragm, or it is measured with a probe tube leading from the vicinity of the tympanic membrane to a calibrated condensor microphone. In either case, thresholds so obtained are referred to as *minimum audible pressures* (M.A.P.).

108

With the open-ear method the sound pressure is measured in a free sound field at the place of the listener but in his absence. Thresholds so obtained are referred to as *minimum audible field* pressures (M.A.F.).

Each of these two arrangements has advantages and disadvantages. The closed-ear arrangement makes it easy to control binaural stimulation. On the other hand, determinations of minimum audible pressures are more liable to error than one might expect. Calculated pressures depend upon known transducer diaphragm excursions, but they are usually so small that they must be estimated by downward extrapolation. Furthermore, the volume of the air enclosed in the external meatus, an important factor in the calculation, typically is assumed to be constant from one listener to another. This assumption is answerable more to convenience than fact. Another difficulty arises because an enclosed column of air in a partially elastic chamber like the external meatus will fail to maintain sinusoidal pressure fluctuations over different frequencies even though the transducer is driven sinusoidally.

The open-ear arrangement is more natural, but the introduction of the listener into the sound field introduces sound shadows which have serious influence on threshold measures, especially at the higher frequencies. Consequently, the position of the head with reference to the sound source is very critical. It is now conventional to have the listener face the source (0° azimuth) with a distance of one meter between the source and the binaural axis. Beside the matter of head position, it is essential with free field measures to eliminate all reflected sounds since they would cause pressure nodes through selective reinforcement and interference with the progressive waves from the source. Their elimination is difficult in practice and requires especially built anechoic chambers.

ABSOLUTE THRESHOLDS

The effects of the open- and closed-ear arrangements on threshold determinations are clearly evident in the summary data shown in Fig. 6.1. The closed-ear (M.A.P.) function is a composite of several independent determinations (*1, 7, 23, 24, 27*), each of which was obtained under monaural listening conditions. Whether or not the threshold is lowered with binaural stimulation is equivocal. Several experimenters have reported that binaural listening improves sensitivity very slightly and a few have reported no difference compared to the monaural condition. The largest

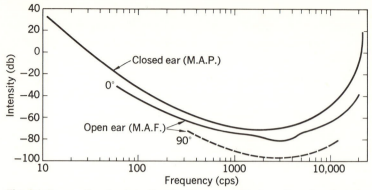

Fig. 6.1 Composite absolute threshold curves obtain under closed- and open-ear arrangements. The closed-ear function is for monaural listening and is based on the results of five independent studies (1, 7, 23, 24, 27). The open-ear function at 0° azimuth is for monaural and binaural listening and is based on three studies (6, 18, 25). The open-ear function at 90° azimuth is based on selected data from Sivian and White (18). Intensity is given in decibels relative to 1 dyne/cm².

and most consistent difference was reported by Holway and Upton (9) who found that the binaural threshold was from 3 to 6 db lower than the monaural threshold, with the greatest difference occurring in the frequency range of maximum sensitivity.

The open-ear (M.A.F.) function at 0° azimuth is also a composite (6, 18, 25), and it represents both monaural and binaural listening. The wavy appearance of the function in the region of 4000∿ is the result of the influence of a single curve obtained by Sivian and White (18) who suggest that it may have been due to diffraction of the sound waves around the head of the listener. The open-ear (M.A.F.) function at 90° azimuth (dashed line) was obtained from the data of Sivian and White for their best listeners. It probably comes close to the ultimate limit for the best listeners under the most favorable listening condition, and it reveals clearly the importance of head position within the sound field.

Comparison of the curves for minimum audible pressure and minimum audible field (0° azimuth) suggests that the sound pressure at threshold, as measured in a free field at the place previously occupied by the listener's head, is actually less than the pressure developed at the tympanic membrane when he listens. For example, the M.A.F. pressure for a 1000∿ tone is about −73 db (re: 1 dyne/cm²), yet from the M.A.P.

function we know that the pressure at the tympanic membrane at threshold for the same tone is 6 db greater (—67 db). We have previously reported that the external meatus has a natural resonance in the frequency range of maximum sensitivity and that sound pressure at the tympanic membrane can be augmented 6 to 8 db by resonance. We conclude that the M.A.F. curve is probably spuriously low in the range between 1000 and 4000∿ because the actual pressure developed at the tympanic membrane is augmented through resonance. If this be so, which seems likely, then the M.A.P. threshold curve is the truer one for the middle frequencies. Meatal resonance also might account for the irregularity of the curve in this frequency range.

For the lower frequencies the closed-ear arrangement may show pressures that are spuriously high so as to overcome the low-frequency noise which occurs when the external meatus is closed (5). Wever and Lawrence (32) state that the tympanic membrane and associated structures are better matched to the impedance of the open air than to the impedance of a limited volume of air trapped in the meatus. If so, we would be led to conclude that the M.A.F. threshold curve is the truer one for low frequencies. Part of the difference between these two threshold curves across all frequencies may be due to the intra-aural muscles which are activated by tactual stimulation of the pinna and meatal entrance. Such stimulation would occur generally only with the closed-ear arrangement, and its effect would be to make the ear appear less sensitive.

Apart from the differences just described, both threshold curves show the normal human ear maximally sensitive to the frequencies between 1000 and 3000∿. Sensitivity falls off above and below this frequency range. If the threshold for a 1000∿ tone is taken as an arbitrary reference, then sound pressure has to be increased almost one-hundredfold to reach threshold at 100 and 15,000∿, and one-thousandfold at 40 and 18,000∿. While individual differences are not shown in Fig. 6.1, it should be remembered that even for a well-motivated listener, absolute thresholds vary by as much as 5 db from one minute to the next (2, 12), and prolonged listening, especially to high frequency tones, can reduce sensitivity by as much as 20 db (23).

TERMINAL THRESHOLDS

Unlike the absolute threshold, the terminal intensive threshold does not vary appreciably with frequency. Discomfort occurs more or less uniformly for all frequencies when sound pressure reaches 40 db above 1 dyne/cm² (17). Sensations of tickle and pain occur when the intensity is raised another 20 db (1, 25). It is not possible to establish very precise terminal thresholds because the subjective criteria of non-auditory sensations which define the upper limit, such as tickle, feeling, or pain, do not occur suddenly.

The normal intensitive range between the absolute and terminal thresholds for a 1000∿ tone is about 140 db, which represents a ten-millionfold change in pressure. From the absolute threshold curves shown in Fig. 6.1, it is clear that this range is shortened progressively for the high and low tones. For example, a 100∿ tone requires an intensity at threshold which is 40 db more intense than for a 1000∿ tone. Therefore, the intensitive range at 100∿ is 100 db.

DIFFERENTIAL INTENSITY DISCRIMINATION

The smallest detectable change in the intensity of a tone is the difference threshold. It may be expressed as the absolute amount of change (ΔI) that is just noticeably different, or it may be expressed as the relative change ($\Delta I/I$). There are three important factors which influence the magnitude of ΔI: the level of I for which ΔI is determined; the frequency of the stimulating tone; and the manner in which the two tones to be compared are presented.

The early work on differential sensitivity led Wundt to conclude that $\Delta I/I$ was constant (Weber's Law) at 0.33. The first man to study differential sensitivity over extensive ranges of both intensity and frequency was Knudsen (10), who reported in 1923 that $\Delta I/I$ was not constant. Furthermore, he reported a $\Delta I/I$ value of 0.1 for the middle frequencies and thereby showed differential sensitivity to be considerably better than the earlier reports had indicated. Even though his apparatus was far superior to that of earlier experimenters, his method has been criticized by Licklider (11). Knudsen used pure tone stimuli and changed their intensity by switching abruptly the voltage level which drove the transducer. Since abrupt switching distorts the purity of the tone by spreading energy to other frequencies, his listeners might have been assisted in their discriminations of intensity by other tonal attributes.

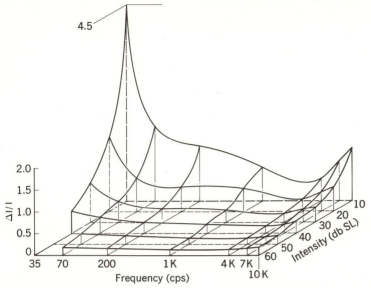

Fig. 6.2 Values of ΔI/I for pure tones as a function of frequency and intensity. Data from Riesz (14).

In an attempt to minimize such distortions, Riesz (*14*) devised a method which allowed the changes in intensity to occur more gradually. A single transducer fitted to one ear was driven by the combined output of two oscillators mis-tuned by 3∿. For example, the output from one oscillator set at 1000∿ was adjusted to give a clearly audible tone. Then the output of the second oscillator (1003∿) was increased until the listener first detected a fluctuation in loudness (beats). When two tones of nearly the same frequency are presented simultaneously, the effect is to hear a single tone of fluctuating loudness rather than two tones, each of constant loudness. He took as the difference threshold the calculated difference between maximum and minimum intensities when changes in loudness were first noticed.

The relative difference thresholds (ΔI/I) obtained by Riesz are given as a function of frequency and intensity in Fig. 6.2. Note that intensity is expressed in decibels relative to absolute threshold, and that for graphic clarity the intensity coordinate is reversed. There is little support for Weber's law, for if it held, the contoured surface would have been a horizontal plane. Instead, it may be seen that regardless of frequency

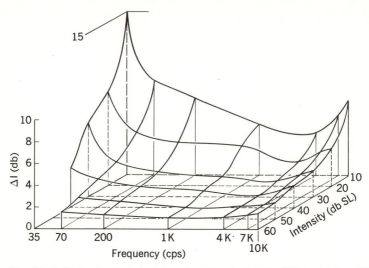
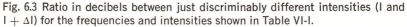

Fig. 6.3 Ratio in decibels between just discriminably different intensities (I and I + ΔI) for the frequencies and intensities shown in Table VI-I.

the discrimination improves (the relative jnd grows smaller) as intensity rises. The improvement is negatively accelerated as a function of intensity, but it continues to the highest levels studied. The effects of frequency on ΔI/I are more complicated. Intensity discrimination is best at about 2500∿, regardless of sensation level, but it becomes progressively worse as frequency is raised or lowered.

When intensity discrimination is considered in terms of relative jnd's (ΔI/I), as in Fig. 6.2, the enormous differences in sensitivity often are not fully appreciated. However, the differences in discrimination are made obvious when the changes (ΔI's) are given directly in sound pressures. Since the observations of Riesz were in relative energy units, it is necessary to convert them in order to obtain values of ΔI in sound pressure. This can be done, as follows. From the closed-ear sensitivity function (M.A.P.) of Fig. 6.1 one can calculate the intensity in dynes/cm² for each frequency at each sensation level studied by Riesz. From these values of I and the empirical ΔI/I ratios reported by Riesz, the ΔI for each frequency at each sensation level can be computed. The results of such computations are given in Table VI-I. It is clear that the difference between two just noticeably different intensities is extremely varied. For example, a 35$\wedge$ tone 40 db SL must have its intensity raised by 50 dynes/cm^2 in order to be perceived as just discriminably louder, whereas a 1000$\wedge$ tone at the same level above threshold (40 db SL) must have its intensity increased by only 0.009 dyne/cm^2 in order to be judged just noticeably louder. The data of Table VI-I can also be expressed in terms of the ratio in decibels of two just discriminably different intensities, as shown in Fig. 6.3. Here we see that a 1000$\wedge$ tone at 10 db SL is just discriminably different from one at 14.6 db SL; at 30 db SL from one at 31.9 db SL; and at 60 db SL from one at 61 db SL.

The amount of sound pressure that must be added to a given pure tone to make it just noticeably different is most simply shown when ΔI is plotted as a function of I where both are given in dynes/cm^2 on linear coordinates. Based upon converted data from the experiment of Riesz

Table VI-I Intensity Discrimination

Values of I and ΔI in dynes/cm^2 for each of seven frequencies at each of six intensity levels above absolute threshold. Values of I were determined from Fig. 6.1, and values of ΔI from $\Delta I/I$ determinations of Riesz (14).

| | | INTENSITY | | | | | |
| | | 10 db SL | | 20 db SL | | 30 db SL | |
		I	ΔI	I	ΔI	I	ΔI
	35$\wedge$	3.160	14.200	10.000	17.000	31.600	28.440
	70$\wedge$	0.250	0.425	0.794	0.585	2.510	1.200
FREQUENCY	200$\wedge$	0.016	0.020	0.050	0.028	0.158	0.047
	1000$\wedge$	0.001	0.001	0.005	0.002	0.014	0.004
	4000$\wedge$	0.002	0.001	0.006	0.002	0.018	0.004
	7000$\wedge$	0.004	0.004	0.013	0.005	0.040	0.012
	10,000$\wedge$	0.010	0.012	0.032	0.016	0.100	0.032

| | | 40 db SL | | 50 db SL | | 60 db SL | |
		I	ΔI	I	ΔI	I	ΔI
	35$\wedge$	100.000	50.000	—	—	—	—
	70$\wedge$	7.940	2.780	25.120	6.028	79.400	13.498
FREQUENCY	200$\wedge$	0.501	0.125	1.585	0.317	5.010	0.752
	1000$\wedge$	0.045	0.009	0.141	0.017	0.446	0.054
	4000$\wedge$	0.053	0.008	0.166	0.023	0.562	0.079
	7000$\wedge$	0.126	0.026	0.398	0.064	1.259	0.201
	10,000$\wedge$	0.316	0.088	1.000	0.190	3.162	0.601

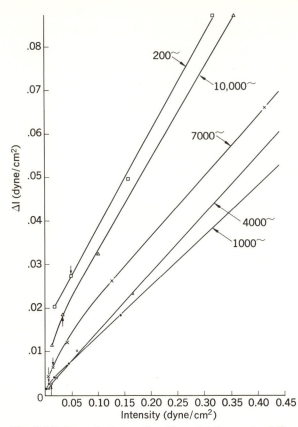

Fig. 6.4 Values of ΔI as a function of I for each of five frequencies plotted in dyne/cm² on linear coordinates. The arrows on each function represent intensities which correspond to 20 db SL. Differences in slope (s) and intercept show intensity discrimination to be best for pure tones of the middle frequencies. Data from Table VI-I.

(Table VI-I), Fig. 6.4 shows the relationship between I and ΔI for the frequencies 200, 1000, 4000, 7000, and 10,000$\sim$. The extreme values of I were omitted from the graph because their range was too great to be represented conveniently on linear coordinates. The arrows on each function represent an intensity corresponding to 20 db SL. They differ according to frequency because the absolute sensitivities also differ (see Fig. 6.1). Once intensity exceeds the absolute threshold by about 20 db, ΔI increases as a linear function of I, at least up to moderate levels (80 db SL).

Beside the linear relationship of I and ΔI (except near absolute threshold), two other important facts are evident from the functions shown in Fig. 6.4. First, for any value of I, ΔI is smaller for the middle frequencies than it is for the extreme frequencies. Second, the slopes of these functions appear to be grouped in two classes, with the extreme frequencies (200∿ and 10,000∿) showing a much greater change in ΔI for a given change in I than is the case for the middle frequencies. Let us consider now some of the implications these facts hold for the role of the cochlear potential in intensity discrimination.

Relationship of ΔI to Cochlear Potential (CP). Recall that the magnitude of the CP is a linear function of sound intensity except at the upper limit where the function becomes negatively accelerated. Fig. 6.5 shows

Fig. 6.5 Intensity functions showing the magnitude of the cochlear potential in microvolts as a function of stimulus intensity in decibels for each of five frequencies. Zero db equals 1 dyne/cm².

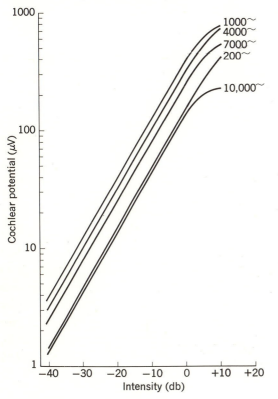

the relationship between CP and I in the form of intensity functions for each of five frequencies. These data were obtained from the ear of a cat in our laboratory, and they are representative of the higher mammals. Note that on log-log coordinates (Fig. 6.5) each function has a slope of approximately 1.0. However, when these same data are plotted on linear coordinates (Fig. 6.6) the slopes may be seen to vary for each frequency while each function remains linear. Accordingly, a standard arbitrary increment in intensity (ΔI) results in a different increment in the cochlear potential for each frequency, as shown by the shaded rectangles.

Instead of using a standard arbitrary value of I, what we should like

Fig. 6.6 Plot of data from Fig. 6.5 on linear coordinates to show that slope of intensity function varies with frequency. The intensity range from 0.1 to 1.0 dyne/cm^2 corresponds to the range from —20 to 0 db on Fig. 6.5. Note that a fixed increment in intensity (ΔI) leads to different increments in the cochlear potential (shaded rectangles) as a function of frequency.

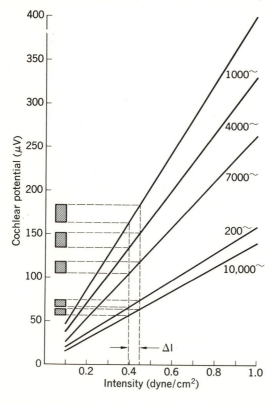

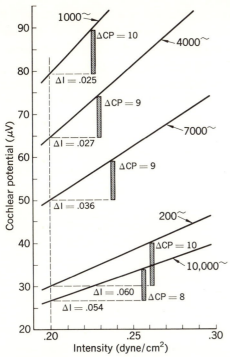

Fig. 6.7 Plot of data from Fig. 6.6 on expanded coordinates. To an arbitrary value of I (0.2 dyne/cm²), values of ΔI from Fig. 6.4 are added to show that ΔI values result in a constant increment in CP (9 μv ±1) across the five different frequencies.

to do is substitute empirical values of ΔI for each frequency shown in Fig. 6.6 in order to determine what effects they would have upon the CP.

It would be best to determine the relationship between ΔI and ΔCP where psychophysical and electrophysiological data were obtained on the same sample of listeners. Unfortunately, that is not possible since we are wanting some of the necessary cochlear potential data on normal human ears. Nevertheless, we know that in man the CP is a linear function of intensity, and we know that the slope of this relationship varies with frequency in essentially the same way as that shown for the cat in Fig. 6.6. Therefore, we shall examine the relationship with the data at hand.

To illustrate the manner in which the relationship between ΔI and CP was determined, consider Fig. 6.7. Here the magnitude of the CP, as recorded from the cat, is plotted as a function of intensity for each of five tonal frequencies. By reference to Fig. 6.4 it is possible to determine the magnitude of ΔI for each of these five frequencies when I equalled 0.2 dyne/cm². For example, for a 1000∿ tone at 0.2 dyne/cm², the average human listener detects a just noticeable difference in loudness when intensity is increased by 0.025 dyne/cm² (ΔI). When ΔI is added to I, we see that the effect is to augment the CP by 10 microvolts. Again, with reference to Fig. 6.4, we find that a 200∿ tone at 0.2 dyne/cm² has a ΔI of 0.060 dyne/cm². When ΔI is added to I, we see that the effect is to augment the CP by the same amount (10 μV). From Fig. 6.7, we can conclude that for each of the five sampled frequencies a just noticeable difference in loudness is equivalent to a constant change in the magnitude of the CP ($\Delta CP = 9 \mu V \pm 1$). This occurs because the values of ΔI vary inversely with the slope of intensity functions.

Nine similar analyses were made for other values of I between 0.1 and 1.0 dyne/cm², and on the basis of them we can state a general principle: for any given intensity between 0.1 and 1.0 dyne/cm², *a just noticeable difference in loudness is equivalent to a constant change in the magnitude of the cochlear potential, regardless of frequency.* Analyses which would allow an extension of the range of intensities over which this principle operates have not been made, but there is no reason to believe that it would not operate at levels below 0.1 dyne/cm². However, it would not hold for intensities very much greater than 1.0 dyne/cm², because it is here that the intensity functions begin to depart from linearity, and they do so at different rates depending upon frequency.

The significance of this principle is made plain in Fig. 6.8, where values of ΔI and ΔCP are plotted for the same combinations of frequency and intensity. The upper curved surface represents ΔI and should be read against the right ordinate scale (dyne/cm²). The lower planar surface represents ΔCP for each corresponding ΔI and it should be read against the left ordinate scale (microvolts). Whereas ΔI changes across intensity and frequency, ΔCP changes only with intensity. As mentioned previously, the remarkable interaction of ΔI and the slopes of CP intensity functions serves to negate the influence of frequency. It should be noted that the more or less constant value of ΔCP across frequency oc-

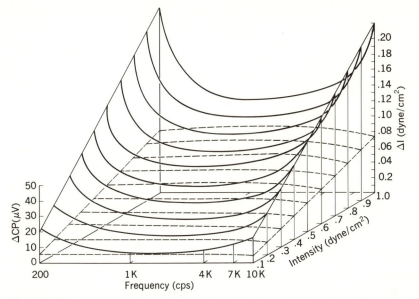

Fig. 6.8 The upper curved surface outlined by the solid contour lines gives values of ΔI in dyne/cm² for each of five frequencies at each of ten intensities, and it should be read against the right ordinate. The lower planar surface outlined by the dashed contour lines gives values of ΔCP in microvolts for the same combinations of frequency and intensity, and it should be read against the left ordinate.

curs only when intensity is held constant. If one were to plot ΔCP's equivalent to ΔI's for different tones all of the same *sensation level,* then ΔCP would vary because intensity would also vary. Therefore, we conclude that it is better here to conceptualize intensive discrimination in terms of constant sound pressures rather than in terms of constant sensation levels.

Needless to say, the relationship between ΔI and ΔCP described here must be taken with caution because the ΔI values were obtained from human listeners whereas the ΔCP values were obtained from the cat. Accordingly, the absolute values of ΔCP shown in Fig. 6.8 cannot be assumed to be valid for the human. On the other hand, enough is known about the CP in the human to suggest that values of ΔI would interact with the slopes of CP intensity functions so as to result in a relationship of the same sort as that shown in Fig. 6.8.

Frequency Thresholds

The frequency limits of hearing are generally stated to lie between 20 and 20,000∿ for normal young human ears. Sounds may vary in frequency from zero indefinitely upward, but any particular ear shows sensitivity within a limited range. When considering the limits we do well to distinguish between the perception of pitch and simple detection. When detection is the sole criterion, the ear is stimulable both above and below these limits, assuming sufficient intensity. Let us consider the evidence for detection.

UPPER LIMIT OF DETECTION

From the previous discussion of intensive ranges, it should be remembered that at very high frequencies the absolute and terminal thresholds essentially converge. Frequency detection, therefore, resolves into a problem of intensity. The stronger the intensity, the higher is the frequency limit. At moderate intensities (80 db SPL) the limit is often no higher than 18,000∿, but it cannot be extended indefinitely, assuming adequate intensity, because there is a final practical limit imposed by pain. High tones reach painful intensities at about 23,000∿. The upper limit is defined, therefore, as the *terminal frequency at which hearing occurs in the absence of pain.* Whether or not hearing occurs for frequencies beyond 23,000∿ is a matter for conjecture since few systematic explorations with humans have been done under stimulus conditions which arouse pain. However, based on electrophysiological experiments with anesthetized preparations, it appears fairly certain that the receptor organ functions at frequencies considerably higher than the limits suggested from behavioral data. The cochlea, therefore, probably does not represent the limiting factor, and the suggestion that the mass of the ossicles is too great to be overcome at vibration rates higher than 23,000∿ is probably wrong (8). In a number of species, single-unit studies support the claim that the auditory nervous system can code frequencies at least as high as 30,000∿, but whether or not this occurs in man is unknown. It seems likely that the practical upper limit of 23,000∿ is imposed both by pain and a failure of the auditory nervous system. Although some benefit for auditory theory would accrue from an experimental separation of these two factors, we shall have to be content with the observations at hand.

Beside the danger of injury to the listener's ear, there are technical problems in studying high tones. The production of pure tones of the required frequency and intensity is physically difficult. The early attempts to generate high tones with whistles were unsatisfactory because of their erratic performance and their low frequency hiss. By utilizing the old Koenig bars and the principle of magnetostriction, it was possible to develop a better instrument. Certain metals change in length when exposed to a magnetic field, and oscillatory currents sent through a coil surrounding such a metal bar produce longitudinal vibrations at the resonant frequency. The major drawback was a failure to achieve the necessary intensities. The development of specifically designed speakers and amplifiers has proved to be much more satisfactory, but unfortunately most commercially available systems are not designed to operate beyond 20,000∿. Accordingly, they are unsatisfactory for an adequate study of the upper limit of frequency detection. Careful determinations of the upper limit require the elimination of electrical and acoustical transients, matters which have been too often ignored or which have been too costly to avoid.

LOWER LIMIT OF DETECTION

Below 20∿ the temporal separation of energy peaks is too great for listeners to achieve a fused tonal quality. Nevertheless, stimulation continues to arouse an auditory sensation, described as "flutter," down to about 10∿. At 15∿ tactual sensations accompany hearing and they are referred either to the middle ear structures or occasionally to the pinna. Wever and Bray (30) employed a pistonphone to study low tone perception, and they emphasized that the variety of auditory experiences to pure tones of low frequency made it difficult to establish any single authoritative lower limit. At frequencies of 15 to 20∿ their observers reported a "thrusting" effect, due very likely to the high intensities necessary to stimulate the ear. Below 15∿ the stimulus was described as a "pumping noise." In a discussion of the methodological difficulties in studies of low tones, Wever (28) has emphasized the importance of well-trained and experienced listeners.

The work of Brecher (4) and Békésy (1) also indicates that 20∿ is the approximate limit for fused tonal quality. Although Békésy has stated that there are recognizable auditory sensations to tones as low as 1 or 2$\curlyvee$, the enormous intensity levels involved (40 to 60 db above 1 dyne/cm^2) make his conclusion dubious because of the difficulty of converting low frequency sinusoidal currents into undistorted sound and the known amplitude distortions by the ear (aural harmonics) to tones of such great intensity. It appears likely that his listeners responded to high frequency components, since distortions are related more directly to the absolute intensity of a tone than to its level above threshold. This is so because the site of distortion is in the cochlea, whereas sensitivity is primarily a neural affair. For example, as stimulus frequency is reduced and intensity is increased to compensate for decreasing sensitivity, distortion becomes present even when the tone is barely audible. Furthermore, the distortions in the form of overtones grow more rapidly than the fundamental as intensity rises. In fact, the second harmonic grows as the square of the pressure, the third harmonic as the cube, and so on (*31*). The lower limit of frequency detection is confounded more than the upper limit by cochlear distortion processes.

We may conclude this discussion of frequency range with the following: the unimpaired human ear can hear sounds from about 10 to 23,000$\curlyvee$, but the range for pitch is limited to 20 to 20,000$\curlyvee$. The matter of pitch is treated in the next chapter.

DIFFERENTIAL FREQUENCY DISCRIMINATION

The capacity of a listener to detect a change in frequency may be expressed either as the absolute difference in cycles per second between two just discriminably different tones (Δf) or as the relative difference ($\Delta f/f$). Although the duration of the tones, the time interval between them, and the psychophysical method employed all have an effect upon Δf, the two overriding factors that influence differential sensitivity are the frequency and intensity of the tones.

Before we consider the experimental data, a major methodological difficulty inherent in experiments on frequency discrimination should be mentioned, since the manner in which experimenters have handled the difficulty has influenced their results. To measure Δf one must present in succession two tones of slightly different frequencies. One cannot present them simultaneously because, as we know from our discussion of ΔI

(Riesz, *14*), the pressures combine so as to give the perception of one tone of fluctuating loudness. It is well known in psychophysics that the difference between stimuli is most easily detected if the change from one to the other is abrupt, and herein lies the problem. Abrupt initiation and termination of tones is always accompanied by a spread of energy along the frequency scale because a sound generator can neither go into nor out of sinusoidal movement instantaneously. The consequence is that the purity of tones is compromised, and often to an extent that is difficult to know. The early work on frequency discrimination ignored the problem of transients, but since then, various attempts have been made to minimize them. One way to reduce the abruptness of tonal initiation and termination is to use an electronic switch which controls the rate of voltage application to the speaker. But this increases the interval between the tones to be compared, and thus leads to Δf's which are probably too large.

To minimize the problem of transients while still allowing tones to be presented in close succession, Shower and Biddulph (*16*) devised the novel technique of a "sliding" tone. The tone was first of constant frequency for a short duration, then it changed sinusoidally to the new frequency where it remained constant for another brief period after which it returned to the original frequency. The difference in frequency between the two constant phases was increased until the listener detected a difference. Unfortunately, the pressure changes produced by sinusoidal frequency change include frequencies other than the two representing the constant phases. Nevertheless, the "sliding" tone is probably the best compromise yet achieved to minimize distortion and maximize abruptness. With this discussion of methodology in mind, let us now review the data.

Since every aspect of failure to obtain pure tones serves to improve discriminability, we would expect that the early work would show smaller Δf's than does current work because there were so many uncontrolled cues on which listeners could have made discriminations. This is clearly the case. In 1888 Luft (*13*) with very crude equipment established a Δf of 0.2∿ for a tone of 1000∿. In 1914 Vance (*22*) published the results of a more comprehensive and better controlled study of frequency discrimination. He found the average Δf of fifty listeners for a 1000∿ tone to be 3.0∿, a far cry from Luft's 0.2∿.

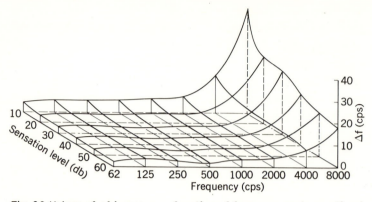

Fig. 6.9 Values of Δf in cps as a function of frequency and sensation level. Converted from Δf/f determinations of Shower and Biddulph (**16**).

The definitive study on frequency discrimination is that of Shower and Biddulph (*16*) whose method has already been described. Based on preliminary work, they settled on a "sliding" rate of 2/sec because it gave keener discrimination than other rates (1 to 5.5). They studied discrimination over an extensive intensity range for selected frequencies from 31 to 11,700∿.

Some of the results of their experiment are shown in Fig. 6.9 where the difference threshold is expressed in absolute terms, Δf, as a function of frequency and sensation level. Note that the sensation level coordinate is reversed for the sake of graphic clarity. From Fig. 6.9 we see that at all frequencies Δf decreases moderately as sensation level rises, and the effect is more pronounced for the high than for the middle and low frequencies. However, the influence of frequency on Δf is much more pronounced. Whereas for any given sensation level Δf remains very nearly constant from 62 to 2000∿, it grows progressively larger with further increases in frequency. If to the data of Shower and Biddulph (*16*) we add the observations of Wever and Wedell (*33*), then the following effects of frequency on Δf may be noted: at a sensation level of 40 db, Δf is about 3∿ for tones of 125 to 2000∿, and by 5000∿ it has risen to 12∿, by 10,000∿ to 30∿, and by 15,000∿ to 187∿. Evidently, man's discrimination of high tones is poor.

The difference threshold data of Shower and Biddulph expressed as

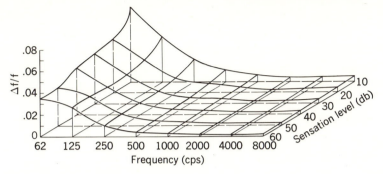

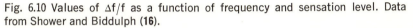

Fig. 6.10 Values of Δf/f as a function of frequency and sensation level. Data from Shower and Biddulph (16).

the relative jnd, Δf/f, are shown in Fig. 6.10. Here it may be seen that the relative jnd grows progressively smaller as frequency rises from 62 to about 1000∿, after which it remains very nearly constant up to 8000∿. Indeed, based upon the partial data of Shower and Biddulph for a 11,700∿ tone and the data of Wever and Wedell (33) for a 15,000∿ tone, Δf/f does not change very much over this higher range. The Δf/f contour for 15,000∿ would look very much like the one shown in the figure for 250∿. The influence of sensation level on Δf/f is moderate. It appears to have its most pronounced effect for the low frequencies, yet even for them, increases in sensation level beyond 40 db do not improve discrimination very much.

Inasmuch as Δf/f is not constant, there is no compelling support for Weber's law. However, it is approximated reasonaly well for the middle and higher frequencies, especially at the higher sensation levels.

Frequency Discrimination and Receptor Processes. Several attempts have been made to map the jnd scale for frequency along the longitudinal extent of the basilar membrane. Wegel and Lane (26) were the first to work out such a map. They assumed that the *place* principle was valid for the entire range of audible frequencies and that any two tones which were just noticeably different in pitch would stimulate "places" on the basilar membrane separated by a constant distance (*constant distance hypothesis*). Based on the Δf observations of Knudsen (10), Wegel and Lane calculated the total number of discriminable pitches and then simply mapped them on the basilar membrane. The lowest pitch was located at the apex and the highest at the base. The number of jnd steps from the lowest pitch to any particular frequency relative to the total number of jnd's was taken to be the fractional distance along the basilar membrane. For example, if there were 300 jnd's between the lowest pitch (20$\curlyvee$) and 800$\curlyvee$, and a total number of 1200 jnd's, then 800$\curlyvee$ was located one-quarter of the way from apex to base (300/ 1200 = ¼). In this way the "places" for each frequency were located on the receptor surface.

The more extensive observations of Shower and Biddulph (16) were treated in a similar manner by Stevens, Davis, and Lurie (21). Their calculations, along with several other lines of evidence on frequency localization, were taken by Stevens and Davis (20) to support the original assumption of Wegel and Lane regarding the constant distance hypothesis.

Steinberg (19) rejected the assumption of constant distances and instead considered each jnd step in terms of a shift across a constant number of ganglion cells (neural shift hypothesis). The density of neural innervation of the human cochlea, measured from the basal end, increases over the first three millimeters from 50 to about 1,100 ganglion cells per millimeter. It remains relatively constant at this level (±10 per cent) over the next twenty-two millimeters where it then begins to decrease linearly over the last seven millimeters to reach a level of about 50 ganglion cells in the final millimeter (29). Steinberg's hypothesis leads to predictions about the spatial representation of discriminable frequencies on the basilar membrane which are different than those made on the basis of the constant distance hypothesis. Whereas both hypotheses are in agreement for the middle frequencies (because constant distances represent shifts across constant numbers of neural elements), they are in disagreement for the low and high frequencies. The distance between two just discriminably different tones of low or high frequency would, according to Steinberg, be farther apart on the basilar membrane than two tones of moderate frequency. Stated differently, there would be fewer jnd's per millimeter at the base and apical ends of the cochlea than there would be in the area between.

There is a better way to consider the relationship between discrimination data and receptor processes which does not require the assumptions

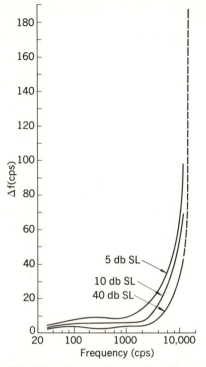

Fig. 6.11 Values of Δf at each of three sensation levels (5, 10, and 40 db) for the frequency range between 31 to 15,000∿. Data from Shower and Biddulph (**16**) and Wever and Wedell (**33**).

made by those whose work has been discussed. Instead of locating the *place* for a given frequency in the fractional manner according to Wegel and Lane or by counting ganglion cells according to Steinberg, we can locate frequencies from direct observations of basilar membrane wave patterns which have been made on the human cochlea. A map of the jnd scale along the receptor surface done in this way allows a direct test of the *constant distance* and the *neural shift* hypotheses. Several steps are required to make such a map and we turn to them now.

The first step consists of determining Δf's from the relative jnd's (Δf/f) reported by Shower and Biddulph (*16*), and the incorporation of additional observations on high frequencies made by Wever and Wedell (*33*). The results are shown in Fig. 6.11 where Δf is shown for each of three sensation levels (5, 10, and 40 db) over a range of frequencies from 31 to 15,000∿. As we know already, Δf for any given frequency decreases as sensation level increases. For example, at 5 db SL a 1000∿ tone is just discriminable from 1009∿ while at 40 db SL it is just discriminable from 1003∿. Therefore, the number of jnd's throughout the frequency range 31 to 15,000∿ varies as a function of sensation level.

The second step consists of calculating the number of jnd's over the same frequency range (31 to 15,000∿) for each of the three sensation levels, beginning with a lower limit of 31∿. The accumulative functions which result are shown in Fig. 6.12, where it may be seen that the total number of jnd's increases from 475 at 5 db SL to 1385 at 40 db SL.

The last step consists of actually mapping the jnd scale along the basilar membrane according to the frequency localizations determined by

Fig. 6.12 Accumulative number of jnd's for pitch between 31 and 15,000∿ for each of three sensation levels. These functions were obtained using values of Δf shown in Fig. 6.11.

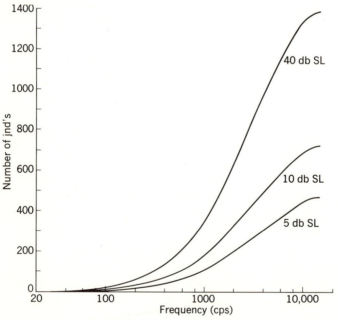

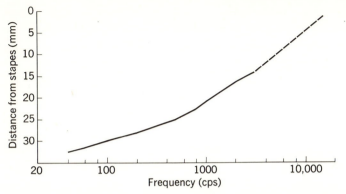

Fig. 6.13 The location of maximum basilar membrane displacement expressed in millimeters from the stapes as a function of stimulus frequency. The dashed line represents an extrapolation to 15,000∿. Data from Békésy (3).

Békésy (*3*) from inspection of anatomical specimens. His data are shown in Fig. 6.13, where the place of maximum membrane displacement is given as a function of stimulus frequency. From Fig. 6.12 we know that for tones 40 db SL there are 100 jnd's between 31 and 300∿. According to Békésy (Fig. 6.13), a 300∿ tone has its "place" located 26.8 mm from the stapes. Therefore, on our map, a place 26.8 mm from the stapes corresponds to 100 jnd's. Again, from Fig. 6.12 we know that for tones 40 db SL there are 400 jnd's between 31 and 1,150∿. Békésy locates this frequency at a place 20.3 mm from the stapes, and on our map this place will correspond to 400 jnd's. In like manner the jnd scale for each of the three sensation levels was mapped in steps of 100 jnd's and the results are shown in Fig. 6.14. The different slopes of these contours simply reflect the fact that near threshold (5 db SL) there are fewer jnd's spread along the membrane than is the case at higher sensation levels. Between 15 and 20 mm there are 110 jnd's at 5 db SL, 180 at 10 db SL, and 325 at 40 db SL. It is obvious, of course, that there can be no *absolute* constant distance between just discriminably different tones since the distance between "places" at 40 db SL is approximately one-third of that at 5 db SL. Of much greater significance, however, is the fact that these contours are not linear as they would have to be if the constant distance hypothesis were correct. For each sensation level shown, the distance between the location of discriminable tones be-

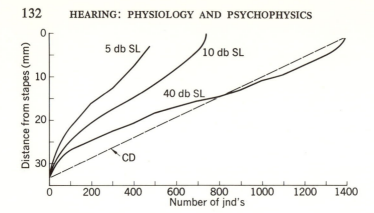

Fig. 6.14 Three contours (5, 10, 40 db SL) showing the relationship between accumulative jnd's and localization of their corresponding frequencies on the basilar membrane. If the "places" corresponding to any two just noticeably different pitches were always separated by a constant distance, then the contours would have been linear, as shown for 40 db SL by the dashed line, CD. Instead, the figure shows that the distance between two just noticeably different pitches varies as a function of sensation level **and** the region of the basilar membrane involved.

comes progressively larger as the basal and apical regions are approached. The straight diagonal line (CD) represents the contour predicted by the constant distance hypothesis for tones 40 db SL. The obtained contour is more consistent with the neural shift hypothesis in that the contour is linear where neural density is contant but the slope of the contour increases as the basal and apical regions are approached, as predicted by Steinberg.

The analysis shown in Fig. 6.14 must not be taken as proof of the spatial localization of jnd's unless the membrane wave patterns, observed by Békésy and included in the analysis, are assumed to embody some very local action of functional significance to frequency coding. Therefore, we do well here to recall the arguments advanced in the previous chapter regarding the difficulties of maintaining a functional place principle, especially for the middle and lower frequencies. Moreover, all available evidence suggests that membrane displacements become broader with increased intensity. Yet frequency discrimination improves. What we still need to know, of course, is the exact nature of frequency coding shown in Fig. 6.14.

References

1. Békésy, G. von. Ueber die Hörschwelle und Fühlgrenze langsamer sinusförmiger Luftdruckschwankungen, *Ann. Physik,* 1936, *26,* 554-566.
2. Békésy, G. von. A new audiometer, *Acta Oto-Laryngol.* (Stockholm), 1947, *35,* 411-422.
3. Békésy, G. von. The vibration of the cochlear partition in anatomical preparations and in models of the inner ear, *J. Acoust. Soc. Amer.,* 1949, *21,* 233-245.
4. Brecher, G. A. Die untere Hör- und Tongrenze, *Pflüg. Arch. ges. Physiol.,* 1934, *234,* 380-393.
5. Brogden, W. J., and G. A. Miller. Physiological noise generated under earphone cushions, *J. Acoust. Soc. Amer.,* 1947, *19,* 620-623.
6. Fletcher, H., and W. A. Munson. Loudness, its definition, measurement and calculation, *J. Acoust. Soc. Amer.,* 1933, *5,* 82-108.
7. Fletcher, H., and R. L. Wegel. The frequency-sensitivity of normal ears, *Phys. Rev.,* 1922, 2nd series, *19,* 553-565.
8. Geldard, Frank A. *The Human Senses,* New York: Wiley, 1953, p. 118.
9. Holway, A. H., and M. Upton. On the psychophysics of hearing: III. The locus of the stimulus threshold, cited in S. S. Stevens and H. Davis, *Hearing,* New York: Wiley, 1938, p. 52.
10. Knudsen, V. O. Sensibility of the ear to small differences of intensity and frequency, *Phys. Rev.,* 1923, *21,* 84-102.
11. Licklider, J. C. R. Basic correlates of the auditory stimulus, Chapter 25 in *Handbook of Experimental Psychology,* S. S. Stevens (Ed.), New York: Wiley, 1951, p. 998.
12. Lifshitz, S. Fluctuations of hearing threshold, *J. Acoust. Soc. Amer.,* 1939, *11,* 118-121.
13. Luft, E. Ueber die Unterschiedsempfindlichkeit für Tonhöhen, *Philos. Stud.* (Wundt), 1888, *4,* 511-540.
14. Riesz, R. R. Differential intensity sensitivity of the ear for pure tones, *Phys. Rev.,* 1928, *31,* 867-875.
15. Rosenblith, W. A., and G. A. Miller. The threshold of hearing for continuous and interrupted tones, *J. Acoust. Soc. Amer.,* 1949, *21,* 467.
16. Shower, E. G., and R. Biddulph. Differential pitch sensitivity of the ear, *J. Acoust. Soc. Amer.,* 1931, *3,* 275-287.
17. Silverman, S. R., C. E. Harrison, and H. S. Lane. Tolerance for pure tones and speech in normal and hard-of-hearing ears. OSRD Report 6303, Central Inst. Deaf., St. Louis, 1946.
18. Sivian, L. J., and S. D. White. On minimum audible sound fields, *J. Acoust. Soc. Amer.,* 1933, *4,* 288-321.
19. Steinberg, J. C. Positions of stimulation in the cochlea by pure tones, *J. Acoust. Soc. Amer.,* 1937, *8,* 176-180.

20. Stevens, S. S., and H. Davis. *Hearing,* New York: Wiley, 1938.
21. Stevens, S. S., H. Davis, and M. Lurie. The localization of pitch perception on the basilar membrane, *J. Gen. Psychol.,* 1935, *13,* 297-315.
22. Vance, T. F. Variations in pitch discrimination within the tonal range, *Psychol. Monog.,* 1914, *16,* 115-149.
23. Waetzmann, E., and L. Keibs. Hörschwellenbestimmungen mit dem Thermophon und Messungen am Trommelfell, *Ann. Physik,* 1936, *26,* 141-144.
24. Waetzmann, E., and L. Keibs. Theoretischer und experimenteller Vergleich von Hörschwellenmessungen, *Akust. Zeits.,* 1936, *1,* 3-12.
25. Wegel, R. L. Physical data and physiology of excitation of the auditory nerve, *Ann. Otol. Rhinol. Laryngol.,* 1932, *41,* 740-779.
26. Wegel, R. L., and C. E. Lane. Auditory masking of one pure tone by another and its possible relation to the dynamics of the inner ear, *Phys. Rev.,* 1924, *23,* 266-285.
27. Wegel, R. L., R. R. Riesz, and R. B. Blackman. Low frequency thresholds of hearing and of feeling in the ear and ear mechanism, *J. Acoust. Soc. Amer.,* 1932, *4,* 6.
28. Wever, E. G. Studying hearing, Chapter 8 in *Methods of Psychology,* T. G. Andrews (Ed.), New York: Wiley, 1948.
29. Wever, E. G. *Theory of Hearing,* New York: Wiley, 1949.
30. Wever, E. G., and C. W. Bray. The perception of low tones and the resonance-volley theory, *J. Psychol.,* 1937, *3,* 101-114.
31. Wever, E. G., C. W. Bray, and M. Lawrence. A quantitative study of combination tones, *J. Exper. Psychol.,* 1940, *27,* 469-496.
32. Wever, E. G, and M. Lawrence. *Physiological Acoustics,* Princeton, N. J.: Princeton University Press, 1954, p. 57.
33. Wever, E. G., and C. H. Wedell. Pitch discrimination at high frequencies, *Psychol. Bull.,* 1941, *38,* 727.

7

Pitch and Loudness

In the previous chapter we dealt especially with absolute, terminal, and differential sensitivities to intensity and frequency. Here we shall treat pitch and loudness, the two basic dimensions of tonal experience. Special attention is paid to the psychological scales for these dimensions and to their relationship to the physical parameters of sound.

Pitch

Pitch is a qualitative dimension of hearing which varies primarily as a function of frequency. It is most often described on a high-low dimension, but the origin of this description is uncertain. There are three hypotheses as to why pitch is commonly described in this manner. First, some observers report that the pitches of high frequency tones give the impression of localization higher in space than the pitches of low frequency tones. Second, musical notation places notes on the staves so that one of a higher frequency always appears above one of a lower frequency. Third, use of the words high and low to characterize pitch may be no more than a reference to the relationship of the frequencies which give rise to different pitches. Of course, the latter hypothesis assumes that listeners know this relationship.

Whatever the reason for describing pitch on a high-low dimension, it is interesting to note that we do not describe the hue of visible light on a long-short dimension even though wavelength is the relevant physical parameter for hue. It is psychologically meaningless to state that green is longer than blue and shorter than red.

135

The difference in the manner of describing hue and pitch is more than an idle curiosity. Although the wavelength of visible light can vary continuously, the receptor process codes it discontinuously, thus leading to discrete primary hues. They may, of course, appear mixed, but aqua is typically described in terms of its psychological primaries; namely, as a blue-green. On the other hand, while the frequency of sound also can vary continuously, coding in the auditory system maintains the continuum. Psychologically and physiologically there are no primary pitches with those between sensed as mixtures. This difference is important because *although pitch is a qualitative dimension it also has numerical properties*. While no one would claim that red has twice the hue of blue, observers can, with good agreement, adjust the frequency of a comparison tone to have twice the pitch of a standard tone. Here, perhaps, we see the manner in which physiological processes influence the dimensions of experience.

DIFFERENCES BETWEEN PITCH AND FREQUENCY

The two terms, *pitch* and *frequency,* often are confused, and in some disciplines, such as physics, they are used interchangeably. Here, however, it is imperative to keep them separate. Pitch relates to sensation while frequency describes one of the physical properties of sound. The differences between them are made clear by four examples. First, a pure tone with a frequency of 18,000∿ leads to a sensation of pitch only if it is heard, and whether or not it is heard depends on the upper limit of frequency sensitivity of the ear as well as the intensity of the tone. Second, two pure tones of different frequency, for example, 18,000 and 18,100∿, will be identical in pitch if the differential sensitivity of the auditory system is insufficient to allow their discrimination. Third, pitch varies as a function of intensity even when frequency is constant. Fourth, as revealed through psychophysical studies, pitch scales are related to frequency scales only in a complex fashion. If a listener is asked to bisect the pitch interval produced by two standard tones, he does not do so by bisecting the frequency scale.

PITCH OF PURE TONES

When a standard tone is presented to an observer, he can adjust the frequency of a comparison so that its pitch is half as high as that of the

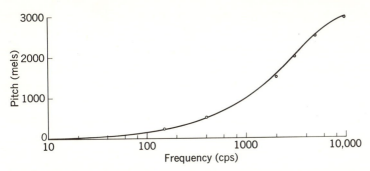

Fig. 7.1 Units of pitch (mels) as a function of stimulus frequency for tones 40 db SL. A standard 1000∿ tone was assigned arbitrarily a pitch of 1000 mels. Tones of 500 and 2000 mels have pitches half as high and twice as high as the standard even though they correspond to frequencies of 400∿ and 3000∿, rather than 500∿ and 2000∿. Data from Stevens and Volkmann (23).

standard. With the *method of fractionation* it has been possible to establish a pitch scale, and by using different standards, an experimenter can determine a pitch-function. In 1937 Stevens, Volkmann, and Newman (*24*) first determined such a function. It was modified later by Stevens and Volkmann (*23*) and their modification is shown in Fig. 7.1. They named the psychological unit of pitch the *mel* and assigned an arbitrary value of 1000 mels to the pitch of a 1000∿ tone. They claim that the numerical significance of the numbers on the pitch scale is that they are related to each other in the same way as the psychological magnitude of the pitches they represent. That is, a pitch of 500 mels is twice as high as a pitch of 250 mels and half as high as a pitch of 1000 mels. Note, however, that the corresponding frequencies do not bear the same numerical relationships.

When considering the pitch-function shown in Fig. 7.1, it is important to recall that its numerical significance derives from the operations which gave rise to it. Failure to appreciate this limitation has led to an important misinterpretation. Thompson (*25*) states that a single mel unit equals Δf at each frequency, but his interpretation demands more of the pitch-function than the operations on which it is based can justify. For example, consider a tone of 10,000∿ (3000 mels) as a standard. To obtain a tone half as high in pitch (1500 mels), the frequency would have to be lowered to 2000∿. Between 10,000 and 2000∿ there are

685 jnd's, as determined from Fig. 6.12. If the standard is changed to 3000∿ (2000 mels), then a tone half as high in pitch (1000 mels) would have a frequency of 1000∿. Between 3000 and 1000∿ there are 490 jnd's. If the standard is changed again to 1000∿ (1000 mels), then a tone half as high in pitch (500 mels) would have a frequency of 400∿. Between 1000 and 400∿ there are 210 jnd's. Clearly, halving pitch is not equivalent to a step across a constant number of jnd's. Neither is the mel scale identical with the cumulative jnd curve as Thompson states.

While the mel scale is of some value in showing a general relationship between pitch and frequency, some question as to its numerical properties can be raised. In our laboratory we have found only limited success with it because judgments of pitch are influenced to a great degree by the particular order of presentation of the standards selected. Furthermore, if mels are to represent a useful *scale,* then not only must N/2 mels be half the pitch of N mels, but N mels must be twice the pitch of N/2 mels. This requirement is not always met by psychophysical data when different references are employed.

OTHER FACTORS INFLUENCING PITCH

Intensity. The intensity of a pure tone influences its pitch. Fortunately for music, intensity does not influence the pitch of the complex tones of musical instruments. The effect with pure tones is of interest to us because of its implications for the coding of pitch. The most widely cited observations dealing with intensive influences on pitch are those of Stevens (*20*) which were based on a single listener. He presented successively two tones of slightly different frequencies and allowed his listener to adjust the intensity of one until its pitch matched the other. He employed eleven standard frequencies ranging from 150 to 12,000∿ and, by the means described, generated a family of *equal pitch contours.* In general, the middle frequencies were shown to have relatively stable pitches regardless of intensity, whereas the low and high frequencies had their pitches shifted progressively downward and upward, respectively, as a function of increasing intensity.

Stevens and Davis (*22*) suggested two different hypotheses to account for the effects of intensity on pitch. One account attributes the effect to the contraction of the middle ear muscles at high intensities. Presumably, this results in an alteration of the resonance characteristics of the ear as a whole. The other hypothesis attributes the effect to a shift in the location along the basilar membrane of the peak amplitude of the cochlear potential (CP) as a consequence of the non-linearity of the CP at high intensities. Both hypotheses run into difficulty because the effect is present and measurable at intensity levels well below those which lead to significant involvement of the middle ear muscles and non-linearity of the CP. Moreover, when a standard tone was presented to one ear, Thurlow (26) found its pitch changed when a tone of the same frequency and intensity was delivered to the other ear. Inasmuch as the effect is binaural, explanations in terms of simple alterations of some peripheral process do not seem adequate.

In his discussion of the evidence for pitch-intensity interaction, Wever (28) concluded that the effect is more illusory than real. For low tones, he suggests that a broader wave pattern in the cochlea occurs either when frequency drops or intensity rises. Accordingly, increased intensity could signal a shift downward in pitch as a result of a confusion of cues. For high tones he suggests that the degree of asynchrony in the first-order neurons increases either when frequency or intensity is raised. Again, there could be a confusion of cues such that an increase in intensity signaled an upward shift in pitch. However, Wever allocates the high frequencies to a place principle, and if *place* is the fundamental cue for pitch, then changes in levels of asynchrony occasioned by increased intensity cannot logically be invoked to explain shifts in pitch.

In an effort to gain a better understanding of the influence of intensity on pitch and to determine the extent to which Steven's single listener was representative of listeners in general, we executed the following experiment. Ten listeners with normal hearing made pitch matches to each of nine standard tones (30 db SL) when the intensity of the comparison equalled 30, 50, and 70 db SL. Each listener heard the standards in random order and separately adjusted the frequency of the comparison to match its pitch to that of the standard. Mean judgments are given in Fig. 7.2A. The intensity of the comparison tone is shown on the ordinate, and the mean change in the frequency of the comparison to effect pitch equality is given on the abscissa. By way of example, consider the contour for the 7000∿ tone shown on the extreme right. When the standard and comparison tones were equally intense (30 db SL), a

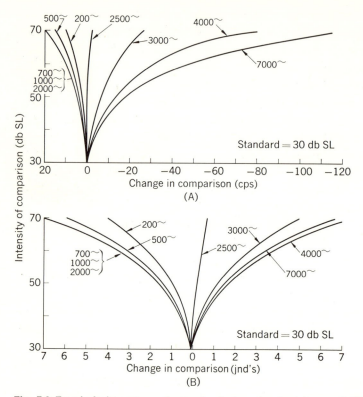

Fig. 7.2 Equal-pitch contours for each of nine standard tones of 200, 500, 700, 1000, 2000, 2500, 3000, 4000, and 7000∿ all at 30 db SL. The intensity of the comparison tone was 30, 50, and 70 db SL, and the changes of the comparison tone at each intensity in order to match the pitch of the standard is shown in cycles per second (A) and in jnd's (B).

pitch match occurred when their frequencies were identical. However, when the comparison was 50 and 70 db SL, pitch matches occurred when the comparison frequency was lowered 18∿ and 115∿, respectively.

With tones below 2500∿ it was necessary to raise the frequency of the comparison to maintain equality of pitch, but the absolute magnitude of the required changes was much smaller than was the case for frequencies above 2500∿. The minimal effect of intensity on pitch was obtained at 2500∿. The asymmetry reflected in the equal pitch contours of Fig. 7.2A is absent in the lower graph (Fig. 7.2B) where the absolute changes in cycles per second are expressed in terms of jnd's. Here it should be recalled that Δf is nearly constant from the lower limit of frequency up to about 2500$\curvearrowleft$. Thereafter, it increases ever more rapidly. This accounts for the symmetry of Fig. 7.2B. When the intensity of the comparison tone exceeded that of the standard by 40 db, the pitch of a 700$\curvearrowleft$ tone was shifted downward about 7 jnd's whereas the pitch of a 7000$\curvearrowleft$ tone was shifted upward about 7 jnd's, even though in terms of absolute frequency change the former involved 20$\curvearrowleft$ and the latter 115$\curvearrowleft$.

Because pitch is perceived as changing continuously as intensity rises, the contours in Fig. 7.2 are shown as smooth even though there are only three mean data points for each one. In general, our observations show the same pattern as those of Stevens except that the influence of intensity on pitch was less pronounced in our listeners.

Duration. The onset of a pure tone is not accompanied instantaneously by a sensation of pitch. Stable and recognizable pitch quality requires some minimal tonal duration, and the establishment of the minimal duration for different frequencies has been of concern because of its implications for coding and auditory theory. Regardless of frequency, tonal durations of a few milliseconds are heard as clicks. As duration is lengthened the click takes on a tonal quality which allows at least some listeners to discriminate among clicks on the basis of what Doughty and Garner (7) call "click-pitch." Still longer durations, usually about a quarter of a second (250 msec), lead to stable pitches. Increases in duration beyond 250 msec do not result in improved discrimination, but reductions in duration lead to poorer discrimination. Békésy (2) found that Δf for an 800$\curvearrowleft$ tone was constant for durations from several seconds down to 250 msec, but Δf doubled at 100 msec and almost tripled at 50 msec. Other experimenters (3, 13, 27) have confirmed this general pattern. Data from these experiments are not entirely consistent in every detail, but this is understandable because of the difficulty of establishing a uniform criterion among listeners. Moreover, the technical problems of presenting pure tones of very brief durations and of specifying their precise character probably make the observations of different experiments not strictly comparable. Nevertheless, it seems clear that there is a critical duration for stable pitch perception, and that below this duration pitch discrimination is adversely affected, finally to be absent for the briefest durations.

How long a given frequency must last in order to produce the experience of a stable and definite pitch, or its *critical duration,* can be expressed in milliseconds or in cycles per second. When the data from the several experiments cited are combined and expressed in both ways, a general principle emerges. Below 1000$\curlyvee$ the critical duration is a fixed number of cycles (6 $\pm$ 3), whereas above 1000$\curlyvee$ the critical duration is a fixed length of time (10 msec).

Here, as in our discussion of frequency discrimination in the previous chapter, we see the possibility that pitch is not coded exclusively according to the *place* or *frequency* principle because neither one operating alone could reasonably give rise to the experimental data on the effects of duration on pitch. That is, if *place* served as the only basis for pitch, then one would expect that some constant time (critical duration) would be required to establish the "place" within the cochlea, regardless of frequency. However, if the *frequency* principle served as the only basis for pitch, then one would expect that some constant number of cycles would be required to establish synchrony between the stimulus frequency and neural discharge rate. Wever (*28*) states that the effects of duration on pitch are quite in line with his *place-frequency* theory. While that is so, the fundamental difficulties of these two principles, as discussed in connection with auditory theory, still remain.

Loudness

Loudness refers to an aspect of auditory experience most often viewed as the psychological correlate of sound intensity. While it is obvious that under usual circumstances loudness grows with intensity, there are exceptions enough to require us to view loudness as a complex function of frequency and wave complexity as well as intensity. Accordingly, loudness should not be used as a synonym for intensity. In passing, we should also note that *volume* also has a special meaning which makes it inappropriate as a synonym for loudness. We shall have more to say about volume in the next chapter.

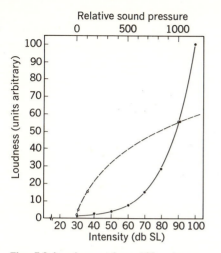

Fig. 7.3 Loudness of an 800∿ tone as a function of stimulus intensity. The loudness was given an arbitrary value of 100 when the intensity of the tone equaled 100 db SL. The solid function, read against the lower abscissa, was obtained with the method of fractionation by Churcher (5). The dashed function, read against the upper abscissa, is another plot of Churcher's data and it shows the growth of loudness as a function of sound pressure.

LOUDNESS OF PURE TONES

Loudness can be measured only by means of the discriminatory responses of listeners. As with pitch, what we should like most to have is a psychological scale for loudness on which the numerical relationships would correspond to sensation magnitudes. Among the psychophysical methods employed to generate a loudness scale, the method of fractionation again has been prominent. The first important work on loudness scaling was done by Churcher (5) and by Churcher, King, and Davies (6). Churcher designated a reference tone of 800∿ at 100 db SL as having a loudness of 100 units. He then determined the intensity in decibels SL for a tone half as loud. Then this tone was halved, and so on. The solid line in Fig. 7.3 gives the form of the loudness scale as determined by Churcher, and it should be read against the lower abscissa. Based on the early work of Fletcher and Munson (10), Fletcher (9) later derived a loudness scale which was almost identical to the one shown.

When loudness is plotted directly against sound pressure on linear co-

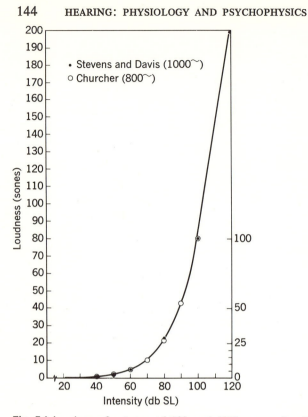

Fig. 7.4 Loudness for tones of 800 and 1000〰 as a function of intensity. The solid circles represent the data of Stevens and Davis (**22**, p. 118) for a 1000〰 tone replotted in modified form where 1 sone is the loudness corresponding to an intensity of 40 db SL. The open circles are from Churcher (**5**) and should be read against the right ordinate.

ordinates a clearer conception of the growth of loudness can be gained. The broken line in Fig. 7.3 represents loudness as a function of sound pressure and it should be read against the upper abscissa. If we arbitrarily set an intensity of 30 db SL as equal to 1 unit of sound pressure, then 50 db SL equals 10 units, 70 db SL equals 100 units, and 90 db SL equals 1000 units. Here we see that at first loudness rises rapidly with sound pressure and then advances progressively more slowly.

It has proved useful to name and adopt a standard unit of loudness. Stevens (*21*) proposed the *sone* as a unit and later Stevens and Davis

(22) suggested that 1 sone be the loudness of a 1000∿ tone 40 db above threshold. The selection of a 1000∿ tone as a referent was suggested out of convenience, and the intensity level of 40 db SL was suggested because of earlier work by Fletcher (8). Both the term *sone* and its reference are now almost universally accepted. With the *sone* thus defined, Stevens and Davis (22, p. 118) determined a loudness function for a 1000∿ tone with the method of fractionation. Their results are shown in modified form by the solid circles in Fig. 7.4. In spite of the fact that Churcher specified a different referent for loudness, his data can be included in the figure (open circles) simply by making the loudness of his referent (100 db SL) equivalent to the loudness obtained by Stevens and Davis for the same intensity. The open circles, however, should be read against the right ordinate. The congruence of the two sets of data is almost perfect, and this gives support to the assertion of Stevens and Davis that the loudness function for a 1000∿ tone is also accurate for other frequencies in the middle range. What data are available indicate that the lower the frequency, the more rapidly does loudness increase with intensity, at least up to moderate levels. Nevertheless, we conclude that the loudness function shown in Fig. 7.4 is approximately correct for the frequencies between 500 and 4000∿. As plotted, the function is positively accelerated; but if intensity were expressed in sound pressure units on a linear scale, then loudness would appear as a negatively accelerated function.

OTHER FACTORS INFLUENCING LOUDNESS

Frequency. We have already stated that loudness is not simply a function of intensity. The influence of frequency on loudness becomes apparent when two tones of different frequency are matched for loudness and their respective intensities are compared. In an effort to establish the degree of influence of frequency on loudness, Fletcher and Munson (10) had listeners make loudness matches between a 1000∿ reference tone and ten other tones over a frequency range from 62 to 16,000∿. Loudness matches were made for each of several intensities of the 1000∿ standard.

The data of Fletcher and Munson could be plotted in any of several ways, but our purpose here is served best when the intensity of the comparison tone judged equal in loudness to the standard is given directly in

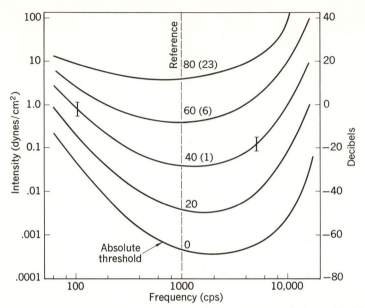

Fig. 7.5 Equal loudness contours showing the changes in intensity (dynes/cm²) required to maintain a constant loudness for different frequencies. Comparison tones were matched to a 1000∿ reference tone at 20, 40, 60, and 80 db SPL. The numbers on each contour give the loudness-level in phons, and the parenthetical numbers give loudness in sones (from Fig. 7.4). Data from Fletcher and Munson (10). Probable errors (vertical bars) from Steinberg and Munson (19).

sound pressure. Fig. 7.5 gives some of the results of their experiment in the form of *equal loudness contours*. The contours represent changes in intensity required by the average listener for loudness to remain constant as frequency changes. For example, consider the function obtained when the 1000∿ standard tone had an intensity 40 db above threshold ($I = 0.04$ dyne/cm²). Here we see that for a 100∿ tone to be judged equally loud, its intensity had to be increased to about 1 dyne/cm², an increase of 28 db. The vertical bars on this function at 100∿ and 5000∿ give the magnitude of the probable error (6 db) for about 100 listeners who made loudness matches between each of these frequencies and a 1000∿ standard, and they come from an experiment by Steinberg and Munson (*19*). A 6 db error is equivalent to a sound pressure ratio of 1:2. Clearly, individual differences are great, but they do not obscure the general relationship observed. As frequencies rise or fall from the middle region, their intensities must be progressively increased to maintain equality of loudness.

Since each one of the contours given in Fig. 7.5 represents combinations of frequency and intensity which produce equivalent loudnesses, it has proved useful to adopt a unit of measure to express the fact of equality and to indicate the manner in which such functions as these differ in *loudness-level*. It is not possible to specify the intensity level in decibels (re $= 0.0002$ dyne/cm²) for an equal loudness contour as a whole because, as Fig. 7.5 shows, intensity varies across frequency. Neither is it possible to specify an equal loudness contour as a whole in terms of sensation level since that also varies across frequency. Instead, equal loudness contours are said to have a *loudness-level* equal to the intensity of a standard reference tone of 1000∿ expressed in decibels with reference to 0.0002 dyne/cm². The unit for loudness-level is the *phon* and for the reference tone of 1000∿ it has the same value as its intensity in decibels (SPL). Consider again Fig. 7.5. The contours presented are identified by the intensity in decibels of the 1000∿ reference tone, but these values also represent the loudness-level of each contour in *phons*. Any sound which is judged to be as loud as a 1000∿ tone 20 db SPL has a loudness of 20 phons. Any tone equal in loudness to a 1000∿ tone 60 db SPL has a loudness of 60 phons, and so on. *The loudness-level in phons of any tone is equal to the intensity in decibels SPL of a 1000∿ tone judged equal in loudness.*

We should note here that the *phon* is not the same as the *sone*. The phon is only a convenient way of expressing the loudness-level of any particular tone in terms of the intensity of a 1000∿ reference tone of equal loudness. The psychophysical judgment required here is one of equality rather than one of scaling. Further, a 1000∿ tone 40 db above threshold is, by definition, equal to 40 phons and 1 sone. The relationship between these two units is actually given in Fig. 7.4 because Stevens and Davis used a 1000∿ tone whose intensity was expressed in terms of the same reference. Accordingly, the abscissa may also be read as *phons*. For the sake of comparison, the number of sones corresponding to each loudness-level (phons) is given in parentheses in Fig. 7.5.

Duration. Auditory fatigue will be considered in the next chapter. We shall treat here the effects of tones of brief duration.

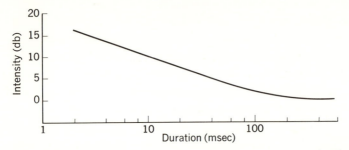

Fig. 7.6 Equal loudness contour for middle frequency tones showing the changes in intensity required to maintain a constant loudness as a function of tonal duration. Intensity is expressed in decibels relative to a standard tone of long duration. Summary of five studies (1, 2, 12, 15, 17).

Several studies have shown that duration influences loudness (*1, 2, 4, 12, 14, 15, 17*). While one study (*14*) dealt with the influence of duration on the absolute threshold and another employed "clicks" rather than tones (*4*), most have employed tones with intensities well above threshold (*1, 2, 12, 15, 17*). A summary of these observations is shown in Fig. 7.6 for tones of the middle frequencies. This, too, is an equal loudness contour because it shows the changes in intensity required as a function of tonal duration in order to keep loudness constant. As durations become progressively briefer than 200 msec, intensity must be increased to maintain equality of loudness.

Whether the effect of tonal duration on loudness is due to receptor or neural processes is still to be determined, but the latter alternative seems more likely because the time course of the integration is too long to be assigned to any known receptor process. On the other hand, the course of integration is consistent with the kind of summation which has been so well established in nervous activity. Lifshitz (*15*) has concluded that within the period of summation (up to 200 msec) time is interchangeable with intensity. However, the relationship of time and intensity shown by Munson's data (*17*) led him to reject their interchangeability and, instead, to view adaptation (neural equilibration) as the primary factor responsible for the effect of duration on loudness. In either case, it is clear that sounds do have a cumulative effect within the first 200 msec.

Complexity. Complex tones are perceived as louder than pure tones of equal sound pressure. This matter has been studied by Fletcher and Munson (*11*) and Pollack (*18*), and from their observations we know that the growth in loudness (sones) with intensity is much more rapid for complex sounds than for pure tones. For example, a "white noise" 60 db SPL was judged to be twice as loud as a 1000∿ tone of the same intensity.

How loud a complex tone is judged to be depends, in part, upon the spectral distribution of its components. When the components are widely separated, the loudness of the tone is equal to the sum of the loudnesses of the components heard separately. However, when the components are close in frequency, the loudness is less than the sum of the individual loudnesses but still greater than that of a pure tone of the same sound pressure. The important point is that the loudness of a complex sound is not always the sum of the components. Failure to find simple additivity has led to speculation that loudness may depend somehow on *place* along the basilar membrane. That is, when the frequency components comprising a complex sound are close together, the cochlear or neural processes which underlie loudness may overlap and thus result in a nonlinear addition. According to this view, the loudness of complex sounds would be the sum of the loudnesses of the components only when the cochlear or neural processes giving rise to loudness did not overlap. Interest in this possibility led to the concept of the critical band.

CRITICAL BAND

Consider a pure tone of 1000∿. If we add other frequencies to it so as to include all those between 900 and 1100∿, then we have a complex sound with a known spectrum. In this example we define the sound as having a *bandwidth* of 200∿ with a *center frequency* of 1000∿. Since it is possible to manipulate bandwidth around a center frequency while holding total sound pressure constant, one can determine the loudness of a complex sound as a function of bandwidth. This may be done most easily by using a pure tone of the center frequency as a comparison with its intensity adjusted so as to match the loudness of the complex sound. Fig. 7.7 shows the effect of bandwidth on loudness for a complex sound with a center frequency of 1000∿ and a constant sound pressure of 60

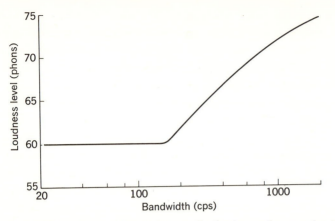

Fig. 7.7 The effects of bandwidth on the loudness of a complex tone of constant sound pressure (60 db SPL) with a center frequency of 1000∿. Loudness is invariant with bandwidths up to 160∿, after which further increases in bandwidth lead to increases in loudness. Loudness level in phons was determined by having six listeners adjust the intensity of a pure tone of 1000∿ so as to match the loudness of the complex tone.

db SPL. Up to a bandwidth of 160∿ the loudness of the sound is not affected. Bandwidths greater than 160∿ result in increases in loudness. Thus, for a center frequency of 1000∿, 160∿ constitutes its *critical bandwidth* because it represents the limits within which loudness is invariant.

Different center frequencies yield different critical bandwidths. When considered in absolute terms, they grow increasingly broader as the center frequency rises. For example, the critical bandwidth for a center frequency of 200∿ is 100∿, for 1000∿ is 160∿, and for 5000∿ is 1000∿. If the limiting frequencies which define each of these critical bandwidths are located on the basilar membrane by reference to Békésy's observations shown in Fig. 6.13, it appears that *a critical bandwidth is equivalent to a constant distance along the membrane of approximately 1.2 mm.* That is, the limiting frequencies of 920∿ and 1080∿ for a center frequency of 1000∿ are the same distance apart on the basilar membrane as 4500∿ and 5500∿, the limiting frequencies for a center frequency of 5000∿. This equivalence obtains for all center frequencies except those below 200∿ and above 16,000∿ in which cases the limiting frequencies are separated by more than 1.2 mm, as would be expected from our discussion of jnd mapping in the previous chapter.

The evidence on loudness obtained from studies of critical bandwidths, along with the equality of distances between their limiting frequencies when projected upon the basilar membrane, suggests a strong link between *place* and the coding of loudness. If this link were established clearly, it would signify a very substantial change in the role of *place* in auditory theory. In an effort to clarify this link a conceptual model is shown in Fig. 7.8. On the left, three center frequencies (*cf*) with non-overlapping but adjacent critical bandwidths (cbw) are depicted. The shaded rectangles represent each of four complex sounds. The areas of the rectangles are equal and represent constant sound pressure. The upper three complex sounds have bandwidths less than or equal to the critical bandwidth whereas the bottom one exceeds the critical bandwidth. If one assumes that loudness is based upon receptor or

Fig. 7.8 Schematic conceptualization of the relationship of critical bands to loudness. See text for explanation.

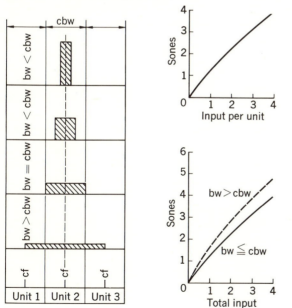

neural processes which have spatial limits equal to those found for critical bands, then each of the three adjacent critical bands shown in the figure can be thought of as a loudness unit. We know from studies of loudness scaling that loudness grows as a negatively accelerated function of sound pressure, and this relationship is shown in the upper right graph of Fig. 7.8 where loudness in sones is plotted as a function of input per loudness unit. As long as sound pressure is constant and bandwidth is less than or equal to the critical bandwidth, only one loudness unit is involved. The upper three rectangles have constant areas (sound pressures), each equivalent, let us say, to 4 units of sound pressure. The bottom rectangle also has an area equal to 4 units of sound pressure, but it is spread over three loudness units rather than one. The lower right graph of Fig. 7.8 illustrates the consequence. The solid line represents the growth in loudness as a function of sound pressure when the input is restricted to one loudness unit: that is, the bandwidth is less than or equal to the critical bandwidth. In such cases four units of sound pressure give a loudness of 4 sones. The dashed line represents the case where the critical bandwidth is exceeded and more than one loudness unit is involved. Loudness units 1 and 3 each have an input equal to 1 which is equivalent to 1.25 sones each, while unit 2 has an input equal to 2 (2.25 sones). The total input is still 4, but the total loudness exceeds 4 units (1.25 + 1.25 + 2.25 = 4.75). It is clear from this conceptualization that the reason loudness increases once a complex sound exceeds a critical bandwidth is that loudness has an underlying process with spatial characteristics *and* that loudness is a negatively accelerated function of sound pressure.

That the processes which give rise to loudness may have a spatial character is not unreasonable in the light of current knowledge from electrophysiological studies of other sense modalities. The size of receptive fields in vision has been correlated with the diameter of the arborized dendritic endings of the bipolars beneath them (*16*). Perhaps loudness coding is based upon something analogous to this.

Relation of Critical Bands to Pitch. Beside loudness, critical bands also hold a curious and remarkable relationship to pitch. Over most of the auditory frequency range (the extremes excepted) a critical band is equivalent to a constant number of *mels*. The number of *mels* within a

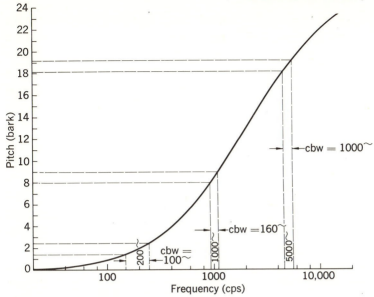

Fig. 7.9 The relationship between pitch (1 bark = 100 mels) and critical band-widths (cbw) for each of three center frequencies (200, 1000, and 5000∿). Between the limiting frequencies for each cbw there are 100 mels.

critical bandwidth depends upon the particular function one uses to derive them. If we use the mel scale shown in Fig. 7.1 and the critical bandwidths already given for center frequencies of 200, 1000, and 5000∿, we see that there are approximately 100 *mels* in each critical band. When a critical band is used in reference to pitch it is defined as 1 *bark* which is equivalent to 100 *mels*. Fig. 7.9 summarizes the relationship. Note that 1 *bark* equals the critical bandwidth (cbw) for the three center frequencies shown. The function is so drawn that the *cbw* for any center frequency may be obtained in the same manner. It should be noted here that although critical bands represent uniform steps along the pitch scale, they do not represent a constant number of jnd's. Within the critical bands for center frequencies of 200, 1000, and 5000∿ there are 40, 52, and 72 jnd's respectively (see Fig. 6.12).

From our discussion of critical bands it is plausible to consider the principle of *place* as playing two different roles in hearing. First, pitch may be coded by a finely spaced series of places while loudness is coded by a much coarser arrangement of places. There does not appear to be an essential contradiction with this dual conception of place, and the neurology of the organ of Corti, being both specific and diffuse, is consistent with it. Still, as attractive as such a conception may be, the serious liabilities noted for the place principle and pitch remain with us.

References

1. Békésy, G. von. Zur Theorie des Hörens; Ueber die Bestimmung des einem reinen Tonempfinden entsprechenden Erregungsgebietes der Basilarmembran vermittelst Ermüdungserscheinungen, *Physik Zeits.,* 1929, *30,* 115-125.
2. Békésy, G. von. Zur Theorie des Hörens. Ueber die eben merkbare Amplituden- und Frequenzänderung eines Tones. Die Theorie der Schwebungen, *Physik Zeits.,* 1929, *30,* 721-745.
3. Bürck, W., P. Kotowski, and H. Lichte. Frequenzspektrum und Tonerkennen, *Ann. Physik,* 1936, *25,* 433-449.
4. Buytendijk, F. J. J., and A. Meesters. Duration and course of the auditory sensation, *Commentationes Pontif. Acad. Sci.,* Rome, 1942, *6,* 557-576.
5. Churcher, B. G. A loudness scale for industrial noise measurements, *J. Acoust. Soc. Amer.,* 1935, *6,* 216-226.
6. Churcher, B. G., A. J. King, and H. Davies. The minimum perceptible change of intensity of a pure tone, *Phil. Mag.,* 1934, *18,* 927-939.
7. Doughty, J. M., and W. R. Garner. Pitch characteristics of short tones: I. Two kinds of pitch threshold. *J. Exper. Psychol.,* 1947, *37,* 351-365.
8. Fletcher, H. Loudness, pitch and timbre of musical tones and their relation to the intensity, the frequency and the overtone structure, *J. Acoust. Soc. Amer.,* 1934, *6,* 59-69.
9. Fletcher, H. Loudness, masking and their relation to the hearing process and the problem of noise measurement, *J. Acoust. Soc. Amer.,* 1938, *9,* 275-293.
10. Fletcher, H., and W. A. Munson. Loudness, its definition, measurement and calculation, *J. Acoust. Soc. Amer.,* 1933, *5,* 82-108.
11. Fletcher, H., and W. A. Munson. Relation between loudness and masking, *J. Acoust. Soc. Amer.,* 1937, *9,* 1-10.
12. Garner, W. R., and G. A. Miller. Differential sensitivity to intensity as a function of the duration of the comparison tone, *J. Exper Psychol.,* 1944, *34,* 450-463.
13. Kucharski, P. La sensation tonale exige-t-elle une excitation de l'oreille par plusieurs périodes vibratoires, une seule période ou une fraction de période? *Année Psychol.,* 1923, *24,* 151-170.

14. Kucharski, P. Sur le loi d'excitation de l'oreille, *Compt. Rend. Soc. Biol.,* 1925, *92,* 690-693.

15. Lifshitz, S. Two integral laws of sound perception relating loudness and apparent duration of sound impulses, *J. Acoust. Soc. Amer.,* 1933, *5,* 31-33.

16. Maturana, H., J. Y. Lettvin, W. S. McCulloch, and W. H. Pitts. Anatomy and physiology of vision in the frog, *J. Gen. Physiol.,* 1960, *43,* 129-176.

17. Munson, W. A. The growth of auditory sensation, *J. Acoust. Soc. Amer.,* 1947, *19,* 584-591.

18. Pollack, I. Studies in the loudness of complex sounds, Ph.D. dissertation, Harvard University, 1948.

19. Steinberg, J. C., and W. A. Munson. Deviations in the loudness judgments of 100 people, *J. Acoust. Soc. Amer.,* 1936, *8,* 71-80.

20. Stevens, S. S. The relation of pitch to intensity, *J. Acoust. Soc. Amer.,* 1935, *6,* 150-154.

21. Stevens, S. S. A scale for the measurement of a psychological magnitude: loudness, *Psychol. Rev.,* 1936, *43,* 405-416.

22. Stevens, S. S., and H. Davis. *Hearing,* New York: Wiley, 1938.

23. Stevens, S. S., and J. Volkmann. The relation of pitch to frequency, *Amer. J. Psychol.,* 1940, *53,* 329-353.

24. Stevens, S. S., J. Volkmann, and E. B. Newman. A scale for the measurement of the psychological magnitude of pitch, *J. Acoust. Soc. Amer.,* 1937, *8,* 185-190.

25. Thompson, R. F. *Foundations of Physiological Psychology,* New York: Harper and Row, 1967, p. 261.

26. Thurlow, W. R. Binaural interaction and the perception of pitch, *J. Exper. Psychol.,* 1943, *32,* 13-36.

27. Turnbull, W. W. Pitch discrimination as a function of tonal duration, *J. Exper. Psychol.,* 1944, *34,* 302-316.

28. Wever, E. G. *Theory of Hearing,* New York: Wiley, 1949.

8

Complex Auditory Phenomena

In this chapter we shall consider the evidence for the existence of dimensions of tonal experience other than pitch and loudness, and then turn to a discussion of auditory fatigue and masking.

Tonal Attributes

There is no dispute over the fact that pitch and loudness are fundamental dimensions of auditory experience. However, it can no longer be argued, as it was a century ago, that the fundamental nature of these two psychological dimenions is derived from their singular relationship to frequency and intensity. Our treatment in the previous chapter made it plain that pitch and loudness are different functions of *both* frequency and intensity. The fundamental nature of pitch and loudness depends upon three conditions: each bears a specifiable dependence upon the physical parameters of tonal stimuli; each produces differential action in the auditory nervous system; and each is independent of the other. These three criteria we shall use to assess several other possible auditory attributes. Except for historical accident, there does not seem to be any reason *a priori* to assume that pitch and loudness constitute the only auditory attributes of tonal experience.

The literature on aesthetics suggests a number of additional attributes, including volume, density, tonality, tonal color, and brightness. In order to determine whether or not any of these proposed attributes is more than an additional way of describing pitch or loudness, we shall consider the available data in the context of our three criteria.

156

VOLUME

Tonal volume pertains to the apparent *extensity* of a tone. In some disciplines, notably physics and engineering, volume is used as a synonym for both sound intensity and loudness; but in psychoacoustics volume refers only to the voluminousness of a sound.

By the turn of the century, casual observers were agreed that tones of low frequency were characterized by most listeners as being more voluminous than tones of high frequency. Furthermore, it was believed that volume grew as a direct function of stimulus intensity. Among these early observers, Carl Stumpf (45) was especially insistent in his belief that tones were discriminable on the basis of their spatiality (volume), but the matter was not investigated in the laboratory until 1916 when Rich (32) attempted the first systematic study.

The results of this first attempt to study tonal volume were confusing, but Rich later improved his method and performed a second experiment in which he determined jnd's for volume as a function of frequency (33). Because of the limitations of his apparatus, Rich employed only a narrow range of frequencies and he ignored the exercise of suitable controls for intensity. Nevertheless, he was able to show that volume was inversely related to frequency. Because his listeners were reliable in their judgments and because they gave many fewer jnd's for volume than would have been the case had they been making pitch discriminations, he concluded that volume was an independent attribute of tones.

A few years later Halverson (17, 18) made further measures of difference thresholds for volume. Unlike Rich, Halverson considered the role of intensity at each of several frequencies, and he found that volume increased regularly with rising intensity for each frequency studied. He also corroborated Rich's findings on frequency: namely, that tones of low frequency are more voluminous than tones of high frequency.

Although these early studies seemed to suggest that volume might be an attribute of tonal experience separate from pitch and loudness, three later studies cast some doubt on the matter. The source of the doubt was a failure of listeners in these later studies to demonstrate agreement on judgments of volume (15, 16, 51). Failure of agreement might have occurred because volume is, in fact, an irrelevant attribute of tones; but the question of relevance is unanswerable from the experiments cited be-

cause insufficient account was taken by these experimenters to the in-
struction of listeners so as to develop an appropriate and uniform manner of judging tonal extensity.

There are two alternatives when gathering psychophysical data on
tasks as complex as judging voluminousness. An experimenter has either
to instruct subjects carefully and then give them practice, or he has to
search for a simpler method sufficient to answer the same question.
Stevens (*40, 41*) chose the second alternative when he had listeners determine *equality* of volume by giving them control over the variable
stimulus. In effect, he demonstrated that a decrease in volume produced
by an increase in tonal frequency could be offset by an increase in
intensity.

A more exhaustive study of the same sort was conducted by Thomas
in 1949 (*46*). He established *equal-volume contours* over a wide range
of frequencies and intensities. His listeners sometimes adjusted the intensity of one tone so as to equate its volume with that of a standard
tone of a different frequency. On other occasions his listeners adjusted
the frequency of one tone so as to equate its volume with that of a
standard tone presented, in turn, at each of ten intensities covering a
range of 80 db.

The two methods, intensity-adjustment and frequency-adjustment, led
to surprisingly similar equal-volume contours, but the latter method gave
more consistent results and it was preferred by the listeners for its relative ease.

The equal-volume contours obtained by Thomas when his listeners
used the method of frequency-adjustment are shown in Fig. 8.1. The
combinations of frequency and intensity that fall on any single contour
represent tones of equal volume, but each contour represents a different
volume. The contours are arranged in order of voluminousness, the left
one being most voluminous, but it is not possible from his experiment to
state quantitatively the volume of one contour in relation to another.

The open circles identify the frequency and intensity of the standard
tone used to generate each contour. For example, consider the middle
contour with its standard stimulus of 1000∿ at 62 db SPL. When the
intensity of the 1000∿ variable tone was increased from 62 to 70 db,
thus increasing its volume relative to the standard, the listeners adjusted
the frequency of the variable tone upwards from 1000∿ to 1300∿,

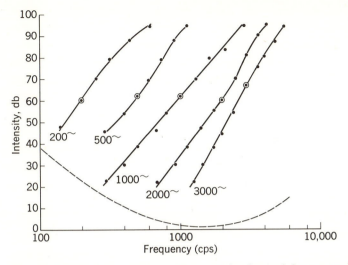

Fig. 8.1 Equal-volume contours. The combinations of frequency and intensity that fall on any single contour represent tones of equal volume. The contours are arranged in order of voluminousness, the left one being greatest. Open circles are the standards used to generate the contours. Intensity is given in decibels with reference to 0.0002 dyne/cm². Data from Thomas (**46**, p. 193).

thereby bringing its volume back to equality with the standard. When the intensity of the 1000∿ variable tone was reduced from 62 to 54 db, thus reducing its volume relative to the standard, the listeners adjusted the frequency of the variable tone downward from 1000∿ to 800∿, thereby restoring volume equality. The other data points along this and the other contours were determined in a similar manner.

Note that for the 200 and 500∿ standards it was not possible to obtain data for intensities very much below the standard because of the limits imposed by the absolute threshold (dashed line). Thomas reported volume data for intensities up to 105 db, but they are not shown in Fig. 8.1 because they were seriously compromised by the limitations of his sound source (PDR-8 headphones).

Based on this experiment we may conclude that equality of volume is described by a linear relationship between log-frequency and log-intensity (decibels). After examination of his equal-volume contours, plotted in terms of *mels* and *sones,* Thomas concluded that the relationship was too complex to conclude that volume was simply a derivative of pitch and loudness.

Gulick (13) has determined subjective scales of tonal volume as a function of frequency at each of two loudness-levels. Six subjects with normal hearing (100 to 10,000∿±5 db) listened binaurally to pure tones from a transducer located one meter away at 0° azimuth while seated one at a time in a soundproof room with soft walls. The volume of the standard 1000∿ tone, 40 db SPL, was arbitrarily assigned a value of 10 *vols*. Subjects manipulated the frequency of a second tone so as to halve and then double the volume of the standard. Frequency changes in the comparison tone were accompanied by intensity changes so as to maintain a constant loudness-level of 40 phons (Fig. 7.5). Multiple references were employed to generate the full volume scale.

In a second session the experiment was repeated with the standard 1000∿ tone set at 60 rather than 40 db SPL. The listeners were unaware (were not told) of this change, and they proceeded under the assumption that the standard equalled 10 *vols*. In the end, each listener made magnitude estimates of the volume of the 60 phon standard with reference to the 40 phon standard so that both scales could be expressed relative to the same volumetric scale.

The results of the experiment are shown in Fig. 8.2 where it may be seen that when loudness is constant, volume decreases as frequency increases. Although low frequency tones are rather enormous compared with those of high frequency, volume is relatively constant between 2000 and 4000∿. The effect of increasing loudness-level from 40 to 60 *phons* is also clearly evident, but the increment in volume is not proportional along the frequency scale. For example, the 60 *phon* function shows a 30 per cent increase in volume at 3000∿ and a 100 per cent increase at 300∿. It should be recalled, however, that the only direct comparison made between the two functions occurred at 1000∿. That the listeners, in making the volume comparison between the two standards, were judging volume rather than loudness appears very likely, for had it been the latter, the functions at 1000∿ would have been different by a factor of about 6 instead of the observed 1.6. The listeners used in this experiment were trained to judge volume, and each was well practiced in preliminary training with three-dimensional visual targets.

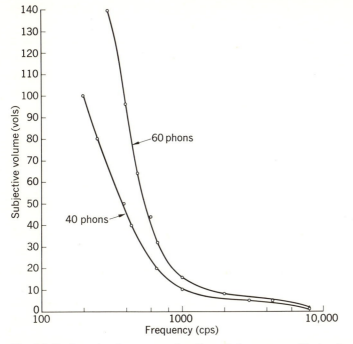

Fig. 8.2 Scales of volume as a function of frequency with loudness-level constant at 40 and 60 phons. Determined by the modified method of fractionation. Standard tone of 1000∿ at 40 db SPL was assigned a volume of 10.

In spite of the fact that judgments of volume are difficult to make, it would appear that volume does bear a specifiable dependence upon the physical parameters of tonal stimuli in a way which is substantially different than pitch and loudness. What remains to be demonstrated, if our three criteria are to be met, is the precise nature of the differential action in the auditory nervous system that could account for volume. Until such evidence is at hand, we are forced to conclude that, although trained listeners can make reliable judgments of tonal volume, volume cannot now be accepted as a fundamental attribute of sound.

DENSITY
Density refers to the apparent hardness or compactness of tones, but the case for density as a fundamental attribute is very much weaker than that

for volume. Stevens (*42, 43*) has reported *equal-density contours* based on experiments in which listeners were allowed to change the intensity of one tone so as to equate its density with another tone of different frequency. Although the frequency range which he studied was very restricted (400 to 600∿), the results suggest that density increases directly with both intensity and frequency. However, its reciprocity with volume raises a question about its independence. Density may be no more than another way of judging voluminousness. Perhaps it would be better, as Osgood has suggested, to think of volume and density as two different ways of considering the single matter of spatiality (*28*, p. 126).

Inasmuch as density has not been the subject of very much research, its dependence on the physical parameters of tones is still tenuous; and since its independence is open to question and nothing is known presently about its relation to nervous activity, there is little to support the claim that density is an auditory attribute. Stevens has argued that density *is* an auditory attribute because it appears to be indepedent of pitch and loudness and because listeners can make density equations. Even if the facts are granted, his argument is wanting if we hold to our three criteria.

TONALITY

Tonality refers to the intimacy of the octave in musical scales, but it applies generally to any two tones when the frequency of one tone is double that of another. A few experimenters have claimed that the perception of pitch carries along with it the property of tonality, and that tonality is responsible for the frequent confusion in octaves. Perceptually, at least, tonality is an anomaly because the pitches of two tones separated by an octave are very discriminable and yet somehow very much alike. Beginning with 256∿ (middle C), the pitches of successively higher notes in the musical scale become increasingly different from middle C except when the octave is reached (512∿). The pitch of the octave is perceived as more similar to middle C than is any other note within the octave, including D which differs in frequency from C by only 24∿. It is because this similarity cannot be accounted for satisfactorily on the basis of pitch that the term tonality has been applied. Licklider (*22*) stated that tonality is characteristic of, and limited to, tones with frequencies below 5000∿. Others have claimed tonality to be essential to absolute pitch discrimination (*1, 26, 27, 31*). Both claims lack experimental support.

It may be that middle C, for example, is endowed with a kind of "C-ness" as a consequence of cochlear distortion in the form of aural harmonics. Recall that at moderate and high intensities, a number of partials can be recorded from the cochlea when pure tonal stimuli are applied. The most prominent harmonic always has a frequency which is double that of the fundamental (stimulus tone). This suggests that the octave may have a kind of *physiological primacy*. Furthermore, electrophysiological studies of single units in the auditory nerve indicate that a neuron that shows itself tuned to a best frequency also shows itself tuned to simple multiples of that frequency. Accordingly, auditory neurons with secondary and tertiary response areas could easily account for tonality and the difficulty of discriminating the octave interval.

Physiological primacy of the octave (actually $x^\wedge \times 2$) does not require that this interval be divided into eight smaller intervals, as in the tempered diatonic musical scale to which we have grown accustomed. Neither does it mean that a scale could not extend beyond the octave for its termination. Although most Western music is written in either the ionian (major) or aeolian (minor) mode, even the less popular modes (dorian, phrygian, lydian, and mixolydian) all contain the octave.

Tonality certainly bears a specifiable dependence upon the physical parameter of frequency. Moreover, there are enough data from physiological studies of receptor processes and auditory neurons to indicate that the octave interval is unique in its effects upon them. Finally, tonality is perceptually distinguishable from pitch and loudness. With our three criteria thus met, we may accept tonality as an auditory attribute.

As for tonal color and brightness, too little is known about them to allow a critical review. Rich (*32, 33*) concluded that brightness was identical with pitch. Later, Boring and Stevens (*4*) suggested that brightness and density probably described a single attribute. At present there is little reason to believe that either tonal color or brightness is an auditory attribute.

CONSONANCE-DISSONANCE

When two or more tones are sounded together, most listeners are able to judge the extent to which the several tones fuse. When they fuse well the tones are said to be consonant, whereas when fusion is poor they are said to be dissonant.

Historically, there have been two major difficulties with the treatment of consonance and dissonance. First, many writers have equated consonance with pleasantness and dissonance with unpleasantness; and second, judgments of consonance and dissonance have been made sometimes to isolated sounds and sometimes to sounds presented in a musical context. We take the view here that *consonance and dissonance are no more than polar opposites to describe the degree of tonal fusion.* Therefore, if fusion is assumed to be a discriminable attribute of complex sounds, then it seems clear that judgments of fusion can only be made satisfactorily when the matter of pleasantness is ignored and when stimuli are presented in isolation. This is an important observation to make because there is now ample evidence that when dissonance is judged along a pleasant-unpleasant dimension, it is heavily influenced by musical context and it is not always unpleasant (*8, 9, 38*).

Explanations of fusion have been of two sorts. One of them has assumed that fusion is a physiological matter. Galileo (*10*) explained fusion in terms of the vibration patterns of the tympanic membrane. According to him, fusion failed whenever discordant vibration patterns of the tympanic membrane kept it in "perpetual torment" as a consequence of its bending simultaneously in two directions. Today this explanation appears inadequate in view of Békésy's data on vibration patterns in the tympanic membrane as a function of the frequency of pure tones presented singly (*3*). He demonstrated that tones above 2400∿ resulted in complex patterns similar to those to which Galileo had alluded. Therefore, if Galileo were correct, any combination of pure tones with at least one of them above 2400∿ ought to be characterized as dissonant. This is not so.

Another physiological explanation was offered by Helmholtz (*20*), who stated that dissonance was due to the beating of partials which led to a "disagreeable discontinuity" in excitation. By use of sirens developed by Cagniard de la Tour, Helmholtz conducted experiments on tonal fusion from which he concluded that the octave gave the best fusion, with the perfect fifth (frequency ratio 3:2), the perfect fourth (4:3), and the major third (5:4) showing decreasing amounts of fusion, in that order. The least fusion occurred with the minor second (16:15). In general, mathematical computations of the frequencies of the partials of two fundamental tones bearing the ratios specified show his observations on fusion to be consistent with the explanation he offered.

The second sort of explanation of fusion ignores sensory and neural processes and, instead, considers it merely a matter of custom, ever-changing according to musical styles. If the degree of fusion of several tones depends on learning, then fusion cannot be considered as an auditory dimension. Rather, it must be viewed as an associated non-auditory attribute. Here again, the confusion of pleasantness with fusion makes the choice between the two kinds of explanation less than obvious. If one accepts consonance-dissonance as a fusional dimension, then a physiological explanation in terms of receptor and neural processes is clearly more germane than would be the case if consonance-dissonance were considered as a dimension of pleasantness. Current data on fusion are insufficient to meet our three criteria for an auditory attribute, and pleasantness, perhaps an associated non-auditory attribute, is illustrative of a class of non-auditory associations which listeners can and do make to complex tones in musical context (*36, 37*) and in isolation (*14*).

NON-AUDITORY ATTRIBUTES

There are a number of associations listeners can make to tonal stimuli. Some involve the application of attributes from some other sense modality, such as using hue to describe pitch (*21*), while others involve cognition (*14*). The latter kind can be exceedingly complex.

In Fig. 8.3 may be seen two illustrative semantic profiles obtained in an experiment by Gulick, Patterson, and Lawrence (*14*). In this experiment listeners rated four different musical dyads (two-tone chords) against each of the ten dimensions shown in the figure. The profiles for all dyads studied were significantly different from each other. When the experiment was replicated after a two-week delay, it became clear that the listeners were very reliable in their judgments (reliability coefficient = 0.90). Surprisingly, the profiles of musically naïve and musically sophisticated listeners proved to be alike. Accordingly, whatever is involved in forming unique associations to tones, it cannot be a product of direct musical training.

Note that the major-second dyad, generally accepted as lacking fusion, was described as hard, rough, dark, sad, tense, hollow, sour, unpleasant,

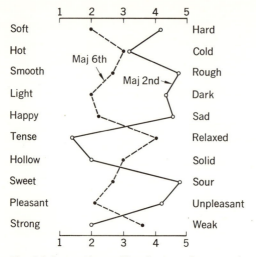

Fig. 8.3 Semantic profiles for a major-second and major-sixth dyad. The lower tone in each dyad had a fundamental frequency of 256∿. Data from Gulick, Patterson, and Lawrence (14).

and strong. On the other hand, the major-sixth dyad, generally accepted as having fusion, was described as soft, smooth, light, happy, relaxed, pleasant, and weak.

The results of this experiment shed some light on our previous discussion of consonance and dissonance. If, as proposed, lack of fusion *is* dissonance (major-second dyad) and fusion *is* consonance (major-sixth dyad), then we see from these profiles why the dimension of pleasantness-unpleasantness has found its way into the literature on tonal fusion. Inasmuch as there are many nonauditory dimensions which listeners can use reliably to describe tonal stimuli, there does not appear to be any compelling reason to consider any one dimension as more important than another.

Auditory Fatigue and Masking

In spite of the fact that both auditory fatigue and masking refer to a reduction in sensitivity to one acoustic stimulus as a consequence of another, it cannot be said of them that they are alike. Not only do the methods of their demonstration differ, but so, too, do their underlying physiological processes differ. Whereas fatigue is a temporary loss in sensitivity to one stimulus *following* exposure to another stimulus, masking is a loss in sensitivity to one stimulus *during* exposure to another stimulus. Herein lies the major methodological difference: fatigue is sequential, masking is concurrent.

As far as the underlying physiological processes are concerned, it seems clear that auditory fatigue rather literally comes about from a fatiguing of sensory or neural processes. The acoustic system is either temporarily incapable of responding, or it requires more energy in order to respond. On the other hand, masking apparently occurs whenever that portion of the acoustic system which normally responds to one stimulus is simultaneously activated by another stimulus.

Needless to say, the experimental conditions that have been employed in studying fatigue and masking are both varied and numerous. Since we cannot treat all of them, we shall restrict our attention to those matters that help to clarify the general case.

FATIGUE

The reduction in the sensitivity of the auditory system as a direct result of stimulation may be demonstrated either as an upward shift in the absolute threshold for a given stimulus, or as a reduction in loudness.

In the latter case, the reduction in loudness is usually noted by comparing the loudness of a fatiguing stimulus presented to one ear with its loudness when presented momentarily to the other ear. This procedure poses three difficulties. First, unless interaural loudness equations have been obtained, it cannot be concluded that the difference in loudness between the ears is due to the fatiguing of one ear. This difficulty can be quite serious because the loudness reduction produced by a fatiguing tone of low intensity to one ear is small and of the same order of magnitude as that found in experiments on right- and left-ear loudness matching under normal conditions. Second, it is impossible to be sure that the introduction of a fatiguing tone to one ear actually leaves the contralateral ear unexposed. Intense tones to one ear certainly reach the other ear through bone conduction. Sound attenuation through the head is about 60 db. Third, if the effects of fatigue on loudness are brought about, even in part, by central neural factors, as contrasted with receptor or peripheral neural factors, then the effects would not demonstrate themselves fully with this method. When fatigue is produced with stimuli of low to moderate intensity, only the first difficulty is encountered. However, when high intensities are employed, all three are encountered, and often to an extent unknowable. Yet, in spite of these difficulties, the procedure of cross-matching for loudness has provided some interesting results which have helped us to understand auditory fatigue.

Threshold Shifts: Pure Tones. The extent to which the absolute threshold for a pure tone is elevated through auditory fatigue depends upon the nature of fatiguing stimulation, especially its intensity and duration. The simplest case is shown in Fig. 8.4, where the elevation of the threshold in decibels for a 1000∿ tone is shown as a function of the duration and intensity of the same tone used to produce fatigue. These data were obtained by Caussé and Chavasse (6). From this experiment it may be seen that fatigue increased with the duration of the prior exposure to the 1000∿ tone as well as with its intensity (10 and 40 db SL). One possible conclusion to draw from these data is that auditory fatigue can arise generally with levels of stimulation near threshold. However, additional data from the same experiment show that this is so only for the higher frequencies, those between 1000 and 10,000∿. Tones below 500∿ did not result in fatigue when they were of low or moderate intensity.

The effect of the frequency of a fatiguing tone on the threshold for the same tone is shown in Fig. 8.5. Here the intensity of each fatiguing tone

Fig. 8.4 The effect of exposure to a 1000∿ tone at 10 and 40 db SL for different durations on the threshold for the same tone. Threshold shift is given in decibels with reference to pre-exposure level. Data from Caussé and Chavasse (**6**).

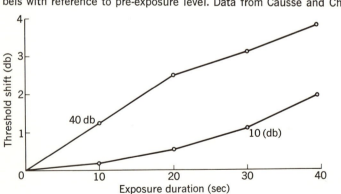

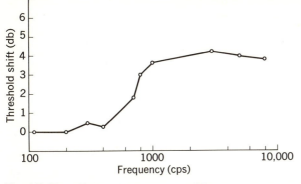

Fig. 8.5. The effects of exposure to different pure tones at 30 db SL for about 30 sec on the threshold for the same tones. Threshold shift is given in decibels with reference to pre-exposure level. Tones below 500∿ produced practically no fatigue. Data from Caussé and Chavasse **(6)**.

was 30 db SL. The dependency of fatigue on frequency is less pronounced than shown in Fig. 8.5 when the intensity of the fatiguing tone is great *(25)*, but even under these conditions the high tones lead to greater fatigue than the low tones. It is possible, of course, that fatigue with exposure to low tones of great intensity actually results from a temporary injury to the receptor *(49)*. We shall have more to say of this later.

Loudness Matching: Pure Tones. We turn now to consider the second way in which fatigue can be demonstrated. As the ear is exposed to sound, not only is there an elevation of the absolute threshold for that sound, but its loudness also declines with time. For a 1000∿ tone of moderate intensity, Wood *(50)* found that its loudness declined over a two-minute period to become fairly stable thereafter. A portion of the results of his experiment is given in Fig. 8.6. A 1000∿ tone was presented to one ear for durations varying from a few seconds to two minutes. Immediately upon its termination his listeners adjusted the intensity of the same tone, now presented for a brief interval to the other ear, so as to produce a loudness match. The intensity of the test tone, in decibels with reference to the fatiguing tone, is given on the ordinate. As the duration of the exposure increased, it was necessary to reduce the intensity of the test tone in order to effect a match in loudness.

Let us now say a word about the effect of an exposure to one pure tone on the loudness of tones of other frequencies. In general, it may be said that a fatiguing tone spreads its effects so as to reduce the loudness of tones of nearby frequencies both above and below itself. The amount of fatigue decreases regularly as the discrepancy in frequency between the fatiguing and test tones increases (*6, 11, 47*), as shown in Fig. 8.7. These data come from an experiment by Thwing (*47*) in which the fatiguing tone (1000∿ at 80 db SPL) was heard for each of four durations. Two durations are included in the figure, one and five minutes, and the major result of a lengthened exposure was a greater amount of fatigue for nearby frequencies. The more remote frequencies appear not to have been affected very much by duration.

It is difficult to establish with certainty the frequency limits above and below the fatiguing tone beyond which loudness remains unaffected. However, if an arbitrary intensity shift, for example −10 db, is taken as a criterion value, then the width of the fatigue effect increases with the intensity and the duration of the fatiguing tone. The case of duration is shown in Fig. 8.7 by the arrows.

The width of the fatigue effect also bears a relation to the frequency of the fatiguing tone. When measured as the *absolute* frequency range within which a matching intensity change of −10 db or more is required to produce a loudness match, the width increases as the frequency of the

Fig. 8.6 Reduction in the loudness of a 1000∿ tone as a function of its duration. See text for explanation. Data from Wood (**50**).

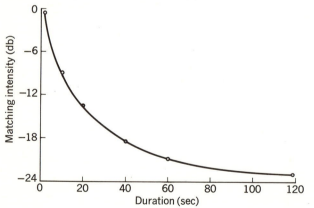

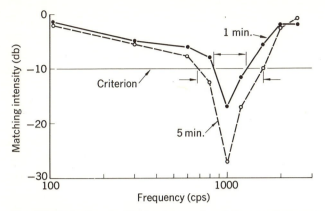

Fig. 8.7 Reduction in the loudness of certain pure tones as a consequence of exposure to a 1000∿ tone at 80 db SPL for 1 and 5 minutes. See text for explanation. Data from Thwing (**47**).

fatiguing tone rises. However, when these same limiting frequencies are projected on the basilar membrane according to their *place,* then the longitudinal extent of the fatigued area along the basilar membrane decreases as the frequency of the fatiguing tone rises.

Loudness Matching: Noise. Much of what has been considered in connection with tonal stimuli applies as well to noise. As expected, the amount of auditory fatigue produced by noise is directly related to its intensity and duration. However, when these two factors are held constant, fatigue can be shown to bear a significant relation to bandwidth. In an experiment by Carterette (*5*), the decline in loudness from exposure to noise was found to be a direct function of bandwidth, as shown in Fig. 8.8. Each bandwidth had an over-all intensity of 90 db SPL, and each was more or less centered at 1500∿. Clearly, more fatigue occurred when the available energy was spread out along the spectrum than occurred when it was more concentrated. This is a curious result. If the function shown in Fig. 8.8 were to remain linear, then we should expect that a tone of 1500∿, essentially of zero bandwidth, would lead to the least amount of fatigue. However, Carterette found that a 1500∿ tone heard under the same conditions as the noise showed the greatest fatigue

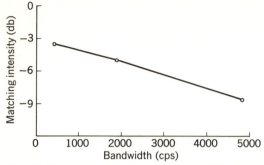

Fig. 8.8 Reduction in loudness of three different bandwidths of noise (440, 1880, and 4800⌒) after 7 min. of stimulation at an intensity of 90 db SPL. Data from Carterette (5).

(—18 db). Similar results have been obtained by others (39), and so we must conclude that the amount of auditory fatigue is not a simple function of the spread of energy within the spectrum.

Recovery. Recovery from fatigue has been shown to follow an exponential course with time (30, 47). It proceeds rapidly at first, and then tapers off. Under usual circumstances, when the exposure is to stimuli of below injurious intensities, normal threshold sensitivity and loudness are restored within a minute after the cessation of the fatiguing stimulus. When very intense stimuli are employed for long durations, the result is a general impairment of acuity which can last for hours. In the extreme, normal sensitivity may never return, as in the case of the "stimulation deafness" experiments cited in Chapter 5.

The Locus of Fatigue. It seems quite likely that auditory fatigue is not due to contractions of the middle ear muscles. Any attenuation of sound transmission on their account would not be restricted to the particular frequency of the stimulating tone, but rather it would show itself more or less uniformly for all stimuli. Therefore, psychophysical data are not consistent with what would be expected if the middle ear muscles were involved. Furthermore, since the muscles act in concert bilaterally, they could only lead to bilateral fatigue. Based on the loudness matching experiments already cited, we know that fatigue can be limited to one ear.

Finally, auditory fatigue has been demonstrated when the intensity of the stimulation is too near absolute threshold to cause middle ear muscle reflexes.

There is also evidence that fatigue probably does not result from any peripheral sensory process because it does not occur in the cochlear potential. One study of the CP recorded from cats showed the CP to be constant (± 2 db) during continuous stimulation with a $1000\curlyvee$ tone (75 db SPL) for periods as long as 96 hours (29). Accordingly, auditory fatigue must occur later than all the processes which lead to the generation of the electrical trigger potential.

Wever (49) and Small (39) both argue that fatigue is an early neural affair. Continuous stimulation is known to diminish the rate at which a given nerve fiber responds, and if, as we suppose, loudness is coded by the total number of impulses per unit time, then loudness certainly should decline during stimulation. Moreover, as intensity rises and fibers thereby are forced to fire earlier and earlier in their relative refractory periods, their excitability becomes impaired and the effects of forcing are cumulative.

The fact that fatigue seems limited under low and moderate intensity levels of tones of high frequency (see Fig. 8.5) supports the theory of Wever (49). According to him, the total population of neural elements available to code the loudness of tones of low frequency is very large because he does not hold to the *place* principle for low tones. As a consequence, the loss of some neural elements through neural fatigue is not especially noticeable since others can act for them. Only at very high intensities would one expect to find evidence of fatigue with low tone stimulation. On the other hand, with *place* operating for the high tones, the population of neural elements available to code the loudness of a high frequency tone is necessarily reduced. Fatigue, therefore, is more likely to occur with stimulation from high tones.

It is possible, of course, that the low tones do not lead to fatigue simply because the excitations in the nerve fibers are so well separated in time that the fibers can always recover. However, if fatigue were only a matter of forcing, and the population of neural elements remained more or less constant for each tonal frequency, as with the *place* theory of Békésy (2), then auditory fatigue should increase regularly with frequency. That it does not is clear from Fig. 8.5. Accordingly, Wever's theory seems better able to account for the data, particularly in view of the fact that fatigue rises in the frequency range where volleying gives way to *place*.

MASKING

As previously noted, masking is a temporary loss in sensitivity to one stimulus during simultaneous exposure to another. It is measured as the amount by which the threshold of one stimulus is raised by virtue of the presence of a second stimulus (masker).

Ipsilateral Masking. Masking, as measured in the laboratory, usually refers to the situation wherein both tones impinge upon the same ear. *Direct masking* occurs when threshold shifts are noted for tones in the same general frequency region as the masker, whereas *remote masking* occurs when threshold shifts are noted for tones of a different frequency region. The distinction is a little arbitrary, but we shall define remote masking as a threshold shift for any tone with a frequency outside the critical bandwidth of the masker.

Wegel and Lane (*48*) have studied tonal interrelations in masking by measuring the magnitude of threshold elevations (db, SL) for a number of frequencies between 400 and 4000∿, determined in the present of a masking tone of 1200∿ at 44 and 80 db SL. Their results are shown in Fig. 8.9. The elevation of thresholds for tones of different frequencies may be seen to be approximately symmetrical when the masker had an intensity of 44 db SL, and the range of the masking effect was limited between 600 and 2400∿. However, the more intense masker (80 db SL) gave rise to asymmetrical masking with the upper frequency limit extended indefinitely. From these data we may conclude that pure tones of moderately high intensity will mask other tones of a higher frequency more readily than those of a lower frequency. Furthermore, the degree of masking does not fall off regularly with increasing frequency, but rather reaches periodic maxima as the harmonics are approached. This is shown in the figure by the scallops in the upper curve at 2400 and 3600∿, the first and second harmonics of the masking tone.

What appears to be happening is that the masking tone of 1200∿ leads to the generation of aural harmonics which are sufficient in ampli-

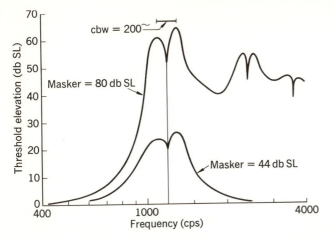

Fig. 8.9 The elevation in threshold (db SL) for various frequencies during continuous stimulation by a 1200∿ tone at 44 and 80 db SL. Masking is both direct and remote as shown by the critical bandwidth for a 1200∿ tone (cbw = 200∿). Data from Wegel and Lane (48).

tude to act as maskers. Again we see that the auditory nervous system is coded according to the character of the trigger potential rather than by the character of the sound impinging on the ear. In our treatment of the electrical activity of the cochlea (Chapter 4), we noted in Fig. 4.7 that the increase in the magnitude of the aural harmonics with intensity is more rapid the higher the order of the harmonic. This being so, we would predict that the rate of growth in masking as a function of the intensity of the masker would be more rapid near the harmonic frequencies (in this case, 2400 and 3600∿) than it would be near the fundamental frequency (1200∿). The data of Wegel and Lane agree with this prediction.

A number of studies have been made of the loudness function (sones) under different levels and kinds of noise (19, 23, 34, 44). In contrast to the normal loudness function obtained with a 1000∿ tone, the presence of a constant masking noise alters the loudness function for a 1000∿ tone only at the lower intensities. That is, in the presence of a masking noise, the loudness of the tone grows more rapidly than normal with increases in its intensity until a moderate level is attained, after which its growth has the same slope as that found without masking. We shall return to this matter when we consider auditory recruitment in the next chapter.

Contralateral Masking. Auditory thresholds can be elevated in one ear during contralateral stimulation, but the masking effects so obtained are greatly reduced compared to the ipsilateral condition. Contralateral masking apparently depends primarily upon direct stimulation of one ear by sound conducted to it across the head. However, there is some evidence that masking can arise in one ear as a consequence of activity in the olivocochlear bundle which is initiated by contralateral stimulation (7).

Masking and Critical Bands. Scharf (35) has reviewed the concept of the critical band and its relationship to the masking of pure tones. When the thresholds for different pure tones were determined in the presence of bands of noise, the degree of masking of the tones followed one of several patterns, depending upon the bandwidth of the noise and its over-all intensity. With bands narrower or equal to a critical bandwidth and of low intensity (below 50 db SL), the amount of masking for a pure tone increased as its frequency approached the center frequency of the noise, beginning either from above or below the center frequency. However, when the masking noise exceeded the critical bandwidth, then the level of masking for a pure tone first increased as the frequency approached the center frequency of the noise, but it did not reach a single maximum at the center frequency as before. Instead, the level of masking remained invariant over a range of frequencies centered within the noise (12). This suggests that the extent and pattern of threshold shifts for pure tones depends upon the bandwidth of the noise, and that a widening of the noise spectrum does not lead to greater masking, but rather to the same maximum level of masking of pure tones over a range of frequencies centered within the noise spectrum.

The Locus of Masking. In our earlier discussion of cochlear distortions we indicated that the CP resulting from one tone is reduced in magnitude upon the introduction of a second tone. This we referred to as interference, and it was accounted for in terms of the diversion of energy into combination tones. Since interference occurs with any two tones, whereas masking depends on the particular frequencies of the two tones, we cannot consider interference and masking as due to the same sensory process. On the other hand, it is difficult to argue that interference does not influence masking even though it cannot account fully for it.

There is evidence that masking arises through the action of first-order cochlear neurons. The view of masking according to Wegel and Lane is that a tone is masked when its action on the basilar membrane is exceeded at its *place* by the action of another tone. This would suggest that masking occurs when the stronger of two tones pre-empts the neural units normally responsive to the weaker tone. Their conception is probably too simple in view of the direct inhibiting effects of certain tones on the response rates of particular cochlear fibers, as described in Chapter 4. While the work of Dewson (7) suggests that efferent connections may be involved in phenomena of masking, the work of Lowy (24) indicates that central neural connections are not necessary to masking.

References

1. Bachem, A. Note on Neu's review of the literature on absolute pitch, *Psychol. Bull.*, 1948, *45*, 161-162.
2. Békésy, G. von. Zur Theorie des Hörens; Die Schwingungsform der Basilarmembran, *Physik Zeits.*, 1928, *29*, 793-810.
3. Békésy, G. von. Ueber die Messung der Schwingungsamplitude der Gehörknöchelchen mittels einer kapazitiven Sonde, *Akust. Zeits.*, 1941, *6*, 1-16.
4. Boring, E. G., and S. S. Stevens. The nature of tonal brightness, *Proc. Natl. Acad. Sci.*, 1936, *22*, 514-521.
5. Carterette, E. C. Loudness adaptation for bands of noise, *J. Acoust. Soc. Amer.*, 1956, *28*, 865-871.
6. Caussé, R., and P. Chavasse. Études sur la fatigue auditive, *Année Psychol.*, 1947, *43-44*, 265-298.
7. Dewson, J. H., III. Efferent olivocochlear bundle: some relationships to noise masking and stimulus attenuation, *J. Neurophysiol.*, 1967, *30*, 817-832.
8. Disererns, C. Reactions to musical stimuli, *Psychol. Bull.*, 1923, *20*, 173-199.
9. Edmonds, E. M., and M. E. Smith. The phenomenological description of musical intervals, *Amer. J. Psychol.*, 1923, *34*, 387-391.
10. Galileo, G. *Dialogues Concerning Two New Sciences*, trans. by H. Crew and A. de Salvio, Evanston, Ill.: Northwestern University Press, 1950, p. 100.

11. Gardner, M. B. Short duration auditory fatigue as a method of classifying hearing impairment, *J. Acoust. Soc. Amer.,* 1947, *19,* 178-190.
12. Greenwood, D. D. Auditory masking and the critical band, *J. Acoust. Soc. Amer.,* 1961, *33,* 484-502.
13. Gulick, W. L. Previously unpublished.
14. Gulick, W. L., W. C. Patterson, and Sharon McH. Lawrence. The meaning of musical dyads, *J. Aud. Res.,* 1967, *7,* 435-445.
15. Gundlach, R. H. Tonal attributes and frequency theories of hearing, *J. Exper. Psychol.,* 1929, *12,* 187-196.
16. Gundlach, R. H., and M. Bentley. The dependence of tonal attributes upon phase, *Amer. J. Psychol.,* 1930, *42,* 519-543.
17. Halverson, H. M. Diotic tonal volumes as a function of phase, *Amer. J. Psychol.,* 1922, *33,* 526-534.
18. Halverson, H. M. Tonal volume as a function of intensity, *Amer. J. Psychol.,* 1924, *35,* 360-367.
19. Hellman, R. P., and J. Zwislocki. Loudness functions of a 1000-cps tone in the presence of masking noise, *J. Acoust. Soc. Amer.,* 1964, *36,* 1618-1627.
20. Helmholtz, H. L. F. von. Lecture delivered in Bonn, Winter, 1857, in *Popular Scientific Lectures,* A. J. Ellis (trans.), New York: Appleton, 1873.
21. Langfeld, H. S. Note on a case of chromaesthesia, *Psychol. Bull.,* 1914, *11,* 113-114.
22. Licklider, J. C. R. Basic correlates of the auditory stimulus, Chapter 25 in *Handbook of Experimental Psychology,* S. S. Stevens (Ed.), New York: Wiley, 1951.
23. Lochner, J. P. A., and J. F. Burger. Form of the loudness functions in the presence of masking noise, *J. Acoust. Soc. Amer.,* 1961, *33,* 1705-1707.
24. Lowy, K. Some experimental evidence for peripheral auditory masking, *J. Acoust. Soc. Amer.,* 1945, *16,* 197-202.
25. Lüscher, E., and J. Zwislocki. The decay of sensation and the remainder of adaptation after short pure-tone impulses on the ear, *Acta Oto-Laryngol.,* 1947, *35,* 428-445.
26. Neu, D. M. A critical review of the literature on "absolute pitch," *Psychol. Bull.,* 1947, *44,* 249-266.
27. Neu, D. M. Absolute pitch—a reply to Bachem, *Psychol. Bull.,* 1948, *45,* 534-535.
28. Osgood, C. E. *Method and Theory in Experimental Psychology.* New York: Oxford University Press, 1953.
29. Rahm, W. E., Jr., W. F. Strother, and W. L. Gulick. The stability of the cochlear response through time, *Ann. Otol. Rhinol. Laryngol.,* 1958, *67,* 972-977.

30. Rawnsley, A. I., and J. D. Harris. Studies in short duration fatigue: II. Recovery time, *J. Exper. Psychol.*, 1952, *43*, 138-142.
31. Révész, G. *Zur Grundlegung der Tonpsychologie,* Leipzig: Veit, 1913, pp. 4-75.
32. Rich, G. J. A preliminary study of tonal volume, *J. Exper. Psychol.*, 1916, *1*, 13-22.
33. Rich, G. J. A study of tonal attributes, *Amer. J. Psychol.*, 1919, *30*, 121-164.
34. Richards, A. M. Monaural loudness functions under masking, *J. Acoust. Soc. Amer.*, 1968, *44*, 599-605.
35. Scharf, B. Special Report, *Critical Bands,* Syracuse, N. Y.: Lab. Sensory Com., Syracuse University, Report LSC-S-3, Aug. 1966.
36. Sippola, B. C. Semantic differential analysis of music, paper read at East. Psychol. Assoc., Philadelphia, April, 1964.
37. Solomon, L. N. Semantic approach to the perception of complex sound, *J. Acoust. Soc. Amer.*, 1958, *30*, 421-425.
38. Solomon, L. N. Semantic reactions to systematically varied sounds, *J. Acoust. Soc. Amer.*, 1959, *31*, 986-990.
39. Small, A. M., Jr. Auditory adapation, Chapter 8 in *Modern Developments in Audiology,* J. Jerger (Ed.), New York: Academic Press, 1963.
40. Stevens, S. S. The volume and intensity of tones, *Amer. J. Psychol.*, 1934, *46*, 397-408.
41. Stevens, S. S. The attributes of tones, *Proc. Natl. Acad. Sci.*, 1934, *20*, 457-459.
42. Stevens, S. S. Tonal density, *J. Exper. Psychol.*, 1934, *17*, 585-592.
43. Stevens, S. S. The relation of pitch to intensity, *J. Acoust. Soc. Amer.*, 1935, *6*, 150-154.
44. Stevens, S. S. Power group transformations under glare, masking, and recruitment, *J. Acoust. Soc. Amer.*, 1966, *39*, 725-735.
45. Stumpf, C. Konsonanz und Konkordanz, *Z. Psychol.*, 1911, *58*, 321-385.
46. Thomas, G. J. Equal-volume judgments of tones, *Amer. J. Psychol.*, 1949, *62*, 182-201.
47. Thwing, E. J. Spread of perstimulatory fatigue of a pure tone to neighboring frequencies, *J. Acoust. Soc. Amer.*, 1955, *27*, 741-748.
48. Wegel, R. L., and C. E. Lane. The auditory masking of one pure tone by another and its probable relation to the dynamics of the inner ear, *Phys. Rev.*, 1924, *23*, 266-285.
49. Wever, E. G. *Theory of Hearing,* New York: Wiley, 1949, pp. 319-326.
50. Wood, A. G. A quantitative account of the course of auditory fatigue, Unpublished thesis, University of Virginia, 1930, cited in F. A. Geldard, *The Human Senses,* New York: Wiley, 1953, pp. 134-135.
51. Zoll, P. M. The relation of tonal volume, intensity, and pitch, *Amer. J. Psychol.*, 1934, *46*, 99-106.

9
Sound Localization

In the middle of the last century the question as to whether or not space was knowable through acoustic stimulation gathered serious debate. Although a few early psychologists proposed that man was immediately and directly aware of an auditory space, most denied the existence of this kind of awareness by arguing that acoustic stimuli had no spatial extent (size and volume). Furthermore, unlike the visual and tactual receptors, with hearing there was no conscious recognition of spatiality in patterns of stimulation impressed upon the auditory receptor (6). For the majority, auditory space was assumed to be derived from, or mediated by, the association of sound sources with their visual or tactual localization.

The early debate about auditory space centered on the empiricistic-nativistic problem, but after the turn of the century when this problem came to hold less currency in psychology, the topic of auditory space lost significance. With concern for the philosophical issue of the immediacy of man's perception of auditory space thus diminished, there arose in its stead a concern for the empirical facts on man's ability to localize sounds, a concern which continues and probably represents the modern statement of an older and more general interest.

Although the results of psychophysical studies of sound localization are necessary to our understanding of hearing, it is important to realize that they do not actually tell us very much about the character of auditory space. In the light of recent data suggesting that sounds have size and volume, and that the distance of familiar sounds can be judged, it would appear that psychology is about to come full circle in defining the scope of its concern.

In this chapter we shall consider what is known about man's capacity to discriminate the direction from which sounds come to him. Discrimination of direction, of course, is not strictly equivalent to localization since both direction and distance are implied by localization. Nevertheless, according to custom, we shall use localization to mean direction. We shall consider first the history of research on this topic up to 1930 in order to set forth the early hypotheses offered to account for localization. Thereafter, the development of more recent thought will be treated in the context of psychophysical and electrophysiological data.

History of Sound Localization

THE FIRST HUNDRED YEARS

The first important work on human sound localization was that of Venturi which appeared between 1796 and 1801 (*57-60*). Employing listeners with normal hearing and others with severe hearing losses confined to one ear, Venturi set out to determine the extent to which his subjects could discriminate his position as he circled them at forty meters in an open field while playing occasional notes on a flute.

From his observations he advanced an *intensity* hypothesis which stated that it is the simultaneous inequality of sensation magnitude at the two ears that informs us of the true direction of sounds. His hypothesis accounted for the confusion in localization occurring in normal listeners when a sound source is located directly in front or behind them because in these instances there is no inequality of sensation magnitude and accurate localization fails. In addition, his hypothesis accounted for the apparent inability of listeners deaf in one ear to localize sounds.

In spite of the fact that Venturi published his *intensity* hypothesis in three languages, his work escaped the notice of all who followed him except Johannes Müller, who must have been only vaguely aware of Venturi's work since he failed to ascribe the hypothesis to him. Accordingly, for three-quarters of a century the role of intensity in sound localization was merely affirmed by Magendie (*32*), Müller (*37*), and Weber (*66*), finally to be verified experimentally for a second time by Rayleigh (*41*) who, seventy-seven years after Venturi, set out to settle the "conjecture" that intensity was a relevant cue.

Rayleigh observed two kinds of systematic errors of localization. The first kind pertained to front-back confusion when the sound source fell in the median plane. The second kind occurred when the source was located somewhat to the side because, as Rayleigh pointed out, for every position forward of the binaural axis there is a corresponding position behind where the binaural intensity ratio is the same. From these two kinds of errors, Rayleigh concluded that the *binaural intensity ratio* constituted the cue for localization and the errors in localization occurred when the difference was zero (front-back) or when two different positions to the side resulted in the same ratio. He also suggested that intensity differences between the ears was a function of frequency, being largest for high-frequency tones and negligible for tones whose wavelengths were four times the circumferences of the head ($\leqslant 160 \curlyvee$). Thus Rayleigh interpreted *frequency* as a cue only to the extent to which it affected binaural intensity ratios.

After Rayleigh came additional support for the *intensity* hypothesis as others experimented with improved techniques such as Preyer's helmet (*40*), Matsumoto's sound cage (*34*), and Thompson's pseudophone (*53, 55*).

There was another development on sound localization in the last century which dealt with a proposal put forward by Laborde in 1881 to the effect that non-extensive sounds might derive a spatial character and a learned locus through stimulation of the semicircular canals (*29*). Laborde argued that sounds led to reflexive head movements which stimulated the canals and provided a "local sign" similar to that suggested by Lotze (*31*) for vision.

It is important to realize that Laborde's *canal-hypothesis* did not account for how a sound was first located so as to determine subsequent movement of the head and, thereby, a unique "local sign." Laborde considered his hypothesis as pertaining to the older problem of auditory space; yet most of those who argued against it did so because it failed to account for localization. For example, Breuer (*10*) argued that there was no way for the canals to mediate sound direction since sound, once passed through the external meatus, could not excite the three canals differentially. Clearly, Breuer interpreted Laborde to mean that the semicircular canals served to locate sound rather than to give a spatial character to sound through associated "local signs" arising from head movement. Breuer's earlier work (*8, 9*) on the vestibular apparatus was very well known, and his rejection of the *canal-hypothesis* contributed significantly to the brevity of its appearance. Von Kries (*28*), who likewise asked more of the *canal-hypothesis* than Laborde had intended, also argued against it.

During the last century there were two important advances toward our understanding of sound localization. First, the role of binaural intensity differences was established; and second, the importance of head movement was recognized. Improving experimental techniques set the stage for rapid developments during the next thirty years.

LATER DEVELOPMENTS: 1900-1930

In his *Tonempfindungen*, Helmholtz (*17*) wrote that phase differences *might* prove important to an understanding of dissonance, but he concluded that they were not relevant to an appreciation of consonance. His theory of consonance made *phase* unimportant, and because he was rather explicit on phase in this regard, most who followed him seemed prepared to attribute to him the view that man is "phase deaf."

The prestige of Helmholtz and the failure by others to take full account of his views on phase undoubtedly delayed consideration of phase as a cue in the localization of sounds. A *phase* hypothesis was advanced first by Thompson (*54*) in 1878 in connection with his observations on binaural beating, but as Boring noted, "At that time [his] results were not accepted because they seemed to contradict Helmholtz's dictum that phase cannot be perceived" (*6*, p. 388).

The role of phase was not firmly established until 1907 when Rayleigh (*42*) repeated the earlier experiments of Thompson. Rayleigh noted that a 128∿ tone from a tuning fork led through a tube to one ear produced binaural beating with a tone from a slightly mistuned fork led to the other ear. As the tones underwent changing phase relations, the beating tone moved back and forth from right to left. Rayleigh limited phase in sound localization to tones of low frequency for which he believed binaural intensitive differences to be too small to serve as an effective cue.

In 1908, repeating an experiment by More and Fry (*36*), Wilson and Myers (*67*) affirmed the importance of binaural phase differences in the localization of low tones. A small diameter tube formed into a large horizontal circle was interrupted by the listener's head with one end of the tube sealed into each ear. The lengths of the acoustic path to each ear were varied by changing the position of an opening along the circle through which the sound from a single tuning fork entered the tube. With sight occluded, their listeners always localized the source toward the side of the leading phase, up to a phase angle limit of 180°. Although they employed only two frequencies, 320 and 512$\curvearrowright$, their work was important to the belated recognition of the dual basis of localization; namely, binaural intensitive differences for the high and middle tones and binaural phase differences for the low tones.

In the same year Mallock (33) suggested that binaural time differences could provide a basis for localization. A binaural time difference occurs because sound from a source outside the median plane arrives at the nearer ear first. Aggazzotti (1) confirmed the time hypothesis in 1911, and by 1920 this cue was believed to be of major importance. A number of experimenters attempted to determine the least binaural time delay which would shift the perceived locus of a sound source out of the median plane. Klemm (25) reported that a delay of 2 μsec in stimulation to one ear was sufficient to cause the tone's locus to migrate toward the side of earlier stimulation. Von Hornbostel and Wertheimer (19) established the delay at 30 μsec with unambiguous localization occurring only with delays as long as 630 μsec.

Kreidl and Gatscher (27) rejected the *time* hypothesis because they felt that binaural time differences which were briefer than the time difference necessary for the perception of successiveness (about 20 msec) could not have any effect on localization. Others attempted to show how phase and time cues were actually one and the same thing (5, 56). Considering the all-or-none law, Boring (5) argued that phase and time differences in the stimulation of the ears would reduce to time differences in the nervous system. He also indicated how time differences could be the physiological equivalent of intensity. Accordingly, by 1930 there was uncertainty about the number of cues that served sound localization. The number of cues seemed to depend upon whether one described them in terms of the acoustic patterns impressed upon the two ears or in terms of the physiological consequences of stimulation. As we shall learn, recent electrophysiological evidence denies the equivalences which Boring stated and leads us toward a more complex view than his of the physiological processes which mediate localization.

Binaural Stimulus Differences

In considering binaural intensity, phase, and time differences, we shall adopt for their convenience two terms suggested by Stumpf (51). Parameters of stimulation identical in amount at both ears we shall call *diotic*. Those that differ we shall call *dichotic*. Whenever actual sound sources are localized and the sound reaches the ears through air, then intensity, phase, and time all will be dichotic unless the source lies in the median plane. However, when sound is generated from transducers placed over the ears, it is possible with suitable electronic circuitry to restrict dichoticity to one parameter at a time.

In order to understand the complexity of the problem of sound localization, it is important to have a thorough grasp of the nature of binaural differences in stimulation which occur under normal conditions of listening.

INTENSITY

When an actual source lies outside the median plane, the intensity is dichotic because the ears are not equally distant from the source *and* the head casts a sound shadow. These two factors interact in complex ways but it is important to our purpose to distinguish between them.

Binaural Distance. Inequality in the distance of each ear from a source is known as the *binaural distance difference,* and it is important to a consideration of intensity because sound pressure decreases with propagation. The extent to which a binaural distance difference influences dichotic intensity levels depends upon both the azimuth and the distance of the source.

The importance of azimuth is immediately apparent. The binaural distance difference is always zero for sources in the median plane, regardless of their distance from the head. On the other hand, a maximum binaural distance difference occurs for sources which lie in the line of the binaural axis (90° or 270° azimuth).

The importance of the distance of the source from the head is less

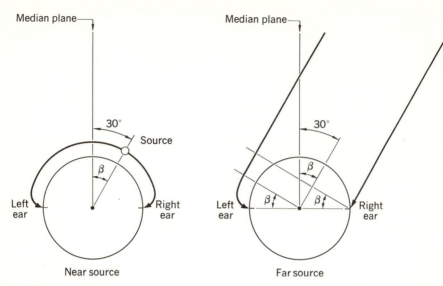

Fig. 9.1 Geometrical considerations of the influence of the distance (near, far) of a source at 30° azimuth on the binaural distance difference. See text for explanation. After Woodworth and Schlosberg (**68**, p. 351).

obvious, but two extremes are depicted in Fig. 9.1. For simplicity we have assumed the head to be spherical with the ears diametrically opposed. With the source at 30° azimuth, the sound must travel twice as far to reach the left ear as it must to reach the right ear when the source is near the head. In contrast, when the source is far enough away to consider the sound as approaching the head on a broad front, then the binaural distance difference represents only a small proportion of the total distance. The greater the distance of a source from the head, the less does a binaural distance difference influence dichotic intensity.

In the case of a source within one meter of the head, the binaural distance difference (D) can be approximated in centimeters by the formula,

$$D = k(2\beta)$$

where k equals the radius of the head (8.75 cm) and the angle β, expressed in radians, equals the azimuth. For a more distant source the formula becomes,

$$D = k(\beta + \sin\beta)$$

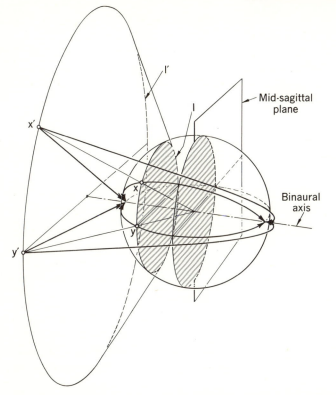

Fig. 9.2 Geometrical considerations showing **circles of identity** for near sources (I) and far sources (I'). The binaural distance difference for all points on circle I (e.g., **x** and **y**) is constant. The same is true for all points on circle I' (e.g., **x'** and **y'**). See text for further explanation.

Both of these general expressions derive from the geometrical arrangements shown in Fig. 9.1, but they are not limited to sources that lie in the horizontal plane. For example, the geometrical considerations apply equally well if one assumes the cross section of the head shown in Fig. 9.1 to be coronal rather than horizontal. The general case is shown in Fig. 9.2. Here it may be seen that sources located near the head at x and y both have the same binaural distance difference because the *difference* in the length of the pathways to the two ears is the same from any point on the circumference of circle l. The same equivalence occurs for more distant sources, as shown by point x' and y' on circle l'. Accordingly, for each direction angle and distance there is a *circle of identity* with its center on the binaural axis and its plane perpendicular to it.

Sound Shadow. In our treatment of binuaral distance we could not have simplified matters by taking *linear* distance differences between a source and the ears because the head does more than hold the ears apart. Linear distances would have served us well enough if we had substituted two microphones for our ears, but the presence of the head in a sound field is sufficient to the production of sound shadows because sound is reflected from it. As mentioned earlier in this book, very little acoustic energy is transmitted into an obstacle like the head whose density and elasticity differ greatly from the surrounding medium.

The reflection of sound depends upon the length of the sound wave relative to the diameter of the head. Whereas the long waves of low frequency tones bend around the head, the short waves of high frequency tones do not. Therefore, the influence of the sound shadow on binaural intensity differences becomes greater as frequency rises.

The combined effect of the head shadow and binaural distance is shown in Fig. 9.3 where the binaural intensity difference in decibels is shown for each of five azimuths for each of four frequencies. The meas-

Fig. 9.3 Differences in intensity in decibels at the ears for pure tones of 250, 1000, 5000, and 10,000∿ at each of five azimuths. Measures were taken 20 cm from the meatal opening on the binaural axis under open-field conditions with the source 2 m from the center of the head. Intensity of each tone equaled 70 db SPL at 2 m with the listener absent. For any azimuth (except 0 and 180°) the binaural intensity difference increased with frequency.

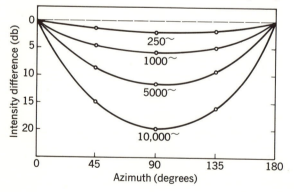

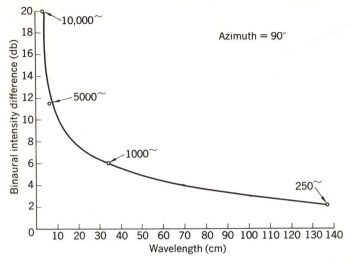

Fig. 9.4 Binaural intensity difference in decibels for pure tones at 90° azimuth as a function of wavelength in centimeters (10,000∿ = 3.44 cm; 5000∿ = 6.88 cm; 1000∿ = 34.4 cm; 250∿ = 137.6 cm). Data from Fig. 9.3.

ures were taken under open-field conditions with the microphone 20 cm from each ear on the binaural axis. The source remained 2 m from the center of the listener's head and in a horizontal plane. For any azimuth out of the median plane, the binaural intensity difference bears an ordinal relationship to frequency, and the difference is greatest at about 90° azimuth.

Sound Shadow and Complexity. The decay function of Fig. 9.4 describes the relationship between the binaural intensity difference (db) and wavelength (cm). Here we see the substantial influence of the head as an acoustical obstacle when sounds of short wavelengths impinge upon it. For wavelengths as short as 3.44 cm (10,000∿) the head causes a 20 db drop in intensity at the farther ear. Even with moderate wavelengths (34.4 cm = 1000∿) there is a pressure ratio of 2 to 1 (6 db) at the two ears under the conditions of measurement described.

Inasmuch as the reduction in intensity that results from the head shadow varies with wavelengths (frequency), we must conclude that complex stimuli undergo changes in complexity as well as over-all intensity: that is, both complexity and intensity are dichotic.

As with binaural distance, there is also a *circle of identity* for binaural intensity and complexity. Whatever are the binaural differences for a source at a given distance and direction, these differences will be invariant at all locations that lie on a circle which includes the locus in question and has its center on the binaural axis and its plane perpendicular to it.

TIME AND PHASE

Binaural distance differences lead to binaural time and phase differences. The extent of the delay in the arrival of the wavefront at the more distant ear is a direct function of the binaural distance difference since the velocity of propagation is constant for a given medium regardless of frequency, intensity, and complexity.

Temporal Difference. If we take the velocity of sound in air to be 344 m/sec, then the wavefront will advance 1 cm in 0.029 msec. Since the maximum binaural distance difference occurs whenever the source is located near one ear (90° azimuth), we can calculate the maximum *binaural time difference* by multiplying the semi-circumference of the head (ear to ear) in centimeters by 0.029. In similar manner, we can calculate the temporal equivalents of binaural distance differences for near and far sources at other azimuths. These equivalents are given in Fig. 9.5. Note that under no circumstance does the binaural time difference exceed 0.797 msec. A source displaced 5° from the median plane gives rise to a binaural time difference of only 50 μsec. We shall consider later the extent to which such brief intervals play a part in sound localization.

Phase Differences. Binaural phase differences occur with tonal stimuli arising from sources outside the median plane, and they are influenced by binaural distance difference *and* frequency. Consider the following example. From Fig. 9.5 we know that a far source at 28° azimuth has a binaural distance difference sufficient to produce a time difference of 0.25 msec. This time difference is constant across frequency, but its equivalence in terms of phase depends upon the frequency of the tone involved. This is illustrated in Fig. 9.6 where pressure changes for each of four different pure tones are shown as a function of time. Note that a binaural time difference at 0.25 msec is equivalent to a phase difference of 90, 180, 270, and 360° for pure tones of 1000, 2000, 3000, and 4000∿, respectively. If the right (nearer) ear is taken as a referent and

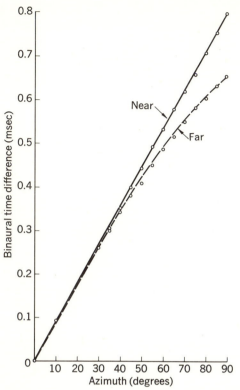

Fig. 9.5 Binaural time difference in milliseconds for near and far sources as a function of azimuth. Calculations are independent of frequency and are based on a propagation velocity of 344 m/sec.

we arbitrarily set the progress of the pressure change at the right ear at 0° phase, then the left (farther) ear may be said to *lag* in phase. From Fig. 9.6 it is apparent that a constant phase difference can only be achieved if the binaural time difference decreases as frequency rises. In our example, a time difference of 0.25 msec gives a 90° phase difference for a 1000∿ tone. If the same phase difference is to occur with a 2000∿ tone, then the binaural time difference has to be reduced to 0.125 msec. In other words, a 1000∿ tone at 28° azimuth and a 2000∿ tone at 14° azimuth both result in a phase difference of 90°. Therefore, if phase differences operate as a cue to the direction of sound (azimuth), then phase differences must interact with frequency since a given phase difference

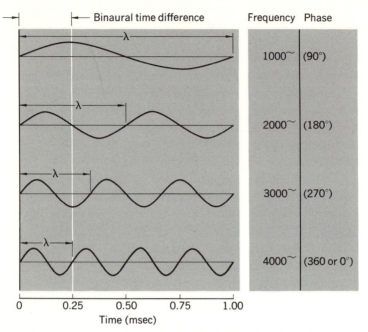

Fig. 9.6 A graphic representation of the relationship between a constant binaural time difference of 0.25 msec and phase angle as a function of the frequency of each of four pure tones. One cycle is denoted by λ.

would signify a different azimuth for every frequency. Furthermore, whenever the time required to complete one cycle (period of the wave) equals the binaural time difference, or some simple fraction of it such as ½, ⅓, ¼, ⅕, and so on, phase cannot serve as an effective cue to localization unless the auditory system keeps track of individual sound waves. For example, if the period of a wave equaled one-third of the binaural time difference, then pressure changes at both ears would be in phase but the ear nearer the source would be three cycles ahead of the other ear. There is little reason to believe that the auditory system can utilize this sort of phase information.

Another complication with phase concerns the difficulty in determining which ear is to be used as a referent in measuring phase. Logically, of course, one would select the ear nearer the source as the referent, with sound at the farther ear considered as lagging in phase. However, with continuous tonal stimulation it is possible that once the farther ear lags by more than 180° phase, it is coded as *leading* the nearer ear. If so, then phase alone would be a poor cue since a listener could not even determine whether the source was to his right or left. The exception to this ambiguity occurs only for tones of low frequency whose half-periods are longer than the binaural time difference, for only then does the nearer ear unambiguously lead in phase.

Psychophysics

Sufficient detail about binaural stimulus differences has been given to allow us now to consider the relationship between the facts of dichoticity and sound localization.

LOCALIZATION OF REAL SOURCES

In Fig. 9.7 several limiting conditions are given. The intensity function

Fig. 9.7 Limiting conditions for intensity and phase. The intensity difference function (solid line) represents the binaural intensity difference in decibels for different frequencies and it should be read against the right ordinate. Data taken from Fig. 9.4. The 180 and 360° phase functions (dashed lines) are **equal phase contours** and they give the time in milliseconds required for tones of different frequencies to go through one-half and one cycle, respectively. They should be read against the left ordinate. Arrows **a** and **b** give frequency limits through which phase can be a cue to localization for each of two binaural time differences. See text for explanation.

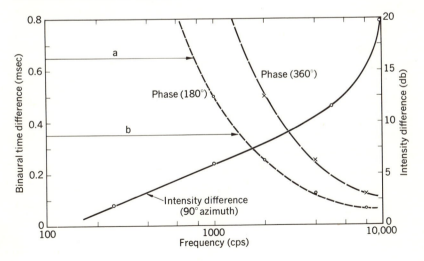

(solid line) represents the binaural intensity difference in decibels for various frequencies, as determined in the manner previously described and shown earlier in Fig. 9.4. Toward our purpose here we need do no more than suggest again that because binaural intensity differences increase with frequency, dichotic intensity must be increasingly effective in sound localization as some function of rising frequency.

The two *equal-phase* contours (dashed lines) shown in Fig. 9.7 give the time in milliseconds required for tones of various frequencies to go through one-half cycle (180° phase) and one cycle (360° phase). Each contour is based on simple calculations of the following sort. A 1000∿ tone goes through one cycle in 1 msec, and one-half cycle in 0.5 msec. A 2000∿ tone goes through one cycle in 0.5 msec and one-half cycle in 0.25 msec; and so forth. From these *equal-phase* contours one can draw several tentative conclusions about the role of phase in localization. Let us consider first the contour for one-half cycle (180°).

We have already suggested that once the farther ear lags the nearer one by a phase angle greater than 180°, the location of a tone becomes ambiguous because there are two locations, one on each side of the head, which would leave phase differences invariant. If we assume, therefore, that 180° represents the limit of unambiguous phase difference, then the contour shown in Fig. 9.7 describes the *upper frequency limit for any given binuaral time difference*. Two examples will clarify the point. We know that sound from a distant source at 90° azimuth will arrive at the farther ear 0.65 msec after it arrives at the nearer one (see Fig. 9.5). This binaural time difference is equivalent to one-half cycle for a 770∿ tone, as shown by arrow *a* in Fig. 9.7. All frequencies below this limit result in phase differences at the two ears of less than 180°. Accordingly, for pure tone sources at 90° azimuth phase can serve as an unambiguous cue only for tones below 770∿. With a source at 40° azimuth, the binaural time difference is 0.35 msec (see Fig. 9.5), and this is equivalent to one-half cycle of a 1400∿ tone, as shown by arrow *b* in Fig. 9.7. Therefore, when a pure tone source is located at 40° azimuth, phase can operate as an unambiguous cue only for tones below 1400∿.

The *equal-phase* contour for 360° represents a different kind of limit. It is possible that between 180° and 360°, phase continues to be coded but with the farther ear leading the nearer one. Though ambiguous by itself, when phase cues are coupled with binaural intensity differences,

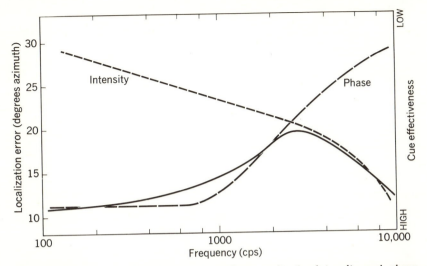

Fig. 9.8 Relative cue effectiveness in arbitrary units for intensity and phase (dashed lines) as a function of frequency. Both are reciprocals of the functions shown in Fig. 9.7 and they should be read against the right ordinate. The solid line, read against the left ordinate, shows mean localization errors as a function of frequency. Data from Stevens and Newman (49).

then phase could conceivably continue to influence localization up to the frequency limit specified by the 360° contour in Fig. 9.7.

We can summarize this discussion as follows: for any given binaural time difference, phase is a powerful cue for localization up to the frequency limit indicated by the 180° contour, a somewhat less effective cue for frequencies between the two contours, and a very weak cue for frequencies beyond the 360° contour.

In Fig. 9.8 the general effectiveness of dichotic intensity and phase (dashed lines, read against right ordinate) as a function of frequency is given. Note that the effectiveness of phase falls off with increasing frequency *before* intensity reaches its greatest effectiveness. Accordingly, one would expect that accuracy of the localization of pure tones would be lowest for frequencies between 2000 and 4000∿. The solid line of Fig. 9.8 represents mean localization errors in degrees as a function of stimulus frequency. These data were obtained by Stevens and Newman (49), and they support the duality hypothesis of localization: namely, dichotic phase for low tones and dichotic intensity for high tones. We shall consider subsequently whether or not phase might better be viewed in terms of binaural time differences.

LOCALIZATION OF APPARENT SOURCES

In the Stevens and Newman study just cited, the sound was generated by a speaker that was moved to various azimuths about the head. As a consequence, and by design, intensity and phase were dichotic. To determine the influence of phase alone, it is necessary to alter the experimental design so as to keep intensity constant. This can be done if sound is delivered separately to the ears by means of transducers affixed to the head.

Phase. With diotic intensity, low tones (below 500∿) are localized in the median plane when there is no phase difference. However, as phase is advanced progressively at the right ear, the apparent location of the source shifts out of the median plane toward the right, finally to be heard as coming from 90° azimuth when the phase difference equals 180°. A further advance in phase (e.g., 200°) shifts the apparent location to the opposite side of the head at 270° azimuth, finally to be heard once again as coming from the median plane when the phase difference reaches 360° (*15, 16*). The same general pattern has been observed by other experimenters who employed tones of higher frequency, but phase differences never resulted in shifts in the apparent location of tones whose frequencies exceeded about 1400∿ (*18, 30*). These data on changing localization as a function of binaural phase differences are open to question because changes in phase necessarily produce changes in binaural time. That is, if the initiation of neural action bears a fixed relationship to phase at each ear, then phase differences can be considered as just another way of producing time differences. Only if phase operated independently of time could we treat binaural phase differences as a primary cue to sound localization.

Temporal Factors. For well-practiced listeners, the binaural phase difference threshold is about 3° for a 100∿ tone (*35*). This is equivalent to a time difference of 83 μsec, and this is approximately the dichotic time threshold value for a detectable shift in the apparent location of a source when the stimuli are clicks and tonal pulses (*64*).

In 1920 von Hornbostel and Wertheimer (*19*) argued that binaural time differences constituted the major basis upon which sounds are localized. They conceptualized phase differences in terms of temporal equivalents. Their arguments were developed more fully by Halverson (*15*) who, in like manner, also favored time differences. His position can be summarized as follows. He assumed that a 180° phase difference was the maximum allowable difference for unambiguous localization. For tones of various frequencies he held constant the binaural phase difference at 180° and had his listeners judge the apparent location of the source. If localization was based on phase differences, then his listeners ought to have localized the source always at the same azimuth. However, his results showed that his listeners actually localized the source at different azimuths for each frequency, and for each frequency that azimuth was selected where the binaural time difference equaled the temporal equivalent of a 180° phase difference. For example, a 1000∿ tone has a half-cycle period of 0.5 msec (see Fig. 9.7, 180° contour). A binaural time difference of 0.5 msec arises from a sound approaching the head from an azimuth of about 60°, and this is where Halverson's listeners located the 1000∿ tone. A high correlation was obtained between the judged locations and those predicted by converting the 180° phase difference into a time difference.

There are two kinds of balancing experiments that lend support to the importance of temporal factors in localization. When sound is led individually to the ears it is possible by dichoticity in one dimension to shift an apparent source out of the median plane and then bring it back by making another dimension dichotic so as to produce an opposite effect. Shaxby and Gage (*48*) found that binaural intensity differences of 6 and 14 db could be balanced by advancing phase at the "weaker" ear; but the amount by which the phase had to be advanced increased with frequency so as to keep the time difference constant for each intensity difference. The conclusion of importance is that intensity differences were balanced by temporal differences which were achieved through phase manipulation. The results of other experiments in which binaural time differences were balanced by intensity differences indicate that rather enormous differences in intensity are required to balance very small time differences (*19, 26*).

Clearly, binaural time differences are extremely important to sound localization, and in the light of psychophysical data, phase differences seem to reduce to time differences.

HEAD MOVEMENT

Thus far we have treated static localization. However, in many listening situations there is relative motion between the listener and the source. In such instances binaural differences go through progressive changes the character of which depends upon particular kinds of relative motion. When transducers are affixed to the head so that sounds can be conducted individually to the ears, it is not uncommon for listeners to localize diotic stimuli inside the head, and this is so whether the head is still or in motion. According to Wallach the *externalization* of a source apparently depends upon changes in binaural differences which are coupled to head movement (*61*). Moreover, head movements have been shown to be critical to accurate location in several experiments by Wallach (*62, 63*), particularly with a source located in the median plane or elevated above the horizontal plane. Head movements around a vertical axis would change binaural differences for sources located ahead or behind but would not lead to differences for sources above or below. In a contrary manner, tilting the head toward the right and left would help to locate sources above or below but not in front or in back.

THE POSSIBLE ROLE OF THE PINNAE

The pinna itself casts a sound shadow when sound approaches the head from the rear. From our earlier discussion of the nature of sound shadows we would expect the shadow to be more pronounced for high than for low tones. This has been demonstrated by having listeners compare the loudness of a tone of constant intensity at a constant distance presented first at 0 and then at 180° azimuth. The judged difference in loudness increased with frequency (*50*). Since pure tones were employed, no information was gained about detectable changes in timbre as a consequence of the removal of high frequency components when the sound came from behind. Nevertheless, note that as long as the source remains at 0 and 180° azimuth any differences in stimulation caused by the pinnae are diotic and not dichotic. Accordingly, the pinnae cannot help to localize sounds in the median plane unless the listener has an opportunity to compare these diotic changes. In the experiment cited, listeners had an opportunity to form a subjective standard of intensity within a few trials since they heard repeatedly the same pure tone coming from ahead and behind. With tones above 3000∿, for which the pinnae cast effect shadows, many fewer errors of location were made than for tones below 3000∿.

Pinna and Monaural Localization. Batteau (*3*) has argued that the pinna gives rise to time delays and stimulus redundancy. Based upon measures taken from an enlarged plastic pinna, he found that a steep wavefront from an acoustic click showed a sequence of delays in sound pressure changes at the meatal entrance. Presumably, these delays occurred from multiple pathways of different length. One redundancy varied with azimuth, and Batteau attributed it to the horizontal dimension of the concha in the pinna since account of this structure predicted the time delay. Corrected for normal ear size, the delay varied linearly from 80 μsec at 0° azimuth to about 15 μsec at 90° azimuth. A second and longer time delay, attributed to the helix of the pinna, varied linearly with elevation. The time delay was about 100 μsec for sounds from above and 300 μsec for sounds from below. From these two time delays Batteau concludes that because of the pinna there is a unique temporal pattern for every locus in space.

The fundamental question, of course, is whether or not Batteau's temporal patterns, or other possible monaural cues, can lead to accurate monaural localization. Based upon some evidence for monaural localization (*4, 23*), Freedman and Fisher (*12*) executed a number of experiments designed to assess the role of the pinna in localization. In one experiment listeners were asked to locate verbally (in one of eight arcs) the direction of pulsed white noise while listening binaurally in each of three conditions: normally, without pinnae, and with artificial pinnae. With free head movement these three listening conditions gave results which were insignificantly different, but with restricted head movement sound localization in the no-pinnae condition was significantly worse. In another experiment listeners were asked to locate verbally (in one of sixteen arcs) the direction of pulsed white noise while listening with both ears unoccluded and with the right ear occluded. For the group of 13 listeners the size of location errors, the direction of errors, and the percentage of errors did not differ significantly between the two listening conditions. Correlations between the true and judged positions were 0.91 in the binaural and 0.89 in the monaural conditions. It would appear that monaural localization of complex stimuli of sudden onset is possible.

Physiological Processes and Localization

TIME-PLACE CONCEPTUALIZATIONS

Most physiological models of localization center around the concept of time. We have referred earlier in our discussion of psychophysics to the view of von Hornbostel and Wertheimer (*19*) regarding the importance of binaural time differences. In a later paper, von Hornbostel (*20*) suggested that binaural intensity differences also were converted into time differences because he believed the latency of neural firing was inversely related to stimulus intensity. Several experiments have now shown this to be so, at least over the intensity range from threshold to 70 db SL (*24, 39*).

At this point it is important to recognize that if *phase* and *intensity* are no more than variations of the *time* hypothesis, at least as far as their effects on the nervous system are concerned, then we must conclude that temporal encoding is exceedingly exact in the auditory system since the range of values upon which localization depends is quite restricted (0-700 μsec).

Neural Place. In 1908 Bowlker (*7*) suggested a central mechanism to transform temporal differences into place differences. A more detailed model of the same sort was proposed by Jeffress in 1948 (*21*). Jeffress envisaged a central neural complex into which tracts from both ears made overlapping synaptic connections such that discrepancies in arrival time of impulses from the ears focused on different loci within the neural complex and thereby triggered different post-synaptic fibers for each time delay. Originally he suggested the medial geniculate nucleus of the thalamus as a suitable site for this neural complex, but later he disavowed this site in favor of the accessory nucleus of the superior olive in the medulla (*22*). Because temporal patterning is altered by synapses, it would be most reasonable to propose that the time-place transformation occurs early in the projection system.

ELECTROPHYSIOLOGICAL DATA

The first possible locus of binaural interaction is in first-order neurons within the cochlea where afferent activity could be influenced by the efferent system triggered through stimulation of the contralateral ear. Galambos, Rosenblith, and Rosenzweig (13) have presented evidence of a cochleo-cochlear pathway in the cat, but the dichotic interval in stimulation of one ear which influenced afferent activity of the other was two long (1.25 msec) to support the view that interaction at the cochlear level mediates localization. Cochleo-cochlear transmission requires about 1 msec whereas localization always depends upon briefer dichotic intervals, often as brief as 100 μsec (65).

There is evidence of binaural interaction in the superior olivary nucleus. To information about the acoustic neurology previously treated in Chapter 3, we can add here that postsynaptic cells in the medial part of the olivary nucleus receive afferent terminals in the form of boutons from *both* cochlear nuclei, but with the boutons of fibers from the homolateral cochlear nucleus located on one side of the postsynaptic cell and boutons of fibers from the contralateral cochlear nucleus located on the other side. Recordings from single units of the superior olive have shown that many of these cells are sensitive to dichotic time delays in that their response rates are a function of interaural delay (14). No binaural interaction has been observed in earlier nuclei of the auditory projections such as the cochlear nuclei.

Axons of postsynaptic fibers of the olivary nucleus ascend via the lateral lemnisci to the inferior colliculi. Although evidence of binaural interaction in the lemnisci is equivocal (47), there is no doubt that it takes place in the colliculi. Erulkar (11) found that 60 per cent of the cells sampled responded to stimulation applied to either ear, with their latency of response influenced by azimuth of the sound source. Moreover, single units have been found in the inferior colliculus of the cat which show regular changes in their rate of response as a function of binaural time differences (44). For example, when stimulating with a 500$\curlyvee$ tone (45 db SPL) for 10 sec, the number of spikes/10 sec recorded from one of these units varied from near zero to over 1000 as a function of the dichotic time interval. If we determine the binaural time delay at which response rate is minimal, then the maximum response rate occurs when the delay is increased an amount equal to half the period of the wave (180° phase). In units of this kind, rate of response appears to be locked to phase rather than to time. However, other single-units were found in which the maximum number of spikes always occurred at a constant dichotic interval, regardless of frequency. These units seem capable of detecting an *absolute* binaural time difference.

While similar evidence of single units tuned to dichotic time is wanting at the level of the cortex, binaural time differences apparently do affect summated response amplitudes. In general, the summated response amplitude from the auditory cortex in one hemisphere is enhanced when the contralateral ear receives prior stimulation, but the time dependency relationships have yet to be worked out in detail (*45, 46*).

ABLATION STUDIES

Although two studies indicate that decorticate cats can localize sounds (*2, 52*), Neff and Diamond (*38*) have shown that bilateral ablations of the auditory cortex of cats impair their ability to localize. In their experiment the normal cats had a localization error of 5° whereas the ablated cats had errors of about 40°. The fact that localization occurred in these and similar experiments has been interpreted by Riss (*43*) as due to a failure to keep the stimulus sufficiently brief to rule out the possibility of localization by means of head movements. He found that cats with bilateral ablations could orient to sounds of long duration but not to sounds of brief duration.

References

1. Aggazzotti, A. Sul più piccolo intervallo di tempo percettibile nei processi psichici, *Arch. Fisiol.,* 1911, *9,* 523-574.
2. Bard, P., and D. E. Rioch. A study of four cats deprived of neocortex and additional portions of the forebrain, *Bull. Johns Hopkins Hosp.,* 1937, *60,* 73-147.
3. Batteau, D. W. The role of the pinna in human localization, *Proc. Royal Soc.,* Series B, 1967, *168,* No. 1011, 158-180.
4. Bauer, R. W., J. L. Matuzsa, R. F. Blackmer, and S. Glucksberg. Noise localization after unilateral attenuation, *J. Acoust. Soc. Amer.,* 1966, *40,* 441-444.
5. Boring, E. G. Auditory theory with special reference to intensity, volume and localization, *Amer. J. Psychol.,* 1926, *37,* 157-188.

6. Boring, E. G. *Sensation and Perception in the History of Experimental Psychology*, New York: Appleton-Century-Crofts, 1942.

7. Bowlker, T. J. On the factors servings to determine the direction of sound, *Phil. Mag.*, 1908, *15*, 318-332.

8. Breuer, J. Ueber die Bogengänge des Labyrinths, *Allg. Wein. med. Zeitung*, 1873, *18*, 598 and 606.

9. Breuer, J. Ueber die Function der Bogengänge des Ohrlabyrinthes, *Med. Jarhb. Wein.*, 1874, 72-124.

10. Breuer, J. Ueber die Function der Otolithen-Apparate, *Arch. ges. Physiol.*, 1891, *48*, 195-306.

11. Erulkar, S. D. The responses of single units of the inferior colliculus of the cat to acoustic stimulation, *Proc. Royal Soc.* (London), Series B, 1959, *150*, 336-355.

12. Freedman, S. J., and H. G. Fisher. The role of the pinna in auditory localization, Chapter 8 in *The Neuropsychology of Spatially Oriented Behavior*, S. J. Freedman (Ed.), Homewood, Ill.: Dorsey Press, 1968.

13. Galambos, R., W. A. Rosenblith, and M. R. Rosenzweig. Physiological evidence for a cochleo-cochlear pathway in the cat, *Experientia*, 1950, *6*, 438-440.

14. Galambos, R., J. Schwartzkopff, and A. Rupert. Microelectrode study of superior olivary nuclei, *Amer. J. Physiol.*, 1959, *197*, 527-536.

15. Halverson, H. M. Binaural localization of tones as dependent upon differences of phase and intensity, *Amer. J. Psychol.*, 1922, *33*, 178-212.

16. Halverson, H. M. The upper limit of auditory localization, *Amer. J. Psychol.*, 1927, *38*, 97-106.

17. Helmholtz, H. L. F. von. *Die Lehre von den Tonempfindungen als physiologische Grundlage für die Theorie der Musik*, Braunschweig: Viewig u. Sohn, 1863, p. 127.

18. Hirsh, I. J. The influence of interaural phase on interaural summation and inhibition, *J. Acoust. Soc. Amer.*, 1948, *20*, 536-544.

19. Hornbostel, E. M. von, and M. Wertheimer. Ueber die Wahrnehmung der Schallrichtung, *SB Preuss. Akad. Wiss.*, 1920, *15*, 388-396.

20. Hornbostel, E. M. von. Das räumliche Hören, in *Handbuch der normalen und pathologischen Physiologie*, A. Bethe (Ed.), Vol. II, Berlin: Springer, 1926.

21. Jeffress, L. A. A place theory of sound localization, *J. Comp. Physiol. Psychol.*, 1948, *41*, 35-39.

22. Jeffress, L. A. Medial geniculate body: a disavowal, *J. Acoust. Soc. Amer.*, 1958, *30*, 802-803.

23. Jongkees, L. B. W., and R. A. van der Veer. On directional sound localization in unilateral deafness and its explanation, *Acta Oto-Laryngol.*, 1958, *49*, 119-131.

24. Kemp, E. H., and E. H. Robinson. Electric responses of the brain stem to unilateral auditory stimulation, *Amer. J. Physiol.*, 1937, *120*, 304-315.

25. Klemm, O. Ueber den Einfluss des binauralen Zeitunterschiedes auf die Localisation, *Arch. ges. Psychol.*, 1920, *40*, 117-146.
26. Klemm, O. Untersuchungen über die Lokalisation von Schallreizen. Ueber den Einfluss des binauralen Zeitunterschiedes auf die Lokalisation, *Arch. ges. Psychol.*, 1920, *40*, 117-146.
27. Kreidl, A., and S. Gatscher. Ueber die dichotische Zeitschwelle, *Pflüg. Arch. ges. Physiol.*, 1923, *200*, 366-373.
28. Kries, J. von. Ueber das Erkennen der Schallrichtung, *Z. Psychol.*, 1890, *1*, 236-251.
29. Laborde, J. -v. Essai d'une détermination expérimentale et morphologique du rôle fonctionnel des canaux semi-circulairs, *Bull. Soc. Anthropol.* (Paris), 1881, *4*, 834-840.
30. Langmuir, I., V. J. Schaefer, C. V. Ferguson, and E. F. Hennelly. A study of binaural perception of the direction of a sound source, OSRD Report 4079, June 1944 (PBL 31014).
31. Lotze, R. *Medicinische Psychologie*, 1852, 325-371.
32. Magendie, F. *An Elementary Compendium of Physiology*, trans. by E. Milligan, 4th ed., Edinburgh: Carfrae, 1831.
33. Mallock, A. Note on the sensibility of the ear to the direction of explosive sounds, *Proc. Royal Soc.* (London), Series A, 1908, *80*, 110-112.
34. Matsumoto, M. Research on acoustic space, *Studies Yale Psychol. Lab.*, 1897, *5*, 1-75.
35. Monnier, A. M., and G. Viaud. Recherches sur l'acuité de la perception binaurale, *Arch. Int. Physiol.*, 1946, *54*, 107-116.
36. More, L. T., and H. S. Fry. On the appreciation of differences of phase of sound-waves, *Phil. Mag.*, 1907, *13*, 452-459.
37. Müller, J. *Handbuch der Physiologie des Menschen*, Coblenz: Hölscher, 1840, Vol. 2.
38. Neff, W. D., and I. T. Diamond. The neural basis of auditory discrimination, in *Biological and Biochemical Bases of Behavior*, H. F. Harlow and C. N. Woolsey (Eds.), Madison, Wis.: University of Wisconsin Press, 1958.
39. Pestalozza, G., and H. Davis. Electric responses of the guinea pig ear to high audio frequencies, *Amer. J. Physiol.*, 1956, *185*, 595-609.
40. Preyer, W. Die Wahrnehmung der Schallrichtung mittelst der Bogengänge, *Arch. ges. Physiol.*, 1887, *40*, 586-622.
41. Rayleigh, Lord (J. W. Strutt). Acoustical observations, *Phil. Mag.*, 1877, *3*, 456-464.
42. Rayleigh, Lord (J. W. Strutt). On our perception of sound direction, *Phil. Mag.*, 1907, *13*, 214-232.
43. Riss, W. Effect of bilateral temporal cortical ablation on discrimination of sound direction, *J. Neurophysiol.*, 1959, *22*, 374-384.
44. Rose, J. E., N. B. Gross, C. D. Geisler, and J. E. Hind. Some neural mechanisms in the inferior colliculus of the cat which may be relevant to

localization of a sound source, *J. Neurophysiol.*, 1966, *29*, 288-314.

45. Rosenzweig, M. R. Cortical correlates of auditory localization and of related perceptual phenomena, *J. Comp. Physiol. Psychol.*, 1954, *47*, 269-276.

46. Rosenzweig, M. R., and W. A. Rosenblith. Some electrophysiological correlates of the perception of successive clicks, *J. Acoust. Soc. Amer.*, 1950, *22*, 878-880.

47. Rosenzweig, M. R., and D. Sutton. Binaural interaction in lateral lemniscus of cat, *J. Neurophysiol.*, 1958, *21*, 17-23.

48. Shaxby, J. H., and F. H. Gage. The localization of sounds in the median plane, *Med. Res. Council Spec. Rept.* (London), Series 166, 1932.

49. Stevens, S. S., and E. B. Newman. The localization of pure tones, *Proc. Natl. Acad. Sci.*, 1934, *20*, 593-596.

50. Stevens, S. S., and E. B. Newman. The localization of actual sources of sound, *Amer. J. Psychol.*, 1936, *48*, 297-306.

51. Stumpf, C. Binaurale Tonmischung, Mehrheitsschwelle und Mitteltonbildung, *Z. Psychol.*, 1916, *75*, 330-350.

52. Ten Cate, J. Akustische und optische Reaktionen der Katzen nach teilweisen und totalen Extirpationen des Neopallismus, *Arch. Néerl. Physiol.*, 1934, *19*, 191-264.

53. Thompson, S. P. Phenomena of binaural audition, *Phil. Mag.*, 1877, *4*, 274-276.

54. Thompson, S. P. Phenomena of binaural audition, *Phil. Mag.*, 1878, *6*, 383-391.

55. Thompson, S. P. The pseudophone, *Phil. Mag.*, 1879, *8*, 385-390.

56. Trimble, O. C. The theory of sound localization: a restatement, *Psychol. Rev.*, 1928, *35*, 515-523.

57. Venturi, J. B. Considérations sur la connaissance de l'étendue que nous donne le sens de l'ouïe, *Mag. Encycl.* or *J. Lett. Arts*, 1796, *3*, 29-37.

58. Venturi, J. B. Betrachungen über die Erkenntnis der Entfernung, die wir durch das Werkzeug des Gehörs erhalten, *Arch. Physiol.*, 1800, *5*, 383-392.

59. Venturi, J. B. Betrachungen über die Erkenntniss des Raums, durch den Sinn des Gehörs, *Mag. neu. Zustand Naturkd.* (*Reil's Arch.*), 1800, *2*, 1-16.

60. Venturi, G. (J. B.). Riflessioni sulla conoscenza dello spazio che noi passiamo ricavar dall'udito, in *Indagine Fisica sui Colori*, Modena: Società Tipolgrafica, 1801.

61. Wallach, H. Ueber die Wahrnehmung der Schallrichtung, *Psychol. Forsch.*, 1938, *22*, 238-266.

62. Wallach, H. On sound localization, *J. Acoust. Soc. Amer.*, 1939, *10*, 270-274.

63. Wallach, H. The role of head movements and vestibular and visual cues in sound localization, *J. Exper. Psychol.*, 1940, *27*, 339-368.

64. Wallach, H., E. B. Newman, and M. R. Rosenzweig. The precedence effect in sound localization, *Amer. J. Psychol.*, 1949, *62*, 315-336.

65. Walsh, E. G. An investigation of sound localization in patients with neurological abnormalities, *Brain*, 1957, *80*, 222-250.

66. Weber, E. F. Ueber den Mechanismus des Gehörsorgans, *Ber. Sächs. Ges. Wiss.*, 1851, 29-31.

67. Wilson, H. A., and C. S. Myers. The influence of binaural phase differences in the localization of sound, *Brit. J. Psychol.*, 1908, *2*, 363-385.

68. Woodworth, R. S., and H. Schlosberg. *Experimental Psychology*, revised ed., New York: Holt, 1954.

10
Deafness and Audiology

In the foregoing chapters we have attended primarily to the actions of the normal auditory system, and our treatment of discriminative sensitivity and scaling has been limited to the normal listener. Now we turn to consider several forms of pathology. In so doing, our understanding of hearing will be extended as we examine the way in which certain kinds of impairments bear upon the principles we have seen to operate under normal conditions. We shall begin by considering the common types of deafness and associated pathologies, after which we shall review the methods used to measure impairments of hearing.

Deafness

Deafness takes many forms. The most widely recognized and least frequently occurring form is a complete failure of the auditory system to be sensitive to acoustic energy. For reasons which will become plain, total deafness holds less interest for us here than other less severe forms of impairment. The former condition does not allow us to make useful inquiry into the processes of hearing because there is little or nothing with which to compare the normal processes. On the other hand, selective impairments that leave the system partly operative afford us a good opportunity to study the functional significance of particular structures and processes. Needless to say, deafness in all its forms is of major concern to those who wish to understand its influence on the psychological adjustment of individuals so afflicted; but this matter is beyond the scope of this book and is, therefore, left to another arena.

We shall define deafness as *any significant impairment of sensitivity which is of moderate to long duration.* Losses in sensitivity that last a few days or more are considered here as forms of deafness, whereas impairments of very short duration, such as those described as auditory fatigue in the previous chapter, do not qualify. Note that our definition is an operational one in that deafness hinges on the presence of a reduced sensitivity rather than on the conditions that give rise to the reduction. Moreover, the definition implies that some forms of deafness can be temporary. This is a worthy observation because it is often assumed that all deafnesses are permanent.

Whereas the forms of deafness could be classified by their severity (*total* or *partial*) or their duration (*temporary* or *permanent*), commonly they are classified according to the site of the pathological condition believed to effect the deafness. Although the site of an abnormality in a particular individual is sometimes difficult to establish with certainty, the common manner of classification is useful to our present purpose which is to organize simply what is known about deafness so that we can examine the tenability of the principles believed to operate with normal hearing. We shall consider later the methods used to localize pathological sites when we treat audiological techniques.

There are three major sites where abnormalities can lead to impairments of hearing. First, there may be an abnormality or pathological condition in the external or middle ear which effectively interferes with the conduction of sound into the cochlea. This form we shall call *conductive deafness.* Second, there may be some abnormality or pathological condition within the cochlea itself which alters sensory processes so as to reduce their effects upon the auditory nervous system. This form we shall call *sensory deafness.* Finally, the site of the abnormality or pathological condition may be within the nervous system, in which event we shall call this form *nerve deafness.* The severity and nature of the abnormal condition obviously determine the extent and duration of the hearing impairment, and there are cases in which several or all of these sites are involved in a single individual.

CONDUCTIVE DEAFNESS

The circumstances which lead to conductive deafness are numerous, but they always affect the mechanical aspects of the ear and the conduction of sound into the cochlea.

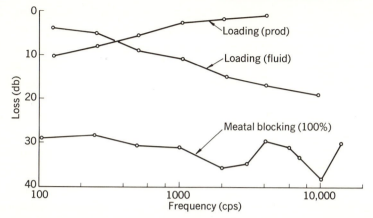

Fig. 10.1 The effects of meatal blocking and two forms of tympanic membrane loading on the human absolute threshold for tones between 100 and 15,000∿. Loss of sensitivity is given in decibels relative to the normal threshold. Data from references **7, 13, 30, 31.**

Meatal Blocking. The simplest form of conductive deafness is a *blocking* of the external auditory meatus. The loss in sensitivity thus produced is not especially noticeable until the blocking is extensive, except when the blocking agent is in contact with the tympanic membrane, in which case the effects are more pronounced. From our earlier discussion (Chapter 2) of the nature of distortions arising from asymmetrical vibratory systems, we would expect that the asymmetrical loading of the tympanic membrane would both reduce absolute sensitivity and change the normal pattern of frequency discrimination. This seems to be the case, as we shall see.

Whereas foreign bodies occasionally serve as blocking agents, especially in curious children, the most common agent is an accumulation of ear wax (cerumen). In both cases the impairment is corrected easily, and afterward normal sensitivity returns.

The loss of sensitivity due to blocking is usually measured as an upward shift of the absolute threshold. When the external meatus in the human was blocked purposely with wax (*13*) or petrolatum-soaked cotton (*7*), the loss of sensitivity amounted to about 34 db (±4 db) for all tones between 100 and 14,000∿, with the higher frequencies showing a slightly greater loss of sensitivity than the lower ones, as shown by the bottom function in Fig. 10.1.

There are occasional instances of malformation of the external meatus which are apparent at birth. When the malformation is limited to the external meatus, which is rare, the condition is correctable through surgery. Usually, however, a developmental deformity includes the ossicular chain as well as the meatus, and therefore the restoration of normal hearing under these circumstances is made more difficult. When both the external meatus and the ossicular chain are malformed, the losses for all tones are of the order of 60 db or more (*55*).

Tympanic Membrane: Loading. We have already mentioned that a blocking agent in contact with the tympanic membrane leads to greater hearing losses than those occurring when the agent is located more distally. When contiguous, the agent not only is an obstacle in the path of the sound, but it also impedes the outward excursion of the membrane and thus constitutes a loading. A more common form of loading occurs from the inside of the membrane as a consequence of accumulated fluid produced by inflamed mucous membranes within the middle ear. In extreme cases the middle ear cavity is filled entirely with fluid and, although its presence certainly impedes the movement of the ossicles, there is little doubt that its main effect is on the membrane (*51*, p. 348).

Most experimental studies of membrane loading in man have involved the application of small loads from the outside. While this method does not match exactly the conditions of loading found in most clinical cases, it has the advantage of convenience. Typically, a listener used in these experiments placed his head so that the external meatus was vertical, and then a weight of a few grams, a small amount of mercury, a small amount of viscous oil, or a prod was introduced into the meatus. The hearing loss thus brought about differed depending upon the method of loading. When a prod was employed, the stiffness of the ossicular mechanism apparently was increased. Therefore, its effects were mainly on the low tones. On the other hand, when the membrane was loaded with a fluid, the mass of the moving mechanical system increased. Accordingly, the loss in sensitivity occurred primarily with the high tones (*13, 30, 31*). The effects of these two kinds of loading also are shown in Fig. 10.1.

Tympanic Membrane: Perforation. Another simple form of conductive deafness results from a perforation of the tympanic membrane. When

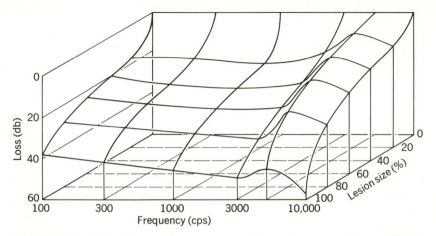

Fig. 10.2 The effects of tympanic membrane lesions in the cat on the magnitude of the cochlear potential (CP) as a function of frequency. Lesion size is given in per cent relative to the whole membrane. Losses in the CP are given in decibels relative to the no lesion condition. Data from Payne and Githler (35).

perforation is the result of a penetrating object, the lesion usually occurs in the posterior region of the membrane because of the curvature of the meatus. Those produced by sudden pressure changes generally are located in the anterior or inferior quadrant.

The effects of lesions in the tympanic membrane have been measured in man by comparing the sensitivity of the injured ear with that of the normal ear (5). They also have been measured in the cat by means of the cochlear potential (35). From both kinds of studies it is clear that the effects of lesions are complex and that the impairment resulting from perforation depends primarily upon the size of the lesion. In Fig. 10.2 are shown some of the results of a study by Payne and Githler (35) in which the effects of the size of lesions were investigated systematically in the cat. Here it may be seen that all perforations were accompanied by a loss of conduction as reflected in a reduced cochlear potential given in decibels relative to normal. For each frequency, the loss increased with the size of the lesion, but small lesions produced proportionately greater losses for the low than for the high tones, whereas with large lesions the effects with frequency were reversed. Similar results for low tones were obtained by Békésy (*3*) when he measured ossicular displacement in cadaver specimens before and after making a 1 mm² lesion in the tympanic membrane. He found that with such small lesions the reduction in the movement of the ossicles was limited to frequencies below 400∿.

Payne and Githler also studied the effects upon sound conduction of the locus of a lesion. They found that perforations in the posterior region of the membrane had more serious effects upon the conduction of sound than did perforations of the same size in the anterior region, but the differential effect was occasionally reversed, depending on the frequency of the stimulating tone.

The impairment of hearing following perforation results primarily from a reduction in the effectiveness with which the tympanic membrane communicates its motion to the ossicular chain. Its effectiveness is reduced because its surface area is made smaller and because lesions allow sound to pass directly into the middle ear where pressure changes occurring at the inside surface of the membrane can reduce the influence of pressure changes occurring outside. Lesions at or near the site of the membrane attachment to the manubrium have more deleterious effects than those of comparable size but of different location. When the membrane is absent, or when it is virtually inoperative as a diaphragm, the transformer action of the middle ear is lost entirely and sound then must act directly upon the cochlear windows. In such cases the absolute sensitivity of the ear is impaired greatly. Furthermore, the natural resonance characteristics of the external and middle ears will be altered, and this, in turn, will alter the relative sensitivity of the ear. For example, consider again the surface shown in Fig. 10.2. The middle ear of the cat has a resonance frequency near 5000∿ (*51*, p. 346). Therefore, perforations in its tympanic membrane ought to change the vibratory characteristics of the ear (as a whole) so as to favor the frequencies near 5000∿ since resonance in the middle ear cavity would now be more influential. That this probably occurred is shown by the prominent ridge along the 5000∿ contour.

We may conclude from the foregoing discussion, that lesions in the tympanic membrane lead to complex changes in auditory sensitivity. In extremely rare instances there may be noted an actual enhancement of sensitivity, but it is limited to a few isolated frequencies and it amounts to no more than 1 or 2 db. The usual result of perforation is a general loss of sensitivity for all frequencies with the severity of the impairment determined by the size and location of the lesion and the frequency of the stimulating tone.

Small lesions in the tympanic membrane heal themselves. Larger lesions require treatment, usually in the form of surgical packing placed in the external meatus. The packing serves as a mechanical support, and it reduces the danger of infection within the middle ear by forming a protective sterile barrier. Lesions of any size greatly increase the probability of middle ear infections, the consequences of which can be both more serious and more lasting than the lesion itself.

Middle Ear Infections. Infections of the middle ear are the most common cause of conductive deafness. There are three ways in which infections work to reduce sound conduction across the middle ear: through air pressure imbalance, through membrane loading, and through adhesion.

With reference to the first of these, *air pressure imbalance,* recall that under normal circumstances air is admitted to the middle ear cavity from the pharynx by way of the Eustachian tube which opens during the act of swallowing. By this means, air pressure exerted against the tympanic membrane from the inside (middle ear) is made approximately equal to that exerted from the outside (external meatus). However, pressure equalization fails to occur whenever the Eustachian tube remains closed because the tissues of the middle ear absorb air and means for its replacement are wanting. The usual cause of closure of the air duct is a swelling of the membranous lining of the Eustachian tube brought about by infections of the throat, but occasionally the infections occur first within the middle ear, particularly if the tympanic membrane is perforated. Regardless of the origin of the infection, once the air duct is closed, air pressure in the middle ear is reduced relative to the external meatus. This pressure imbalance causes the tympanic membrane and its ossicular attachments to be displaced inward with the result that a new resting position is established as the null around which the system vibrates. This, in turn, changes the vibration characteristics of the conductive mechanism.

The effects on sound conduction of a partial vacuum (negative pressure) in the middle ear have been studied extensively in the cat by means of the cochlear potential. In each of four experiments a loss of conduction was noted, and it was expressed as a reduction in the magnitude of the

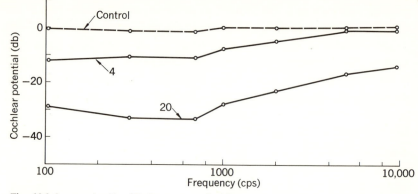

Fig. 10.3 Losses in the CP for tones of different frequency as a function of a pressure imbalance of 4 and 20 inches of water between the meatus and the middle ear of the cat. See text for explanation. Data from Rahm **et al.** (**36, 37**) and Wever **et al. (50, 53)**.

cochlear potential in decibels relative to a criterion response (50 μV) obtained under normal pressure conditions (*36, 37, 50, 53*). Summary data are presented in Fig. 10.3 for each of two levels of pressure imbalance, 4 and 20 inches of water. In two of these studies (*36, 50*) both positive and negative pressures were investigated. The results indicated that a negative pressure of 4 inches of water had the same effect on sound conduction as a positive pressure of like amount. The same relationship held with the larger pressure. Accordingly, the two functions shown in Fig. 10.3 actually describe conduction losses produced by pressure imbalances of the specified amount, regardless of their direction relative to normal pressure.

Note that when the pressure difference was of a moderate amount (4 inches), the losses were confined to the frequencies below 5000∿, whereas when the pressure difference was made greater (20 inches), losses occurred for all frequencies studied (100 to 10,000∿). From both conditions it is clear that pressure imbalances affect the conduction of the low tones to a greater extent than they affect the high tones. Furthermore, regardless of frequency, the losses produced in the condition of the larger pressure difference exceeded those produced in the smaller by about 20 db.

In one of the experiments (*37*) the external meatus was sealed so that pressures above and below normal could be varied simultaneously in the external meatus and the middle ear cavity, within the range from —20 to + 20 inches of water. As long as the average pressure acting on the inner surface of the tympanic membrane equaled the average pressure acting on its outer surface, sound conduction remained normal. This is shown by the control function in Fig. 10.3. Accordingly, we may conclude that *losses in sound conduction are due to the relative pressures between the external meatus and the middle ear cavity and not to the absolute pressures.*

The second influence of middle ear infection on sound conduction concerns a fluid loading of the tympanic membrane. As mentioned, inflammation of the mucous membranes can lead to an accumulation of fluid within the middle ear. Known as *serous otitis media,* this condition may come about with respiratory infection although it is related occasionally to an allergic reaction. The impairment of hearing brought about by serous otitis media may be noticed either with high or low tones, depending on the amount of fluid loading and the amount of pressure imbalance which the fluid brings about. As we have seen already, fluid loading shows up especially with high tones whereas pressure imbalance interferes most with the low tones.

If the fluid is allowed to remain, then *chronic otitis media* may occur. Suppuration (pus formation) leads to various tissue changes, including the formation of new connective tissue that can become fibrous in nature. When tissue changes of this sort take place, the movement of the ossicular chain is impeded or prohibited by *adhesions* between the ossicles and the walls of the middle ear. This constitutes the third way in which middle ear infections influence sound conduction to the cochlea. Adhesions can raise the auditory threshold for all frequencies by 60 db (± 10). In cases of long-standing chronic otitis media, the suppurative processes can erode the ossicular chain.

Ossicular Chain Fixation. Fixation of the ossicular chain is the last form of conductive deafness we shall consider. Although fixation can occur from the accumulation of semifluids and adhesions, as in chronic otitis media, the most serious form of fixation is *otosclerosis,* a disease of the bone apparently unique to the human middle ear. The disease is found more often in women than men, and it has been estimated that about 7 per cent of the adult population has otosclerosis. The disease impairs hearing only when it leads to a fixation of the stapes. In the absence of stapes fixation otosclerosis often goes undetected.

The cause of the disease is unknown, but it seems to be related to a vascular abnormality that leads to chemical changes in the bone. In its early stages, otosclerosis involves a partial decalcification of the bony wall of the middle ear cavity which is followed by the production of sclerotic bone, usually in more abundant quantity than is required simply to repair the damaged bone. When the disease occurs near the oval window, the stapes footplate usually becomes bound to the margin of the window, and as the pathological bone spreads, the fixation increases until the stapes is immobilized.

Partial or total fixation of the stapes interferes most with the conduction of the low tones because the fixation adds stiffness and resistance to the mechanical system. However, impairment on the order of 60 to 80 db can occur for all tones between 100 and 10,000∿ (28, 29). In some instances of otosclerotic deafness, especially in patients of middle age or old age, there is a pronounced absence of sensitivity to the high tones. This could be due to some secondary effects of otosclerosis which involve the cochlea and auditory nerve. However, since there is an independent disorder (presbyacusia) which commonly accompanies old age and which has high-tone deafness as its major symptom, high-tone deafness in older people with otosclerosis probably represents an independent disorder that has been added to the otosclerosis (51, p 358).

The complete mechanical fixation of the stapes in the oval window results in the loss of the transformer system. Of greater importance is the fact that the fluids within the cochlea are immobilized since the round window alone is insufficient to the production of fluid movement even if sounds were to impinge upon it (48). As a consequence, the sensory processes that depend on the relative motions of the structures of the organ of Corti to movements of the cochlear fluids are virtually absent. If normal or near-normal hearing is to be regained, then two requirements must be met. First, mobilization of the cochlear fluids must be achieved, and second, the middle ear must be restored so that its transformer action can operate.

In 1938 Lempert (27) developed a successful procedure to meet the first requirement. His procedure involved the making of a new window (fenestra) in the lateral semicircular canal near the vestibule. With the inoperative oval window thus replaced, the new window and the round window once again could allow fluid movements through their reciprocal actions. The new window was covered with a tissue flap taken from the wall of the external meatus. The ossicular chain was removed, except for the otosclerotic footplate, and the tympanic membrane, freed from its bony sulcus except at its anterior-inferior quadrant, was diverted medially to divide the middle ear into two chambers. One chamber was continuous with the external meatus and contained the new window. The other contained the round window which was removed somewhat from the influence of impinging sounds by the diverted tympanic membrane. Both the new skin flap and the diverted tympanic membrane were held in place by surgical packing until their attachments were made.

While the fenestration procedure allows the fluids of the cochlea to be mobilized once again, it does not restore the transformer mechanism. Nevertheless, if stapedial fixation from otosclerosis is unaccompanied by other difficulties, then fenestration leads to an immediate improvement in hearing which often brings sensitivity for all frequencies to within 25 db (± 5) of normal. Of course, fenestration does not restore high-tone losses due to some other disorder such as presbyacusia.

A more recent development in corrective surgery for otosclerotic deafness involves the removal of the entire stapes and its replacement with an artificial strut (32). In this procedure access to the middle ear is gained through the external meatus by freeing the tympanic membrane along its posterior boundary. The crura of the stapes are broken at the footplate and the capital is detached from the lenticular process of the incus. Next the footplate is removed by drilling and chipping, after which a small section of vein, taken from the patient's forearm, is placed over the oval window and held in place by a prosthesis of polyethylene tubing beveled at one end to fit in the oval window and fitted at the other end over the lenticular process of the incus. Finally, the posterior portion of the tympanic membrane is replaced to its normal position where it is held with packing until its attachment is made.

The *stapedectomy* not only eliminates the problem of stapedial fixation, but it does so without destroying the transformer mechanism of the middle ear: that is, the otosclerotic and inoperative stapes is replaced by an artificial stapes consisting of a vein flap and a plastic strut. Accordingly, the stapedectomy procedure meets both of the requirements we mentioned early for the restoration of normal hearing.

In summarizing the results of one thousand stapedectomy operations, Myers, Schlosser, and Winchester (*32*) reported that hearing was restored to normal (which they defined as 0 to 15 db residual loss) in 78.3 per cent of the cases. Serviceable hearing (0 to 30 db residual loss) was attained in 91.7 per cent of the cases. Reduction in hearing sensitivity following a stapedectomy occurred in only 1.6 per cent of the cases. From periodic audiometric measures taken over a twelve-month period they also established that there was a strong tendency to continuous improvement rather than regression. Certainly, the successful development of modern microsurgical techniques like the stapedectomy and its variations (*42, 43, 44*) lends testimony to the adequacy of our understanding of the principles of sound conduction.

SENSORY DEAFNESS

So far, our treatment of deafness has been limited to those conditions in which the impairment of hearing was traceable to a reduction in the passage of sound through the conductive mechanism. Here, in this section, we shall extend our consideration to impairments arising directly from injuries to the receptor apparatus, particularly the finer structures of the organ of Corti.

Before considering the major forms of cochlear injury that constitute sensory deafness, it should be said that the distal ends of the acoustic nerve fibers are in such intimate relation with the organ of Corti that a serious dysfunction of cochlear processes can lead secondarily to neural dysfunction. Furthermore, because the normal human cochlea has not been available to us for the experimental inquiries we should have liked most to make, information about the effects of cochlear injuries has come primarily from animal studies and from post-mortem examinations.

Stimulation Deafness. Exposure to intense acoustic stimulation, especially for prolonged periods, can lead to severe impairments of hearing. Long ago audiologists recognized the risks to hearing of certain noisy environments in which men worked, and often the observed hearing losses would be labeled according to the work, for example "boiler-maker's deafness." This kind of labeling implied, unjustly, that there were characteristic hearing losses produced by different noise environments. We know now that the losses due to prolonged exposure are rather more general than had been believed earlier.

Some of the effects of intense sounds upon the ear are straightforward while others are more elusive. In consideration of the first sort we need do no more than recall the *stimulation deafness* experiments cited earlier in connection with our discussion of the *place* principle in auditory theory. From them we learned that injurious intensities actually loosed some of the hair cells from their normal attachments, with the result that these cells were found upon histological examination to be floating freely in the scala media. Other hair cells, those adjacent to the region of most violent injury, were found to have ruptured or to have swollen. When, in these experiments, the regions of injury were mapped along the longitudinal extent of the organ of Corti as a function of the frequency of the injuring tone, different spatial patterns became apparent. As the frequency of the injuring tone was changed from low to high, there was a systematic shift in the site of injury from the apical to the basal end of the cochlea. This led to two conclusions. First, different frequencies have their effects on the receptor surface at different *places;* and second, hearing losses brought about by stimulation deafness are confined to the frequency range about the injuring tone. We have considered elsewhere the severe limitation that other facts impose on the first conclusion (see Chapter 5). Let us consider here the tenability of the second conclusion, for in so doing we shall show up the elusive effects of intense stimulation.

From our earlier treatment of the electrical activity of the cochlea we are now familiar with the general form of the intensity function of the CP. With pure tone stimuli, the CP first rises linearly with intensity but later departs from this form to reach a maximum. If intensity is raised still further, then the response actually falls off and injury results. Afterward, the original function can no longer be obtained and the new one is lower in magnitude, although it continues to have the same slope (1.0 on log-log coordinates). The reduction in the CP to a tone of the injury-producing frequency following overstimulation is precisely what we would expect, given the known structural changes that result from intense stimulation. Of special interest to us, however, is the fact that *following injury by overstimulation with one tone, the cochlear potential is impaired more or less uniformly for all tones.* Smith and Wever (*45*) stimulated

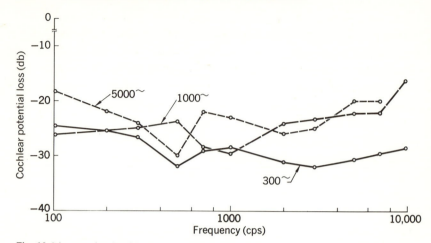

Fig. 10.4 Losses in the CP of the guinea pig brought about by 4 minutes of stimulation with tones of 300, 1000, or 5000∿ at an intensity of 1000 dynes/cm². Note that following injury by overstimulation with one tone, impairments were obtained for all tones. CP given in decibels relative to pre-injury level. Data from Smith and Wever (**45**).

groups of guinea pigs with different pure tones, each at an intensity of 1000 dynes/cm² (134 db SPL) for a period of 4 minutes. The impairments of the CP following injury produced by tones of 300, 1000, and 5000∿ are shown in Fig. 10.4, where the loss in the potential is given in decibels relative to the original level. Apparently the injuries noted histologically by microscopic examination do *not* parallel the functional injuries. Indeed, diminution of the CP is found in many ears in which the hair cells later show themselves to be normal in appearance.

No doubt many of the effects of overstimulation are subtle inasmuch as all but the most severe effects remain undisclosed to visual study with standard histological procedures. Although the loss of nucleic acids and other proteins has been observed in first-order acoustic neurons after trauma produced by intense stimulation, the nature of the early injury process in the hair cells has not been established (*25*). However, there is no reason to think it would be very different. By comparing the electrical activity of the cochlea after overstimulation with that obtained following injury produced by other means, we can draw some tentative conclusions about the injury process.

Injury and Drugs. In the years immediately following the discovery of
the cochlear potential, there were held a number of different views about
its origin. A number of experimenters sought after the physiological basis
of the potential by studying the effects upon it of various chemical agents
applied to the cochlea (*1, 12, 14-16, 23, 24, 49*). More recently, with
the advent of microsurgery for the correction of certain forms of conductive deafness, the interest in drugs has turned to the effects of topical
anesthetics upon the ear (*22, 34, 38-41*). Rather than treat here the details of the effects of different drugs on the CP, we shall instead direct
our attention to a general phenomenon which can serve as the basis for
a brief discussion of cochlear injury.

Fig. 10.5 Intensity functions from the cat to a 1000∿ tone. The control represents the normal relationship. Reduction by overstimulation does not influence
the slope of the function whereas reduction by drugs lowers the slope. Intensity
given in decibels relative to 1 dyne/cm².

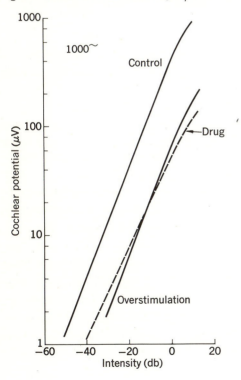

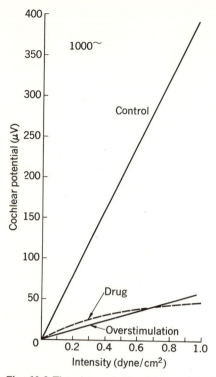

Fig. 10.6 The data of Fig. 10.5 replotted on linear coordinates. The reduced slope of the drug function in the previous figure shows itself here as a negative acceleration.

Brief topical applications of certain drugs (such as procaine hydro-chloride, tetracaine hydrochloride, and chloramphenicol) to the round window membrane of the cat have been shown to result in a reduction of the CP. Whether the CP subsequently showed recovery or a continuing progressive decline depended upon which particular drug was applied and in what concentration. Of particular interest to us here is the fact that the reduction in the potential by drugs was accompanied by a change in the slope of the intensity function. Recall that overstimulation left the slope unchanged. This difference is shown in Fig. 10.5, where stimulus intensity is given in decibels relative to 1 dyne/cm² and the cochlear potential is given in microvolts. As plotted, both coordinates are logarithmic scales, and for the *control* and *overstimulation* functions (solid lines), a 20 db increase in stimulus intensity led to a 20 db increase in the magnitude of the CP. Therefore, both of these functions have a slope of 1.0. However, the *drug* function (dashed line), while showing a similar over-all reduction, had a lower slope. The significance of the slope difference in these two post-injury functions is made plain in Fig. 10.6 where the data shown in the previous figure are replotted on linear coordinates. Note that the relationship between stimulus intensity and the magnitude of the CP remains linear in the case of overstimulation but is negatively accelerated in the case of drug-induced injury.

Apparently these two treatments affect different sensory processes. The relatively simple pattern of diminution in the CP by overstimulation is exactly what one would expect if the total number of active hair cells was reduced. In fact, Alexander and Githler (2) have shown a high correlation ($r = 0.9$) between CP magnitude and the number of normal hair cells remaining after overstimulation. The fact that the intensity function remains linear suggests that the primary effect on the cochlea of intense stimulation is a reduction in the size of the hair cell population and not an interference with the transduction process in those cells which continue to function. However, the absence of linearity after drug application indicates that, in addition to the destruction of some cells, the transduction process itself undergoes modification. In the case of drugs, then, injury is a twofold process.

After exploring this matter further, Gulick and Patterson (21) found that the recovery of the slope of intensity functions occurred independently of changes in the magnitude of the potential. The twofold injury process, one part involving cellular destruction and the other involving a modification of transduction, is reflected in the data shown in Fig. 10.7 where the loss in the magnitude of the CP to a constant stimulus (1000∿ tone) and the change in slope of intensity functions both are given as a function of time. The changes depicted were brought about by a brief application of chloramphenicol to the cat's round window membrane, and the data are based on the effects noted in seven animals. At zero time on the abscissa, pre-drug measures of slope and magnitude were taken, after which the drug was applied for 15 minutes and then removed. Note that the slope decreased over the first two hours from 1.0 to about 0.87 where it then remained unchanged for the next 12 hours. Thereafter, it rose steadily, finally to reach normal once again 26 hours after the ex-

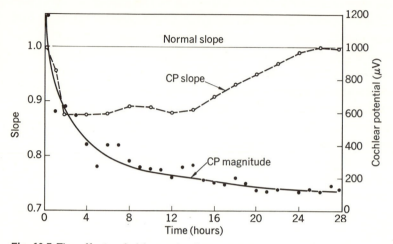

Fig. 10.7 The effects of chloramphenicol applied to the round window of the cat on the magnitude of the CP and the slope of intensity functions through time. Slope should be read against the left ordinate, CP magnitude against the right ordinate. See text for explanation. Data from Gulick and Patterson (21).

periments had begun. However, the restoration of the normal slope was not accompanied by a recovery of normal sensitivity, since the magnitude of the CP continued to decline. Control data obtained with a 15-minute application of physiological saline showed both the slope and magnitude of the cochlear potential to be unaffected over the same course of time.

The effects noted here for chloramphenicol also occur with a number of other drugs, especially sodium chloride, hexylcaine hydrochloride, and tetracaine hydrochloride. From these observations it would appear likely that the cochlea can recover from certain kinds of injury, particularly those involving modification of the transduction processes, but that it cannot recover from other kinds of injury which either immediately or in time lead to cellular destruction.

Ménière's Disease and Tinnitus. When endolymph is formed in excessive amounts, an abnormal positive pressure occurs throughout the scala media and the vestibular system. This disorder is known as *Ménière's disease,* and in its early stages *tinnitus,* or a "ringing" in the ear, is its most common symptom. Apparently, endolymphatic pressure causes a general stimulation of the nerve endings. In its later stages Ménière's disease leads to vertigo accompanied by severe nausea or vomiting. The latter symptoms may be alleviated with several types of medical treatment, including the administration of anti-motion drugs and antihistamines, or in extreme cases, with the partial or total destruction of the non-auditory labyrinth by surgery or cryosurgery (11). With this disease there are impairments of hearing, especially for the low and middle tones.

Tinnitus itself has many causes beside endolymphatic pressure, and it occurs occasionally in the absence of pathology. What is heard may be tonal or noisy in quality and the "sound" is referable to one ear. In some cases it may arise from spasms of the intra-aural muscles or from partial obstruction of a blood vessel. In other cases tinnitus has a neural origin inasmuch as it occasionally persists even after the acoustic nerve is destroyed (6).

Systemic Influences. Impairments of hearing as a consequence of cochlear dysfunction occasionally accompany diseases such as meningitis, measles, mumps, diabetes, syphilis, and myxedema. There are also a number of ototoxic drugs, such as streptomycin, kanamycin, and salicylates, known to have an adverse effect upon the cochlea, especially with protracted use.

Vascular accidents also can have pronounced effects upon the organ of Corti. Whereas a spasm or temporary clot in one of the vessels that supplies the inner ear can result in a temporary loss of sensitivity, prolonged interruption of the normal blood supply to the cochlea can lead to permanent hair cell damage. In particular, a reduction in the flow of blood through the stria vascularis reduces the availability of oxygen that can be transported to the hair cells, and without sufficient oxygen the metabolic processes supporting transduction fail to play their role (52, 54). When the deprivation is severe, the life-supporting processes also fail and the hair cells degenerate.

Oxygen want may also arise through hypoxemia even though circulation to the inner ear is normal. In a study using cats, Gulick (18) reported that the cochlear potential obtained to a constant pure tone stimulus declined in a positively accelerated manner as hypoxemia grew in severity. When hemoglobin saturation in arterial blood was reduced from normal (94-96 per cent to about 50 per cent), the loss in the potential was surprisingly moderate (5 db). However, with further reductions, the losses became progressively more pronounced. Full recovery was noted shortly after the restoration of normal saturation unless hypoxemia had been very severe (less than 35 per cent hemoglobin saturation), in which cases there occurred residual losses of about 15 db. Sensory deafness can occur from oxygen deprivation, but the deprivation has to be severe before permanent damage ensues.

Mild states of hypoxemia have been shown to affect auditory sensitivity in man (*17, 26*). When listeners with normal hearing were tested after breathing a reduced oxygen mixture (10 per cent O_2 by volume, compared with 21 per cent O_2 in air) for about 15 minutes, sensitivity to pure tones was impaired about 5 db (*26*). When cats were respired artificially on the same reduced mixture (10 per cent O_2 by volume), the cochlear potential showed no loss when compared with that obtained during normal oxygen levels (*18*). Per unit volume, cat blood has about two-thirds the concentration of hemoglobin that human blood has, and since hemoglobin is the major determiner of oxygen transport, we would expect the cochlear potential generated in the human ear to be the more resistant to the consequences of breathing diluted air. Accordingly, it would appear that the losses in sensitivity in the human studies cited may have been brought about by the actions of oxygen want on the nervous system rather than on the cochlea.

Finally, we can note in passing that the receptor processes of the ear reach their most efficient levels when the cochlea and the body are of normal temperature. Departures from normal, as with high fevers or prolonged exposure to cold, always have deleterious effects upon the electrical activity of the ear (*10, 19, 20*). When extremes are reached, sensory deafness from hair cell injury may result.

NERVE DEAFNESS

Unlike deafness that results from disorders of the conductive apparatus and the cochlea, impairments due to neural involvements almost always show themselves first as a deafness to the higher tones, those above 4000∿. Moreover, the commonest site of pathology is in the auditory nerve itself, with the frequency of incidence for other sites declining as they become more central. Our attention here will center on those conditions that involve primarily the auditory nerve, of which there are three

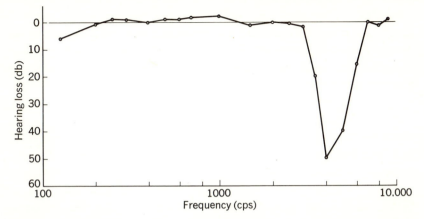

Fig. 10.8 An audiogram showing a tonal dip. Hearing loss is given in decibels relative to the normal threshold. Data courtesy of R. N. Leaton, Psychology Department, Dartmouth College.

common clinical manifestations: the tonal dip, presbyacusia, and clinical high-tone deafness.

Tonal Dip. In an ear that is otherwise normal, there may be evident a loss of sensitivity to tones in a limited region of the audible frequency range. Known as the tonal dip, this limited loss occurs more frequently in men than in women, and it appears with surprising regularity in the frequency range between 3000 and 5000∿. A typical example obtained in our laboratory is shown in Fig. 10.8. The width of the dip generally does not exceed one octave and the losses appear symmetrically about a center frequency, that one showing the greatest loss. The loss in sensitivity characteristically amounts to 30 db (± 10), but occasionally tonal dips reach levels of 70 db below normal.

It has been argued that the tonal dip is the result of overstimulation, but this interpretation is open to debate on several grounds. First, we have already mentioned in our discussion of stimulation deafness that injury produced by overstimulation with a tone of one frequency leads to losses in sensitivity to all frequencies, although not necessarily in equal amount. Second, if the tonal dip were due to overstimulation, one would expect it to appear more suddenly than our audiometric data indicate.

Third, post-mortem studies of the ears of many persons with prominent tonal dips do not show any significant abnormalities in the organ of Corti (*47*, p. 363). Accordingly, the view that overstimulation is a necessary antecedent to the tonal dip does not seem justified. However, there is no question about the fact that overstimulation is sufficient to the impairment of hearing.

An alternative explanation, admittedly speculative, is that the tonal dip occurs because of a failure of the acoustic nerve. Inasmuch as the tonal dip appears in the frequency range of greatest absolute sensitivity, it is here that we would expect first to see the effects of subtle changes in neural action. Furthermore, the coding of intensity is apparently very complex in the frequency range about 4000∿, for here, according to Wever's theory, loudness is coded by the number of impulses within a neural volley while the number of volleys per unit of time serves to code pitch. With the neural elements thus responding near their critical limits insofar as timing is concerned, even subtle changes in the metabolic processes supporting neural action could disrupt the normal firing pattern and lead to selective losses in sensitivity.

Presbyacusia. With advancing age there is generally a progressive loss of sensitivity to the high tones. This is known as presbyacusia. In Fig. 10.9 are shown summary data for men and women that were obtained by Corso (*8*). At age 60 there is a general impairment for all tones, but the losses noted for tones up to 1000∿ are all on the order of 10 db relative to the sensitivity of younger listeners. However, as frequency rises beyond 1000∿, the losses become progressively more severe, particularly for men.

Observations of this sort, so common as to be expected, have led some to propose that presbyacusia is the result of changes in sensory and neural processes *directly* associated with the biological process of aging. On the other hand, presbyacusia could result *indirectly* with age as a consequence of the accumulated influences of occasional infections, acoustic and systemic trauma, or exposure to intense stimulation. The latter alternative is supported by the fact that some fortunate people of advanced age maintain normal hearing. In either case, post-mortem studies of the ears of people who demonstrated the pattern of presbyacusia have shown the sensory apparatus and the neural supply at the

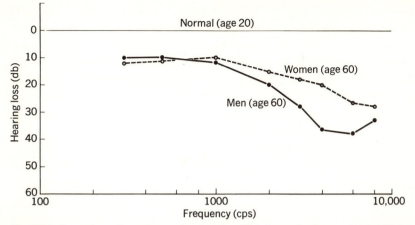

Fig. 10.9 Examples of presbyacusia showing high-tone deafness at age 60 for men and women. Hearing loss is given in decibels relative to thresholds obtained with a 20-year-old group. Data from Corso (8).

basal end of the cochlea to be degenerate. The abnormalities seldom extend toward the apex beyond 12 to 15 mm. It should be noted that the first stage of presbyacusia shows itself as a loss of sensitivity for tones near 4000∿, and as age advances, the losses spread first toward the higher tones and only much later and less markedly to the lower tones.

Clinical High-Tone Deafness. The final form of deafness we shall treat concerns a loss of sensitivity to high tones that is not related to age. Once again, the disorder is most common in men.

High-tone deafness may not be very different in origin from presbyacusia, particularly if we accept the view that age is only indirectly related to presbyacusia. For example, Crowe, Guild, and Polvogt (9) have demonstrated correlations between high-tone deafness and lesions in the basal turn of the organ of Corti and its neural fibers. Lesions limited to the organ of Corti were correlated with an abrupt fall-off of sensitivity to high tones, whereas lesions of the acoustic nerve were correlated with more gradual losses. What brings about the lesions is unknown. Apparently, high-tone deafness occasionally can result from lesions of the acoustic pathways central to the auditory nerve since Crowe, Guild, and Polvogt noted a few instances of high-tone deafness in the absence of any detectable changes in the cochlea or auditory nerve.

Audiology

The measurement of hearing stands as the central function of the audiologist because all of his other activities, whether diagnostic or therapeutic in nature, depend ultimately upon a comparison of the hearing of one person with normative data. Accordingly, here we shall treat briefly a few of the more common techniques of *audiometry* for tones and in so doing mention a related matter, loudness recruitment.

Before beginning a review of methods, it is important to our purpose to distinguish between *psychophysical* and *clinical* audiometry. The former refers very generally to the broad aspects of auditory psychophysics which form our normative data. After all, normal hearing can be defined only by a series of summary statistics that describe what the average listener without any known impairments hears. The whole body of psychophysical data presented in the foregoing chapters serves as the reference against which impairments and deviations show themselves. The normative data represent a slow accumulation of information gathered in laboratories with great care.

In contrast, clinical audiometry has the practical purpose of identifying in individuals impairments of hearing and their probable causes so that suitable treatments and therapies can be administered. Therefore, the methods of audiometry employed in the clinic need be no more precise than is required to gain these ends. This is not to say that careful measurement is unimportant or that it is usually wanting in a clinical setting, but the standard psychophysical methods often are simply impractical.

TUNING-FORK TESTS

Tests of hearing that involve the use of tuning forks have a long history. Yet, despite their essential crudeness, they continue in use because of their convenience and their utility in identifying certain forms of deafness.

Weber Test. When the stem of a vibrating tuning fork is held against the head anywhere along the midline, a person with normal hearing will not lateralize the sound. Instead, he will hear the sound as coming from the median plane or from the center of his head. However, a person with asymmetrical sensitivity of the ears will lateralize the sound, and he will do so differently depending on the form of deafness. If he has a conductive deafness in one ear, lateralization is *toward* the side of impairment. On the other hand, if he has a sensory or neural deafness, lateralization is *away* from the side of impairment. Thus, the Weber test is useful to the early process of diagnosis.

The reason for the lateralization of a bone-conducted tone to the side of the conductive impairment is not understood, but several studies have shown that a temporary blocking of the external meatus increases absolute sensitivity (up to 20 db) to bone-conducted sounds of frequencies below 2500$\curvearrowright$ (*51*, pp. 337-339).

Rinné Test. In this test the stem of a vibrating tuning fork is held first against the mastoid bone behind one pinna until the sound of it just becomes inaudible. Immediately thereafter, the fork is moved so that its prongs are exactly opposite the meatal entrance. With normal hearing, the sound once again becomes audible, whereas with a conductive deafness it remains inaudible.

Schwabach Test. The Weber and Rinné tests do not give quantitative information about a hearing loss, nor do they show losses as a function of frequency. However, in the Schwabach test an effort is made to determine the relative sensitivity of the ear to different tones covering a range of frequencies. The standard measure of sensitivity is the *time* required for the various tuning forks to become inaudible. This measure of sensitivity is fraught with difficulties because the time required to reach inaudibility is influenced both by the sensitivity of the ear and the force with which the tuning forks were struck. Nevertheless, in practical hands the Schwabach test can be useful in identifying losses of sensitivity, especially to high tones.

AUDIOMETERS

An audiometer consists essentially of a pure-tone generator, an attenuator, and a transducer, usually a headphone. In the simpler instruments only certain fixed frequencies are available (for example, 125, 250, 500, 1000, 2000, 4000, and 8000$\curvearrowright$), but in others frequency can be continuously varied. Sound intensity is controlled with an attenuator that changes the voltage to the transducer in such a way that it takes into account the input-output curve of the earphone and the assumed normal threshold. If the attenuator remains at *audiometric zero,* zero on the dial, then the voltage to the transducer does not remain constant with changes in frequency, but rather it varies so as to generate sound pressures according to normal thresholds. On the other hand, if tonal frequency remains constant, then changing the attenuator stepwise increases sound pressure at each step by a constant number of decibels. Stimulus onset is controlled with a special switch designed to eliminate click transients. Although standard procedures for the use of audiometers certainly are established by individual users, the procedures vary rather substantially among users. Yet despite these differences, data obtained with the aid of audiometers are usually plotted in a standard manner, as shown in Fig. 8.8. The *audiogram* is distinguished by the fact that normal hearing (audiometric zero) is depicted as a straight line of zero slope. Because the sound pressure required for absolute threshold varies with frequency, it is easier to specify all these different pressures as 0 db and then plot in decibels the deviations in pressure required by a particular listener to hear each tone. The audiogram for a person of normal hearing thus appears as a straight line. Impairments are noted below this line, especially good sensitivity above it.

Békésy Audiometer. In 1947 Békésy (*4*) described a new audiometer that by now has come into wide use. It consists of a variable-frequency oscillator, an attenuator, transducers (headphones), and a writing device. Unlike the older instruments, the oscillator in Békésy's instrument is made to sweep slowly through the frequencies from 100 to 10,000∿ by means of a mechanical coupling to a motor. Furthermore, sound intensity is controlled by the listener with a switch that determines the amount of voltage delivered to the headphones. Procedurally, the listener depresses the key when he hears a tone and releases the key as soon as it becomes inaudible. In this manner he continually "brackets" the absolute threshold as the oscillator sweeps through the frequency range. The writing device records simultaneously the changes in intensity made by the listener in the form of an audiogram, as shown in Fig. 10.10. The alternation of attenuation is what gives rise to the spiked appearance of the trace. The threshold is assumed to lie in the middle of the envelope

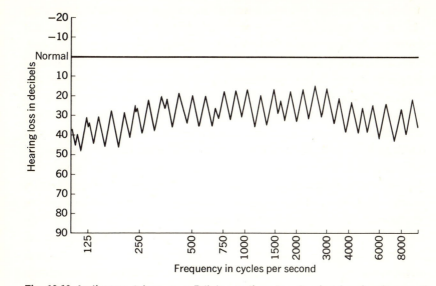

Fig. 10.10 Audiogram taken on a Békésy audiometer showing hearing losses at all frequencies. See text for further explanation.

obtained by connecting the peaks, and the width of the envelope (vertical dimension) is a crude measure of the difference threshold. Envelope width has been of special interest because it has turned out that narrow envelopes indicate a form of hearing impairment that is accompanied by loudness recruitment.

LOUDNESS RECRUITMENT

Loudness recruitment refers to a greater than normal rate in the growth of loudness as a function of intensity, and it seems to accompany both sensory and nerve deafness but not conductive deafness. The phenomenon can best be described by reference to inter-aural loudness matches made by individuals with sensory deafness in one ear. When a frequency is selected that falls in the range of impairment, equality in loudness can only be achieved for a tone near threshold by having the intensity at the poorer ear greatly exceed that at the normal ear. However, when the same tone is well above threshold, the loudness match no longer requires a greater intensity at the poorer ear. Apparently, an impaired ear somehow can catch up to a normal ear. In cases of conductive deafness, loudness in the defective ear remains about the same number of decibels below that in the normal ear, regardless of stimulation level.

Loudness recruitment occurs almost exclusively in cases of high-tone deafness. Wever (47, p. 368) has argued that recruitment is explicable in terms of the spread of action within the cochlea brought about by rising intensity. Cochlear action with high tones at near threshold intensities is sharply peaked and localized. Lesions near the basal end of the cochlea would account for the disturbance in threshold sensitivity. However, with intense stimulation, the action would spread apically so that the hair cells or neural units comprising the lesion would make up a smaller proportion of the total. As a consequence, the influence of the lesion would become less and less noticeable as the stimulation level increased. A phenomenon like loudness recruitment has also been observed in the normal listener in the presence of a masking tone (46).

DIRECTIONAL AUDIOMETRY

As implied in our earlier distinction between psychophysical and clinical audiometry, impairments of hearing can be measured in many ways beside changes in absolute threshold. One such way is to examine the effects of deafness upon sound localization. Nordlund (33) has pursued this matter rather fully, and he has been able to make a strong case for the utility of directional audiometry in the diagnosis of several forms of deafness. His data are especially compelling because the results of directional audiometry are not correlated especially with pure-tone audiograms, and thus additional information is gained. In general, Nordlund found that people with nerve deafness have markedly impaired directional hearing if the lesions lie between the cochlea and the pontile region. Neither nerve deafness from brain lesions nor sensory deafness had marked effects upon directional hearing.

References

1. Adrian, E. D., D. W. Bronk, and G. Phillips. The nervous origin of the Wever and Bray effect, *J. Physiol.*, 1931, *73*, 2p-3p.
2. Alexander, I. E., and F. J. Githler. Chronic effects of jet engine noise on the structure and function of the cochlear apparatus, *J. Comp. Physiol. Psychol.*, 1952, *45*, 381-391.

3. Békésy, G. von. Ueber die mechanisch-akustischen Vorgänge beim Hören, *Acta Oto-Laryngol.*, 1939, *27*, 281-296, 388-396.

4. Békésy, G. von. A new audiometer, *Acta Oto-Laryngol.*, 1947, *35*, 411-422.

5. Bordley, J. E., and M. Hardy. Effect of lesions of the tympanic membrane on the hearing acuity, *Arch. Otolaryngol.*, 1937, *26*, 649-657.

6. Brain, W. R. *Clinical Neurology*, 2nd ed., London: Oxford University Press, 1964, p. 45.

7. Bunch, C. C. *Clinical Audiometry*, St. Louis: Mosby, 1943.

8. Corso, J. F. Aging and auditory thresholds in men and women, *Arch. Environ. Hlth.*, 1963, *6*, 350-356.

9. Crowe, S. J., S. R. Guild, and L. M. Polvogt. Observations on the pathology of high-tone deafness, *Bull. Johns Hopkins Hosp.*, 1934, *54*, 315-379.

10. Cutt, R. A., and W. L. Gulick. Effects of abnormal body temperature upon the ear; heating, *Ann. Otol. Rhinol. Laryngol.*, 1960, *69*, 997-1005.

11. Cutt, R. A., R. J. Wolfson, E. Ishiyama, F. Rothwarf, and D. Myers. Preliminary results with experimental cryosurgery of the labyrinth, *Arch. Otolaryngol.*, 1965, *82*, 147-158.

12. Davis, H., A. J. Derbyshire, M. H. Lurie, and L. J. Saul. The electric response of the cochlea, *Amer. J. Physiol.*, 1934, *107*, 316.

13. Dishoeck, H. A. E. van, and G. DeWit. Loading and covering of the tympanic membrane and obstruction of the external auditory canal, *Acta Oto-Laryngol.*, 1944, *32*, 99-111.

14. Fowler, E. P., Jr., and T. W. Forbes. Effect of certain agents on cochlear effect and hearing, *Proc. Soc. Exper. Biol. Med.*, 1935, *32*, 827-829.

15. Fowler, E. P., Jr., and T. W. Forbes. End organ deafness in dogs due to the application of certain chemicals to the round window membrane, *Ann. Otol. Rhinol. Laryngol.*, 1936, *45*, 859-864.

16. Fowler, E. P., Jr., and T. W. Forbes. Depression in order of frequency of the electrical cochlear response in cats, *Amer. J. Physiol.*, 1936, *117*, 24-35.

17. Gellhorn, E., and I. Speisman. Influence of variation of O_2 and CO_2 tension in inspired air upon hearing, *Amer. J. Physiol.*, 1935, *112*, 519-528.

18. Gulick, W. L. Effects of hypoxemia upon the electrical response of the cochlea, *Ann. Otol. Rhinol. Laryngol.*, 1958, *67*, 148-169.

19. Gulick, W. L., and R. A. Cutt. Effects of abnormal body temperature upon the ear: cooling, *Ann. Otol. Rhinol. Laryngol.*, 1960, *69*, 35-50.

20. Gulick, W. L., and R. A. Cutt. Intracochlear temperature and the cochlear response, *Ann. Otol. Rhinol. Laryngol.*, 1962, *71*, 331-340.

21. Gulick, W. L., and W. C. Patterson. Implications of slope changes in cochlear response intensity functions, previously unpublished.

22. Gulick, W. L., and W. C. Patterson. Effects of chloramphenicol upon the electrical activity of the ear: II. Long term data, *Ann. Otol. Rhinol. Laryngol.*, 1964, *73*, 204-209.

23. Guttman, John. Electrical distrubances in the cochlea produced by sound, *Laryngoscope*, 1933, *43*, 983-985.
24. Hallpike, C. S., and A. F. Rawdon-Smith. The "Wever and Bray phenomenon," a study of the electrical response in the cochlea with especial reference to its origin, *J. Physiol.*, 1934, *81*, 395-408.
25. Hamberger, C. A., and H. Hydén. Cytochemical changes in the cochlear ganglion caused by acoustic stimulation and trauma, *Acta Oto-Laryngol.*, 1945, Suppl. 61, 89 pp.
26. Klein, S. J., E. S. Mendelson, and T. J. Gallagher. Effects of reduced oxygen intake on auditory threshold shifts in a quiet environment, *J. Comp. Physiol. Psychol.*, 1961, *54*, 401-404.
27. Lempert, J. Improvement of hearing in cases of otosclerosis: a new one-stage surgical technic, *Arch. Otolaryngol.*, 1938, *28*, 42-97.
28. Lempert, J. Endaural fenestration of external semicircular canal for restoration of hearing in cases of otosclerosis, *Arch. Otolaryngol.*, 1940, *31*, 711-779.
29. Lempert, J. Fenestra nov-ovalis; a new oval window for the improvement of hearing in cases of otosclerosis, *Arch. Otolaryngol.*, 1941, *34*, 880-912.
30. Lüscher, E. Untersuchungen über die Beeinflussung der Hörfähigkeit durch Trommelfellbelastung, *Acta Oto-Laryngol.*, 1939, *27*, 250-266.
31. Lüscher, E. Experimentelle Trommelfellbellastungen und Luftleitungs-audiogramme mit allgemeinen Betrachtungen zur normalen und pathologischen Physiologie des Schalleitungsapparates, *Arch. f. Ohren-Kehlkopfheilk*, 1939, *146*, 372-401.
32. Myers, David, W. D. Schlosser, and R. A. Winchester. Otologic diagnosis and the treatment of deafness, *Clinical Symposia*, 1962, *14*, No. 2, 39-73, Summit, N.J.: Ciba Pharmaceutical Co.
33. Nordlund, B. Directional audiometry, *Acta Oto-Laryngol.*, 1963, *56*.
34. Patterson, W. C., and W. L. Gulick. Effects of chloramphenicol upon the electrical activity of the ear, *Ann. Otol. Rhinol. Laryngol.*, 1963, *72*, 50-55.
35. Payne, M. C., and F. J. Githler. Effects of perforations of the tympanic membrane on cochlear potentials, *Arch. Otolaryngol.*, 1951, *54*, 666-674.
36. Rahm, W. E., Jr., W. F. Strother, and J. F. Crump. The effects of pressure in the external auditory meatus, *Ann. Otol. Rhinol. Laryngol.*, 1956, *65*, 656-665.
37. Rahm, W. E., Jr., W. F. Strother, G. Lucchina, and W. L. Gulick. The effects of air pressure on the ear, *Ann. Otol. Rhinol. Laryngol.*, 1958, *67*, 170-177.
38. Rahm, W. E., Jr., W. F. Strother, W. L. Gulick, and J. F. Crump. The effects of topical anesthetics upon the ear, *Ann. Otol. Rhinol. Laryngol.*, 1959, *68*, 1037-1046.

39. Rahm, W. E., Jr., W. F. Strother, W. L. Gulick, and J. F. Crump. The effects of anesthetics upon the ear: II. Procaine hydrochloride, *Ann. Otol. Rhinol. Laryngol.*, 1960, *69*, 969-975.

40. Rahm, W. E., Jr., W. F. Strother, W. L. Gulick, and J. F. Crump. The effects of anesthetics upon the ear: III. Tetracaine hydrochloride, *Ann. Otol. Rhinol. Laryngol.*, 1961, *70*, 403-409.

41. Rahm, W. E., Jr., W. F. Strother, J. F. Crump, and D. E. Parker. The effects of anesthetics upon the ear: IV. Lidocaine hydrochloride, *Ann. Otol. Rhinol. Laryngol.*, 1962, *71*, 116-123.

42. Rosen, S. Palpation of the stapes for fixation, *Arch. Otolaryngol.*, 1952, *56*, 610-615.

43. Schuknecht, H. F., T. M. McGee, and B. H. Coleman. Stapedectomy, *Ann. Otol. Rhinol. Laryngol.*, 1960, *69*, 597-609.

44. Schuknecht, H. F., and S. Oleksiuk. The metal prosthesis for stapes ankylosis, *Arch. Otolargynol.*, 1960, *71*, 287-295.

45. Smith, K. R., and E. G. Wever. The problem of stimulation deafness: III. The functional and histological effects of a high-frequency stimulus, *J. Exper. Psychol.*, 1949, *39*, 238-241.

46. Steinberg, J. C., and M. B. Gardner. The dependence of hearing impairment on sound intensity, *J. Acoust. Soc. Amer.*, 1937, *9*, 11-23.

47. Wever, E. G. *Theory of Hearing*, New York: Wiley, 1949.

48. Wever, E. G. Recent investigations of sound conduction: II. The ear with conductive impairment, *Ann. Otol. Rhinol. Laryngol.*, 1950, *59*, 1037-1061.

49. Wever, E. G., and C. W. Bray. Effects of chemical substances upon the electrical responses of the cochlea: I. The application of sodium chloride to the round window membrane, *Ann. Otol. Rhinol. Laryngol.*, 1937, *46*, 291-303.

50. Wever, E. G., C. W. Bray, and M. Lawrence. The effects of pressure in the middle ear, *J. Exper. Psychol.*, 1942, *30*, 40-52.

51. Wever, E. G., and M. Lawrence. *Physiological Acoustics*, Princeton, N.J.: Princeton University Press, 1954.

52. Wever, E. G., M. Lawrence, W. Hemphill, and C. B. Straut. Effects of oxygen deprivation upon the cochlear potentials, *Amer. J. Physiol.*, 1949, *159*, 199-208.

53. Wever, E. G., M. Lawrence, and K. R. Smith. The effects of negative air pressure in the middle ear, *Ann. Otol. Rhinol. Laryngol.*, 1948, *57*, 418-446.

54. Wing, K. G., J. D. Harris, A. D. Stover, and J. H. Brouillette. Effects of changes in arterial oxygen and carbon dioxide upon the cochlear microphonics, USN, Submar. Med. Res. Lab. Rep., 1952, 11(5), 37 pp.

55. Woodman, DeG. Congenital atresia of the auditory canal, *Arch. Otolaryngol.*, 1952, *55*, 172-178.

Glossary

∿	cycles per second
cps	cycles per second
Δ	change
δ	locus in space
m	meter(s)
cm	centimeter(s)
sec	second(s)
msec	millisecond(s)
μsec	microsecond(s)
V	volt(s)
mV	millivolt(s)
μV	microvolt(s)

TERMS

absolute jnd
The least detectable change in intensity (ΔI) or frequency (Δf).

azimuth
Refers to the angular direction of a sound source, in degrees, with straight ahead as zero.

bandwidth (bw)
The width in cycles between the upper and lower cut-off frequencies of a band of noise. Sounds with bandwidths extending over most of the audible spectrum result in "white" noise.

center frequency (cf)
That frequency which is at the center of a bandwidth.

centrifugal
Anatomical term describing the downward, outward, or efferent tracts and nerves. Opposite of centripetal.

cochlear potential (CP)
The electrical potential generated by the hair cells of the cochlea that acts to trigger the auditory nerve.

contralateral
Anatomical term meaning the opposite side with reference to the midline. Opposite of ipsilateral.

238

critical bandwidth (cbw)

The maximum bandwidth of noise for which loudness remains invariant when sound pressure is constant.

cycle ($\wedge$)

One complete set of pressure changes around a reference pressure, including a condensation and a rarefaction.

decibel (db)

Unit of a logarithmic scale of the ratio of two sound pressures.

$$N \text{ (db)} = 20 \log \frac{P}{p}$$

20 db = ratio of 1:10

6 db = ratio of 1:2

dichotic

A different auditory stimulus presented to each ear.

diotic

An identical auditory stimulus presented to both ears.

dorsal

Anatomical term meaning (in man) toward a posterior direction: toward the back. Opposite of ventral.

dyne

A unit of force.

dyne/cm²

Dyne per square centimeter. A unit of sound pressure.

intensity (I)

The magnitude of an auditory stimulus. Measured in pressure units (dyne/cm²).

ipsilateral

Anatomical term meaning the same side with reference to the midline. Opposite of contralateral.

jnd

The just noticeable difference. The smallest change of an auditory stimulus which leads to a discriminable difference.

lateral

Anatomical term meaning to or toward the side. Opposite of medial.

loudness-level

Loudness-level of a sound is equal to the intensity (db SPL) of an equally loud 1000$\wedge$ tone. Measured in phons.

medial

Anatomical term meaning to or toward the middle (midline). Opposite of lateral.

mel

Unit of pitch. One thousand mels equals the pitch of a 1000$\wedge$ tone 40 db SL.

N_1

Refers to the cochlear nerve or its electrical activity. First-order neurons of the auditory nervous projections.

noise

A sound of sufficient complexity as to have no periodicity in pressure changes over time.

phon

Unit of loudness-level. The loudness of any tone in phons is equal to the intensity (db SPL) of an equally loud $1000\curlyvee$ tone.

pure tone

A sound which has a pressure change which is a simple sinusoidal function of time.

relative jnd

The least detectable change in intensity or frequency divided by the intensity $(\Delta I/I)$ or frequency $(\Delta f/f)$ itself.

sensation level (SL)

Sound pressure in db with reference to the pressure required at the threshold of audibility for that sound.

sone

Unit of loudness. One sone equals loudness of a $1000\curlyvee$ tone 40 db SL.

sound pressure level (SPL)

Sound pressure in db with reference to 0.0002 dyne/cm².

spectrum

The distribution of energy among the component frequencies of a sound.

summation potential (SP)

An electrical potential of the cochlea. Probably an artifact although some claim it to have a functional role in hearing.

ventral

Anatomical term meaning (in man) toward an anterior direction: toward the belly. Opposite of dorsal.

vol

Unit of tonal volume (voluminousness). Ten vols equals the volume of a $1000\curlyvee$ tone 40 db SL.

Subject Index

Ablation
  and localization, 202
Absolute just noticeable difference, 114,
    124
  and basilar membrane mapping, 127-
    132
  Δf as a function of f, 125, 126
    effects of intensity on, 125-127
    total number of, 129, 130
  ΔI as a function of I, 114-118
    effects of frequency on, 115-117
  for frequency, 125-127
  for intensity, 112, 114-118
Absolute threshold, 109-112
  and cochlear potential magnitude in
    cats, 100, 101
  as a function of frequency, 108, 109-
    111
  methods of obtaining, 108, 109
  variation of, 111
  with minimum audible field, 108, 109
  with minimum audible pressure, 108,
    109
Acoustic resistance, 33
  and transformer action of middle ear,
    32, 33
  defined, 33
Afferent nerve endings
  and hair cell membrane, 46
  nature of, 44, 45
Aging
  and sensitivity, 228, 229

All-or-none law
  implications for frequency theory, 89,
    90
Amplitude
  and aural harmonics, 63-65
  and overloading, 65
  difference tones, 66-68
  distortions of by the ear, 63-68
    role of Deiters cells in, 65, 66
  interference, 66-68
  modulation, 14
  summation tones, 67
Anesthetics
  effects of topical on cochlear poten-
    tial, 221-224
Anvil. *See* Incus
Apex of cochlea, 34
Arches of Corti, 38
  fulcrum of, 55-60
  shearing force of, 55-60
Attenuation through the head, 167
Attributes of tones. *See* Tonal attributes
Audiogram
  nature of, 231, 232
  with Békésy audiometer, 232, 233
Audiology, 230
Audiometer
  nature of, 231-233
Audiometric zero, 232
Audiometry, 230-234
  audiometers, 231-233
  Békésy, 232, 233

241

Resonance
  and place principle, 87
  determinants of, 19, 20
  direct coupling, 19
  in external meatus, 28
    influence on absolute threshold, 111
  indirect coupling, 19
  limitations of resonance in place theory, 88, 89
  nature of, 19, 20
  relation to damping, 20
Resonance-Place theory of Helmholtz, 87
  and wave complexity, 87
  conception of basilar membrane, 87
  criticism of, 88, 89
  frequency coding in, 87
  intensity coding in, 87, 89
  problem of damping, 88, 89
  resonators in, 87
Response areas
  and best-tuned frequency, 74
  and inhibition, 74, 75, 80-82
  and worst-tuned frequency, 80, 81
  frequency-intensity interdependence, 102, 103
  in higher-order fibers, 74, 75
  nature of, 72-75
  relation to frequency, 73, 74
  relation to intensity, 73, 74
  types of, 73, 74, 80, 81
Resting potentials in cochlea, 53, 54
  endocochlear potential, 53, 54
  intracellular potential, 53
Reticular formation
  acoustic collaterals to, 48
Rinné test, 231
Root-mean-square pressure, 21, 22
  computation of, 22
    in sine waves, 22
Round window
  function of, 34, 36
  relation to oval window, 34

Scala media
  nature of, 34, 35
  volume of, 36
Scala tympani, 34-36
Scala vestibuli, 34-36
Schwabach text, 231
Semantic differential, 165
  and non-auditory tonal attributes, 165, 166

reliability of, 165
Sensation level (SL)
  and frequency discrimination, 126, 129, 130
  and intensity discrimination, 113-115
  defined, 24
Sensory deafness, 218-226
  and cochlear temperature, 226
  and hypoxemia, 225, 226
  defined, 208, 218
  from systemic disorders, 225, 226
  from vascular disorders, 225
  loudness recruitment in, 233
  Ménière's disease, 224, 225
  through drugs, 221-224
  through stimulation, 218-221
  tinnitus, 224, 225
Serous otitis media, 215
Shearing force
  and hair cells, 55-60
Sine wave
  nature of, 13
Single-unit recordings
  and frequency tuning, 72-75, 102, 122
  and localization, 200-202
  in auditory nerve, 72-74
Sliding-tone technique, 125
  effects of rate, 126
Sone
  defined, 144, 145
  distinguished from phon, 147
Sound
  energy of, 14
  in free sound field, 109
  interference of, 19
  nature of, 10, 11
  parameters of, 13-19
  propagation of, 11, 12
  reinforcement of, 19
  sine wave, 13
  velocity in air, 12, 190
Sound pressure level (SPL)
  defined, 24
Sound-producing bodies, 11
  properties of, 11
Sound shadow, 12, 13, 188-190
  and complexity, 189, 190
  role of pinna, 198, 199
Spectral analysis, 16-18
  and audiospectrometer, 25, 26
  and loudness, 149
Spiral ganglion, 41
  as part of cochlear nerve, 41, 42

Author Index

Along with the names of the authors cited in the text appear the page numbers on which specific reference to their work is made. Numbers in italics denote the pages on which the full reference is given.